T0274786

Ashforth's
Curiosities of
Horseracing

Ashforth's
Curiosities of
Horseracing

by David Ashforth

MERLIN UNWIN BOOKS

First published in Great Britain by Merlin Unwin Books Ltd 2022

Text © David Ashforth 2022

All rights reserved, including the right to reproduce this book or portions thereof in any form or by any means, electronic or mechanical, including photocopying, recording, or by any information storage and retrieval system, without permission in writing from the publisher:

Merlin Unwin Books Ltd
Palmers House
7 Corve Street
Ludlow
Shropshire SY8 1DB
UK

www.merlinunwin.co.uk

The author asserts his moral right to be identified with this work.
ISBN 978 1 913159 46 7
Typeset in 11pt Minion Pro by Merlin Unwin Books
Printed by Akcent Media UK

RACECARD

Before You Begin

A sport based on one animal sitting on top of another and trying (usually) to be the first pair to reach a wooden stick is a curiosity in itself. So it's no surprise that horseracing is full of curiosities.

The curiosities in this collection have been chosen to arouse your interest, as they have engaged mine. They are stories of those curious creatures – people, and of horses.

The curiosities are arranged in themes but dip in and out, as the mood takes you. If you get bored with one, try another. Eventually the law of averages should come to your rescue.

I hope the collection will leave you with a benevolent view of an intriguing sport, if you don't have one already.

Dedication

To the friends I have made through this intriguing sport,
some of them very curious.

Chapter

1

Owners

In which Lord Lade
has his teeth filed
• Joe thrives on mincemeat
• Prince Khalid chooses his
curtains • the Duke
of Devonshire promises straw
• Death stretches out its hand.

1 LORD LADE HAS HIS TEETH FILED

For the heirs of wealthy aristocrats, 21 was a golden number. In 1780, Sir John Lade, having survived for the necessary number of years, gained control of the considerable fortune left by his late father.

Lade's uncle was Henry Thrale, a close friend of Dr Samuel Johnson. Johnson quickly deemed Sir John unfit for his inheritance and greeted Lade's 21st birthday with his poem, *To Sir John Lade, On his Coming of Age*. The opening lines were:

> *Long-expected one-and-twenty*
> *Ling'ring year, at length is flown*
> *Pride and pleasure, pomp and plenty*
> *Great Sir John, are now your own.*
> *Loosen'd from the minor's tether,*
> *Free to mortgage or to sell.*
> *Wild as wind, and light as feather*
> *Bid the sons of thrift farewell.....*

Johnson's opinion of Lade did not improve and when Lade asked him, "Mr Johnson, would you advise me to marry?" received the dismissive reply, "I would advise no man to marry, sir, who is not likely to propagate understanding."

Johnson proved a sound judge, as Lade diligently disposed of his wealth by the tried and tested means of racing, gambling, womanising, drinking and dedicated profligacy.

Lord Lade once sat still long enough for Joshua Reynolds to complete a portrait of him with his dog and, unusually, without his whip. Lade was habitually dressed in riding clothes, carrying a whip, as it was never long before he either mounted a horse or a carriage, from which he drove his team of six greys or, often, those of the Prince Regent.

As well as dressing like a coachman, Lade had his front teeth filed, so that he could mimic the loud whistle coachmen made through the spaces in their teeth. Thomas Raikes, a noted dandy, remarked that Lord Lade's "ambition was to imitate the groom in dress and in language."

Lord Thurlow, a former Chancellor, doubtless had Lade's emulation of coachmen in mind when, at a dinner with the Prince Regent, he was appalled to find Lade among the guests. "I have no objection, sir," he told the future King George IV, "to Sir John Lade in his proper place, which I take to be your Royal Highness's coach-box, and not your table."

The bold Lady Lade as seen by George Stubbs (1793).

If Lade's dress and language were not enough to alienate high society, his penchant for excess, outrageous bets and choice of wife did the trick. Lade bet that he could drive the wheels of his phaeton over a sixpenny piece, and that he could drive a four-in-hand rig around Tattersall's small sales yard at Hyde Park Corner.

Notoriously, Sir John once bet the burly Lord Cholmondley that he could carry him from opposite Brighton's Royal Pavilion twice around the Old Steine. When the time came, Lade demanded that Cholmondley strip off, on the grounds that he had bet that he could carry Cholmondley, not his clothes. Unwilling to be seen naked in public, especially as there were women among the spectators, Cholmondley conceded the bet.

Not all his bets were successful and his betting at racecourses was generally disastrous. Lord Lade usually settled his debts quarterly, on a

Monday, enabling him to leave his mark by coining the expression, 'Black Monday.'

Until it was no longer possible, Lord Lade owned and bred many racehorses, including the distinguished grey, Medley, later a successful stallion in America, and Crop, runner-up in the 1781 Derby.

In 1787 he subjected society to a further shock when marrying a woman from such an obscure background that even her name was uncertain. Letitia or Laetitia's maiden surname was either Smith or Derby. According to John Robert Robinson's *The Last Earls of Barrymore, 1769–1824* (1894), she "had been a servant at a house in Broad Street, St Giles, whose inhabitants were not endowed with every virtue."

A relationship with 'Sixteen String Jack' Rann, so called because he wore 16 coloured strings attached to the knees of his silk breeches, ended abruptly in 1774, when the highwayman was executed at Tyburn.

Moving up in the world, Letitia became the mistress of the Duke of York, the Prince Regent's younger brother. Her looks and skill at riding and carriage driving attracted attention, particularly that of Sir John Lade and the Prince Regent.

Robinson wrote, "She was a smart, bold woman and became, under her husband's tuition, as deft a 'whip' as Sir John himself. Lady Lade also became a skilled horsewoman, and regularly attended the Windsor hunt. It was at one of these meetings that she attracted the attention of the Prince of Wales by her bold riding."

The Prince Regent became so well disposed towards Lady Lade that in 1793 he commissioned George Stubbs to paint a portait of her. Appropriately, Lady Lade appears sitting calmly, side saddle, on a rearing horse.

She and Lord Lade were well matched, for Letitia was a disciple in betting and leader in slang. She once challenged a rival lady 'whip' to drive a four-in-hand eight miles across Newmarket Heath for 500 guineas, 'play or pay.' Lady Lade was willing but her rival was not. When it came to swearing, Robinson noted that, "Sir John Lade and his lady were both skilled in 'stable' and other slang." The Prince Regent was prone to say of someone, "he swears like Lady Lade."

Her behaviour did not enamour her to the wives of other aristocrats, many of whom ignored her. In Brighton in 1789 Lady Lade prevailed on the Prince Regent to dance with her, thinking this would improve her standing but, led by the Duchess of Rutland, several ladies promptly left the room. The following day they left Brighton for Eastbourne, in protest.

As Lord Lade's fortune shrank and his debts rose, his racecourse and social appearances diminished until, in 1814, he arrived at the King's Bench debtors' prison. Yet, unlike his inheritance, his luck hadn't vanished completely. He, or his friends, paid for the privilege of being allowed to live not in but in close proximity to the prison, where Lady Lade joined him.

Late that year, enough of Lord Lade's debts were cleared to obtain his release, whereupon the Prince Regent generously bestowed an annuity of £300 a year on him, eventually raised to £500. The payments were disguised as a salary for acting as the Prince Regent's driving tutor, with the bank drafts made out to the 'Reverend Dr. Tolly.'

Lady Lade died in 1825 while her husband lived on at his stud farm in Sussex, defying decades of unhealthy living until expiring, aged 78, in 1838.

Even then, Lord Lade wasn't completely dead, nor Lady Lade, for both were resurrected by William M. Reynolds in *The Mysteries of the Court of London* (1849), by Conan Doyle in *Rodney Stone* (1896), and by Georgette Heyer in *The Corinthian* (1940).

In 2021, Lady Lade reappeared as a racehorse, winning twice for trainer Keith Dalgleish.

2 JOE THRIVES ON MINCEMEAT

Vincent O'Brien was one of the best, arguably the best, trainer of all time. Based in Ireland but twice champion jumps trainer and twice champion Flat trainer in Britain, the trainer of six Derby winners, including the Triple Crown winner Nijinsky, O'Brien achieved the remarkable feat of winning the Grand National three years in succession.

In 1953 O'Brien triumphed with Early Mist, in 1954 with Royal Tan and in 1955 with Quare Times. The first two were owned by fellow Irishman 'Lucky' Joe 'Mincemeat' Griffin, and the celebration Griffin led at Liverpool's Adelphi Hotel after Early Mist's success was without equal, which took some doing.

Before the guest list was expanded to, as Griffin recalled, "whoever was there, Irish or anyone else," there was a formal dinner. The dinner cost Griffin £1,500 (about £45,000 today), partly because he had bay prawns and asparagus flown in from France.

The dinner did not go altogether smoothly, thanks largely to the host having invited an Irish Cabinet Minister and an Irish Senator to join the celebrations, along with the Mayor of Liverpool. At midnight, when the band struck up God Save the Queen, the Minister, who had crossed the threshold into drunkenness, refused to stand up. "I'm not standing up for any fucking English Queen," he shouted. Afterwards, revellers danced through the night to a full orchestra.

Later, in Dublin, a civic reception was laid on for Early Mist and Griffin, with both paraded along O'Connell Street to the Mansion House, where the

Lord Mayor, Andy Clarkin, held a reception for them. There were yet more parties in the Gresham Hotel and Kilcoran Lodge Hotel near Vincent O'Brien's home, with poker games around the clock, paused for trips to the races.

The cost to Griffin was academic or, as he put it, "money was no object at that time. I had so much of it I didn't know what to do with it." He gave £10,000 to Early Mist's trainer, jockey and stable staff.

The prize money for the winner was £9,255 (about £260,000 today) but, encouraged by O'Brien advising him to "have a good bet," Griffin won far more by backing Early Mist at odds from 66-1 down to 20-1, the price at which the horse started. He was said to have won £100,000 (about £2.8 m today), mainly from bets via the English bookmakers Wilf Sherman and Jack Swift.

Two years earlier, aged 35, Griffin had moved into Knocklyon House, near Tallaght, south-west of Dublin, with his wife Peggy and their four (later six) children. It was a 21 room Georgian mansion, complete with ballroom, set in 30 acres. The staff included a cook, nurse, gardener and housemaid, plus a chauffeur to drive Griffin's Buick, Dodge and Hillman cars.

That year, Griffin boasted, "I can make money out of anything," which pleased Peggy, who told one reporter, "Life with Joe is just like a fairy story. This ring came from Amsterdam – it's worth over £1,500."

Griffin's wealth came from mincemeat. After the Second World War, with rationing still in place in Britain, an English friend told him, "Joe, we haven't seen mince pies for years."

Griffin promptly bought a £100,000 shipload of dried fruit on credit from the Greek government after an order from a British grocery chain had been cancelled. He used the fruit to make mincemeat and, exploiting a loophole in restrictions on the import of fruit, sold it in jars to British grocers for £1.2 million. In 1950, his Red Breast Preserving Company bought all Ireland's available stock of dried fruit. At its peak, the company employed 500 workers and was exporting 400 tons of mincemeat a week to Britain at £140 a ton. In 1951 Griffin boasted, then complained, "Last year I sent over £1,500,000 worth of mincemeat, and now you don't want it any more."

The Ministry of Food had recently placed restrictions on the import of mincemeat. Griffin remained confident. "If the British don't want my mincemeat I don't worry," he said. "I'll sell it to the Germans instead."

Royal Tan's success in the 1954 Grand National masked the fact that Griffin's luck had run out. An economic downturn as well as obstacles to exporting his mincemeat to Britain led to the collapse of his company, not helped by Griffin's gambling reverses. A year earlier, following Early Mist's success, bookmaker Jack Swift had signed a cheque to Griffin for a five figure sum; by the time the Grand National came around again, Griffin owed him £56,000.

Before it all went wrong. Joe 'Mincemeat' Griffin leads in Early Mist after winning the 1953 Grand National, ridden by Bryan Marshall.

In July 1954, Griffin petitioned for bankruptcy and Early Mist and Royal Tan passed into the custody of the Official Assignee, who was soon given permission to sell them, together with nine other horses. In November, eight horses were sold at the Ballsbridge Sales, with the Aly Khan buying Royal Tan for 3,900 gns and Vincent O'Brien paying 2,000 gns for Early Mist.

Three months earlier, the first public sitting to deal with Griffin's bankruptcy was held, marking the start of over two damaging years in court. Creditors, including Bryan Marshall, the rider of Early Mist and Royal Tan, claimed a total of £53,656 (about £1.5 m today).

Marshall, it emerged, had come close to refusing to ride Royal Tan. After Early Mist's success in the 1953 National, Griffin had given him £3,500. The usual riding fee at that time was £7. Marshall testified that Griffin undertook to give him the same sum if he won on Royal Tan but that he already owed Marshall £600, which was proving difficult to get. £500 of the £600 related to the unpaid half of the £1,000 retainer Marshall had accepted in August 1953, for Griffin to have first call on his services.

Griffin had sent Marshall a cheque for £600 but it bounced. A day or two before the Grand National, Marshall received another cheque but while staying at the Adelphi Hotel got a message to inform him that the cheque had been stopped. Marshall told Griffin that unless he was paid, he wouldn't ride.

That evening he received an envelope containing £250, followed by an invitation from Griffin to join him for dinner. Griffin told him that he had found another £50 lying on his bed. Marshall agreed to meet him for a drink. Griffin said he would have his money in the morning, which he did, together with another cheque, conditional on him winning the National. Later, Marshall realised that the cheque was for £3,000 rather than the agreed £3,500.

Two weeks after the National, Marshall received £1,000. Griffin explained that he was owed £10,000 by a bookmaker and Marshall would be paid the rest when the bookmaker paid him. During the bankruptcy hearings, Marshall claimed a total of £2,781. Ultimately, judgment was given for just £31 but it was another blow to Griffin's battered reputation.

In July 1955, in Dublin High Court, Mr Justice Budd made clear his frustration with Griffin's failure to supply satisfactory answers during his bankruptcy examination. As a consequence, Griffin had been sent to Mountjoy prison and when he returned to face more questions, Budd sent him back to prison for the same reason.

Among other sins, Griffin was alleged to have failed to disclose the sum of £28,300 received as the result of business dealings with a Colonel Tickler of the St Martin's Preserving Company in Maidenhead, a manufacturer of mincemeat. Griffin had deposited £14,000 of this in the Munster and Leinster Bank.

Having given two different explanations for the deposit, Griffin now, without apology, produced a third. Mr Justice Budd was incensed. He accused Griffin of having no respect for the Court and no consideration for his creditors. It was worse than discourtesy, "it was plain untruth, plain lying, flagrant perjury."

1956 was equally disastrous. Griffin had offered to pay ten shillings in the £ of the £53,656 claimed by his creditors. Griffin said that he had friends in England prepared to put up the money and, to persuade the Court, he produced a letter dated 25 January 1955 purporting to be from Gilbert Reeves, offering to supply £10,000 as evidence of good intent.

When examined again in April 1956, it was suggested that the offer indicated that Griffin must have assets in England. In June, he went missing, a warrant was issued for his arrest and police were sent to Dublin and Shannon airports to look out for him. Griffin soon reappeared, but not at Knocklyon House, which the Official Assignee had sold for £15,300.

The following month Griffin appeared at Dublin District Court charged with having forged the 25 January 1955 letter with the intention of deceiving the High Court. In January 1957 he was given a surprisingly lenient suspended six months prison sentence for the offence.

Speaking in his defence, Mr Noel Hartnett said that Griffin could have wound his business up and still been a wealthy man but "the belief in his luck was almost pathological." He had given personal guarantees to the Red Breast Preserving Company's creditors, "with the result that when the ship sank he sank with it."

The sea bed had yet to be reached. In February 1960 Griffin was charged with having, on Christmas Eve, stolen two cheques valued at fourpence, with forging a cheque and stealing a wardrobe. That June he was convicted of presenting a forged cheque and obtaining £20 by false pretences, for which he received a suspended sentence of 12 months in prison.

Griffin was said to be "in poor circumstances" and they did not improve. In 1966 he was convicted on six charges of having obtained credit by fraud. In 1963 he had obtained goods including weighing machines, a cash register and a refrigerator on credit and never paid for them.

After slithering down the slope to ruin and disgrace, Griffin moved to Britain. He once said, "For me, money is for spending and for making people happy. I have made a lot of people happy. I realise now that a lot of them were just hangers-on."

It was a sad end to so much success and laughter. Peggy, his wife, stuck by him until Joe died in 1992, aged 75. He was buried in Beckenham Cemetery, in Kent.

3 PRINCE KHALID CHOOSES HIS CURTAINS

Every racefan recognised Prince Khalid Abdullah's racing colours and had done for several decades before his death in 2021, aged 83. The colours – green, with a pink sash, white sleeves, pink cap – first entered the winner's circle when Charming Native won a small race at Windsor in 1979. After that, they were worn by the fortunate riders of many top class horses. The list is a long one – from Known Fact, Rainbow Quest and Dancing Brave in the 1980s through to Kingman, Frankel and Enable.

A member of the Saudi royal family, Khalid Abdullah had a gentle, quiet demeanour and his racing colours were muted, too, yet easy to spot. A long time ago, he told me, "I like to see my colours from a distance but I have a problem with my eyes. When I decided to buy horses, Lord Weinstock visited me and said, 'You don't need to find colours, these are your colours', and pointed to the curtains. The curtains were green, white and pink, so he chose the colours for me."

Well done, Lord Weinstock, well done Prince Khalid and well done the curtains. Good choice.

Prince Khalid Abdullah's curtains aboard the mighty Frankel after winning the 2012 Juddmonte International, ridden by Tom Queally.

THE DUKE OF DEVONSHIRE PROMISES STRAW

Modern horseracing could not function without racing colours but in the early 18th century there were far fewer races, over longer distances, dominated by the landed aristocracy. The use of colours was haphazard.

As racing became more popular, the number of runners greater and the distances shorter, this laissez-faire attitude to colours caused confusion and led to disputed results. Initial attempts to encourage the use of coloured jackets were undermined by different owners choosing the same colours while some individual owners used more than one set of colours.

On 4 October 1762, at a meeting in Newmarket, the fledgling Jockey Club resolved that, *"For the greater convenience of distinguishing the horses in running, as also for the prevention of disputes arising from not knowing the colours worn by each rider, the undermentioned gentlemen have come to the resolution and agreement, of having the colours annexed to the following names, worn by their respective riders."*

There followed a list of 19 Jockey Club members, including six Dukes, five Earls, two Knights, one Marquess, one Viscount and a Lord.

The Stewards expressed the "hope, in the name of the Jockey Club, that the above gentlemen will take care that the riders be provided with dresses accordingly."

The Duke of Devonshire and his descendants deserve credit for having continued to race with the "Straw colour" specified in the 1762 resolution right through to the present day. Many owners, however, ignored the Jockey Club's invitation to register their colours. By 1794 only 38 appear to have done so out of about 300 known owners and in 1833 the figures were 150 and 700 respectively.

In some cases, owners had colours but did not register them while some colours continued to be used by more than one owner. In 1808 six owners raced with plain black colours and four with plain white.

By then a 'Registry of Racing Colours' had existed for over 20 years but the proper registration of owners' colours was only established in 1870, with compulsory registration arriving in 1890.

Nowadays owners are presented with a choice of two colour schemes, standard and bespoke.

They have 18 colours to choose from for display on the body, sleeves and cap, with 25 different designs available on the body, such as large spots or a triple diamond. On the sleeves, there are a dozen designs to choose from, including a diabolo, stripes and chevrons. On to the cap, with 10 options, including diamonds or a star.

If that isn't enough, since 2017, for a fee of £5,000, owners can design their own colours, within reason. "The colours must be distinguishable by judges and describable by commentators, as well as clearly identifiable to members of the public."

Once your colours have been registered for five years, they can be advertised for sale. At the time of writing, royal blue and yellow diabolo, striped sleeves, quartered cap are yours for £1,000 while the more distinctive black, white chevrons, black sleeves, white cap is advertised for £9,500.

Personally, I hanker after the colours once worn by horses owned by the notorious 'King of the Ringers', Peter Christian Barrie (see curiosity 82).

5 DEATH STRETCHES OUT ITS HAND

The Hennessy Cognac Gold Cup is one of jump racing's most famous races, or was until 2017, when it became, more mundanely, the Ladbrokes Trophy.

From its creation in 1957, the roll-call of winners was littered with great horses, particularly in its early years, when there were fewer suitable conditions races for the best chasers, who therefore contested the most valuable and prestigious handicaps, of which the Hennessy was very much one.

Mandarin (1957, 1961), Arkle (1964, 1965) and Denman (2007, 2009) all won the Hennessy twice and nine winners also won the Cheltenham Gold Cup, including the same trio of Mandarin (1962), Arkle (1964, 1965, 1966) and Denman (2008). Many Clouds, winner of the Hennessy in 2014, went on to win the following year's Grand National.

It was a great race won by many great horses as well as by a few less great ones, which brings us to Ghofar. In 2002, the racing historian and statistician John Randall cast his cool eye over the list of Hennessy winners and found Ghofar wanting. As he put it, "If the 43 Hennessy winners are assessed on the merit of their best form, Ghofar ranks at the very bottom."

Ghofar's future had looked rosy in 1989, when the David Elsworth-trained six-year-old narrowly beat Brown Windsor to win the Hennessy in record time. It was an exciting race but the wielder of a bucket of cold water could have pointed out that Brown Windsor was giving the blinkered Ghofar 15lb, that the going was fast and the field uncharacteristically small, only eight strong. It was to be more than four years before Ghofar won another race. Not that it matters because Ghofar is incidental to this story. It is his connections that matter.

By virtue of their Hennessy successes, Ghofar and Mandarin were connected. When Mandarin won the 1957 Hennessy he was ridden by an amateur jockey, Mr John Lawrence. Lawrence's sister, Enid, married Hugh Dundas, who was in little danger of becoming a jockey himself, as he was 6ft 4ins tall.

Lawrence, later Lord Oaksey, was a distinguished and much loved racing journalist, broadcaster and fund raiser. In 2011, he resurrected his connection with the Hennessy by breeding and part-owning the winner, Carruthers. None of that matters much, either, because it is Dundas who is the subject of interest.

If Lord Oaksey encouraged his brother-in-law to become a racehorse owner, his encouragement was only partially successful. Dundas was the half-owner of Ghofar but Ghofar's glorious success did not prompt Dundas to expand his portfolio. Ghofar raced on in his colours until 1994, the year before Dundas's death, and thereafter in those of Lady Dundas, but there were no more equine purchases. None of that really matters, either. What matters is Hugh Dundas's life before Ghofar.

Born in 1920, in 1939 he fulfilled his ambition to join the Royal Air Force and become a pilot. The Second World War started that September and in March 1940, aged 19, Dundas flew his first mission in a Spitfire. In August, during the Battle of Britain, he was lucky to escape alive when his plane was shot down by a German Messerschmitt 109. He just managed to force his way out of the cockpit and open his parachute in time.

Winston Churchill had urged soldiers to display "a sincere desire to engage the enemy." It wasn't easy. "When it comes to the point," Dundas observed, "a sincere desire to stay alive is all too likely to get the upper hand. That was the impulse which consumed me at that moment that day. And that was to be the impulse which I had to fight against, to try and try and try again to overcome, during the years which followed."

Hugh 'Cocky' Dundas. In 1944, aged 24, Dundas became the youngest ever Group Captain.

In eight days straddling August and September 1940, the 616 Squadron to which Dundas belonged lost five pilots killed or missing and five others wounded. "Death stretched out its hand to touch me every day," he wrote. "Everybody was frightened and everybody knew that everybody else was frightened." Dundas felt fear but faced it down.

In November 1940 his brother John, also a pilot, was killed. In May 1941, Dundas was shot down again and survived a crash landing. The following year he again managed to crash land without being killed. In 1944, there was a repeat performance.

By then Dundas had set some remarkable records, a testimony to his courage and character. At the end of 1941, aged only 21, he became a Squadron Leader; in 1943, a Wing Commander in charge of five squadrons of Spitfires. Towards the end of 1944, Dundas became the youngest ever Group Captain, aged 24.

That year, his team were flying in support of the Allied invasion of Italy, and facing intense flak on a daily basis. "With good luck," Dundas wrote, "you would get through the barrage unscathed. With only a bit of luck you would sustain a hit but would still be able to fly home.

"With bad luck you would be forced to bale out or to crash land. With no luck at all you would be killed. It was my job to ensure that fear was held within restraint."

In a macabre twist, a consignment of bombs arrived with faulty fuses. In mid-flight, the Spitfires carrying them exploded. One pilot, his nerves in shreds, fired at Dundas's plane.

Dundas led from the front, incredibly brave. Jockeys risk their lives and break their bones but no one is doing their best to kill them on a daily basis, except perhaps for a particularly malevolent novice chaser.

After the war, Dundas eventually became managing director then chairman of BET, an industrial conglomerate. Subsequently he was chairman of Thames Television. In 1987 he was knighted.

The following year, the year before Ghofar won the Hennessy, Dundas's account of his wartime experiences was published. *Flying Start. A Fighter Pilot's War Years* tells a remarkable story. I've given away a lot of books but I've kept the signed copy Hugh Dundas gave me after interviewing him in 1989; a special curiosity.

Chapter

2

Jockeys

In which Liam bares his teeth • Lester licks ice cream and prefers a cheque • Frank goes legless • Seb takes his boots off • Christopher does what he shouldn't • Frankie chews gum • Fred's life ends sadly.

6 LIAM BARES HIS TEETH

Raceriding poses a threat to virtually every part of a jockey's body, including their teeth. Fortunate the jump jockey who retires with as many teeth as he started out with, or avoids smiling in front of a camera to reveal unflattering gaps.

Unusually, Liam Treadwell's smile revealed a set of his own teeth yet led to him displaying a different set a year later.

The smile that triggered the transformation was forced out of him by Clare Balding during a television interview after Treadwell won the 2009 Grand National on 100-1 shot Mon Mome.

With trademark enthusiasm but subsequent regret, Balding said, "Give us a big grin." When the victorious but shy jockey kept his teeth hidden, she galloped on with "No, no, let's see your teeth."

Treadwell's teeth were unusually small with conspicuous gaps between them. "He hasn't got the best teeth in the world," Balding remarked, "but you can afford to go and get them done now."

It was unintentionally insensitive, the BBC received 2,000 complaints and Balding apologised, but the interview turned out to be the proverbial blessing in disguise.

The exchange came to the attention of Dr Thang Nghiem, a leading dental practitioner and co-founder of the Ultrasmile practice in London. Nghiem

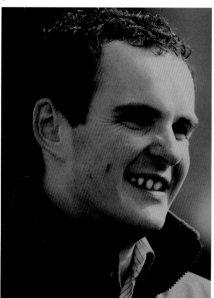

Liam Treadwell's victory on Mon Mome at 100-1 in the 2009 Grand National led to a change of teeth.

offered a complete makeover of Treadwell's teeth without charge. After months of treatment the jockey emerged with a set of teeth anyone would be proud to smile with. "Clare Balding did me a favour when she teased me on television," Treadwell said. "Because of the way my teeth were, I've spent years hiding them and now I'm discovering a new confidence. My teeth are gleaming. It's amazing."

Ultrasmile were smiling, too. Having reported a pre-tax profit of less than £70,000 during the year ended March 2010, six years later the figure had shot up to over half a million pounds. Perhaps Treadwell's teeth helped things along.

There was a sad end to the tale. In 2016 Treadwell suffered a head injury in a fall at Bangor which had lasting effects. The Injured Jockeys Fund gave help, as it has given help to so many jockeys in difficulty, but in 2020, aged 34, Treadwell committed suicide.

Stan Mellor, champion jump jockey from 1960 to 1962 and the first to ride 1,000 winners, also disliked displaying his teeth, the paucity of which prompted Mellor to acquire a false set.

For safety reasons, jockeys were not allowed to wear false teeth when riding so Mellor tucked them up his sleeve, in case of a post-race interview. One day he had a fall and lay on the ground in agony, clutching his arm. Elain, his wife, dashed up. "Have you broken your arm?" she asked. "No," groaned Stan, "they bit me."

Elain once feared that worse had happened. Stan had a fall at Cheltenham. The feeble protective headgear worn by jockeys in those days shot off and rolled away. In the grandstand, Elain screamed out, "Oh my God, his head has come off!"

Stan kept his head until 2020, when he died, aged 83.

7 LESTER LICKS ICE CREAM .....

Colin Fleetwood-Jones was ghosting a weekly column for Lester Piggott in the *Daily Star*, and finding it hard work. It was proving difficult to extract information from the notoriously monosyllabic jockey.

Fleetwood-Jones lived in Sussex and on a day off he drifted across to Brighton for a relaxing afternoon at the races. Walking back to his car after the last race, he heard a familiar voice behind him. "Hello," said Lester, "are you driving back to London? Can I have a lift?"

"I'm sorry, Lester, I only live a few miles away. I was going back home."

"That's a pity," said Lester, "I've got some good stuff for your column."

Fleetwood-Jones took a deep breath. "All right, then."

Lester 'Stoneface' Piggott, a connoisseur of ice cream.

They got into his car, drove down the hill and turned on to the London road. "No," said Piggott, "not that way, go this way."

Puzzled and increasingly irritated, Fleetwood-Jones followed Piggott's directions, turning this way and that through the back streets of Brighton. Eventually his passenger told him to pull in.

Lester got out, crossed the road and disappeared into a small shop. After a few minutes he came back, sat down and started to lick the ice cream he had just bought. "They sell the best ice cream in the country there," he said.

It was too much even for the compliant journalist. "I don't suppose you thought to buy me one?" said Fleetwood-Jones, a touch sharply.

"Oh," replied Lester, looking surprised. "I didn't know you liked ice cream."

8 ..... AND PREFERS A CHEQUE

It was Robert Ellis's dream to have a horse ridden by the great Lester Piggott. In 1973 he had a chance to make his dream come true.

Ellis owned a three-year-old called Pirate Way. On 9 July, ridden by Roger Wernham for trainer Ron Vibert, Pirate Way was unplaced in a six furlong handicap at Windsor. Ellis then went on a business trip to Brazil.

While there, he had a call from Vibert, who told him that Piggott had phoned and asked to ride Pirate Way in a race he was entered for at Nottingham. According to Piggott, the horse had been given a poor ride at Windsor. If Piggott was given the ride, he would win.

Ellis didn't usually allow his horses to run if he was unable to be there to watch but this was different. He gave his permission.

On 19 July, over a mile at Nottingham, Pirate Way, at 7-1, won the Playhouse Handicap with Piggott in the saddle.

Ellis was delighted. As a present for the winning jockey he bought a set of stone ashtrays made in Brazil. A few days after his return, he went to Windsor races and presented the ashtrays to Piggott, telling him how much it meant to have the great man ride one of his horses, and to win on it.

With a distinct lack of enthusiasm, Piggott studied the ashtrays. In the ensuing quiet, Ellis asked if Piggott liked them? "I'd rather have a cheque," said Lester.

Ellis got his cheque book out, walked to the weighing room table and wrote out a cheque. Then he took the ashtrays home with him.

9 FRANK GOES LEGLESS

After the First World War, Frank Wise still had two legs but one of them was wooden. Warfare had also reduced his allocation of ten fingers to seven.

It was a particularly vexing development as Frank, following his father's example, was a keen horseman, a pursuit most easily pursued with a full complement of legs, feet and fingers.

Major Francis Hubert Wise, Frank's father, was a prominent figure in hunting, polo and racing circles in Ireland. Master of the Limerick Hounds from 1899 to 1908, he was also a notable breeder.

When the First World War started, Frank senior went to Canada to purchase horses for the British War Office. By 1917 he was back home, at Rochestown House, Cahir, Co.Tipperary, where he died at the age of 48.

As well as losing a leg and three fingers, Frank junior soon lost the use of Rochestown House, which was burnt down in 1923, during the Irish Civil War. He and his sister moved to the nearby Shamrock Lodge from where, undeterred, Frank, following his father in the possession of a moustache, became Master of the Tipperary Hounds,

In 1928, riding his five-year-old mare Alike, he finished fourth of five finishers in an attritional Irish Grand National. Later that day he won the Fairyhouse Plate on his own Ardfinnan, who won again less than a fortnight later, at Punchestown. The *Sport* newspaper observed, "Mr Frank Wise who, as the majority are aware, wears an artificial limb, is one of the most remarkable horsemen of this or any other era."

As the 1929 edition of the Irish Grand National drew near, *The Irish Times* echoed the *Sport*'s accolade. It remarked that, despite the great handicap of having been badly wounded in the War, Wise was "one of the best amateur riders in Ireland today."

In 1927, his admirable efforts included a remarkable comeback at Powerstown Park (Clonmel). Riding Glengarnock in the Tipperary Hunt Clonmel Harriers Cup, the *Sport*'s correspondent watched as, in a field of four, "Glengarnock made the running until three quarters of a mile from home, when he fell and Jenny took command, with Royal Sheila next. Approaching the straight, Glengarnock, who was remounted, resumed the lead to win by one length."

In 1929, Wise and Alike returned to Fairyhouse for another try at the Irish Grand National – and won easily. According to *The Irish Times*, Alike took up the running going out onto the final circuit and "jumping all the fences in flippant style, she maintained the foremost position and scored a very easy victory." The victory was, the reporter reported, "extremely popular, if one was to judge by the rousing cheers which greeted horse and rider passing the winning post and on reaching the paddock."

The *Sport* glowed with pleasure, believing that *"the success of Alike – or to put it better, the success of Mr Frank Wise – made it a red letter anniversary. Those who did back Alike wanted her to win and those who did not back her were delighted to see her gain such a gallant victory. Not since Loch Lomond's Irish Derby victory (1919) has such a scene of enthusiasm been witnessed as that which signalled Mr Wise's return to scale, the vociferously expressed admiration being, of course, in the main for the rider whose pluck is on a par with that of anyone recorded in history."*

Wise was not alone in being short of a leg. Many limbs were lost during the First World War but Lieutenant Colonel Gerald William Frederick Savile

Frank Wise, minus one leg and three fingers, returns after winning the 1929 Irish Grand National on Alike.

Foljambe, later the 3rd Earl of Liverpool, managed to return from the battlefront intact. That happy state ended, as a local newspaper reported, when Foljambe "had the misfortune to lose a foot as the result of a riding accident at the recent Southwell races. He was riding his own horse, Francis II, and was dragged by his foot getting caught in his stirrup-iron."

Armed with his remaining foot, in 1925 Foljambe rode a memorable double on Bombaria and Lady Biddy at the Melton Hunt NH meeting. Shortly afterwards, less memorably, he was unseated from Lady Biddy, knocked unconscious and taken to hospital with severe concussion.

Concussion was one of several occupational hazards that, before more stringent medical checks were introduced, countless jockeys concealed, denied or downplayed in order to continue riding.

Leading the field in grim determination was the remarkable Beltran de Osorio y Diez de Rivera, the 19th Duke of Alburquerque. From childhood, it was the Spanish monarchist's ambition to ride in the Grand National. Finally, in 1952, aged 33, he did.

Riding Brown Jack III, the Duke fell on the first circuit, at Becher's Brook, broke two vertebrae and was despatched to the nearby Walton Hospital. Four months later, he represented Spain at the Helsinki Olympics, for the Duke was often down but rarely out.

What he needed was a suitable horse and in 1963, aged 44, he reappeared on Jonjo. The pair reached the 21st fence before falling. Unusually, a visit to Walton Hospital was not needed.

That became necessary two years later, after Groomsman fell at Valentine's Brook. The Duke's broken leg brought his career tally of fractures to 22. Utterly undaunted, in 1966 he was back, on L'Empereur, who reached the fourth fence from home before being pulled up.

Hope springing more or less eternal, the Duke bred Nereo and sent him to Fred Winter, who had already won the Grand National four times, twice as a jockey and twice as a trainer. Nereo was the horse the gallant Duke had been waiting for and in 1973, when Nereo was seven and the Duke 54, he tried again. While stablemate Crisp, carrying 12st, jumped magnificently in the lead, only to be cruelly caught by Red Rum, carrying 10st 5lb, the Duke of Alburquerque fought his own battle with a broken stirrup leather. At the eighth fence, the Canal Turn, he finally lost.

The following year Red Rum was back at Aintree, and so was Nereo. More remarkably, so was the Duke of Alburquerque, who had recently had 16 screws removed from his leg and, a week before the National, broke his collar bone in a fall at Newbury.

To Winter's annoyance, the Duke managed to pass a medical inspection. "Fred was furious that I was riding in the race," the Duke recalled, "and his instructions were monosyllabic. Ironically, it was my best performance in the National, when I was in the worst condition. The poor animal had to do everything on his own. He didn't have a jockey on board, but a sack of potatoes."

The 55-year-old potatoes finished eighth. The Duke of Alburquerque had finally succeeded in completing the course. "It gave me enormous satisfaction," he said, "and if I had been in decent shape, we wouldn't have been far away."

A multiple compound fracture of his right leg forced the Duke to miss the 1975 National but in 1976, with another seven screws securing a metal plate in his leg, he partnered Nereo for a third time in the National, falling at the 13th fence. Nereo was unscathed but the Duke was taken to Walton Hospital. The next day, the hospital issued a bulletin, "The Duke's fracture of the right thigh bone and concussion have been dealt with and he is comfortable. It is hoped he will be fit to travel within a few days." "I spent most of my time there unconscious," the Duke remembered, "but when I did wake up, the staff were charming."

Like the poor, wars are always with us and 80 years after Frank Wise won the Irish Grand National when riding with an artificial leg, Captain Guy Disney had his right leg amputated below the knee after his vehicle was blown up during a war in Afghanistan.

Disney belonged to a cavalry regiment and race-riding was one of his impressive list of ambitions. When the British Horseracing Authority initially refused him a licence, Disney filled in the spare time by trekking to the North Pole and then to the South Pole.

In 2015 the BHA relented and Disney, riding with a prosthetic leg, promptly finished third in the Royal Artillery Gold Cup at Sandown Park. Two years later, riding Rathlin Rose, he won the same race and the following month, on the same horse, won the Grand Military Gold Cup, also at Sandown.

In 2018, Disney and Rathlin Rose again won the Royal Artillery Gold Cup and the following year, riding Shanroe Tic Tec, he won an amateur riders' handicap hurdle, again at Sandown.

Frank Wise would have been proud of him.

10 SEB TAKES HIS BOOTS OFF

The thing about Seb Sanders' racing boots was that he wasn't wearing them. He'd worn them for the previous 25 years but on 1 September 2015, at Goodwood, at the age of 43, he didn't.

At about quarter to five, to everyone's surprise, Sanders walked into the parade ring before the Clancy Docwra Charity Stakes without his boots on. He mounted Langley Vale without them on, rode to the start without them on and raced back bootless, finishing fourth of nine to Pettochside.

Everyone except Sanders was puzzled and the racecourse stewards wondered whether or not he had committed a riding offence. After studying the rules, they decided that he hadn't.

Sanders declared himself puzzled that everyone else was puzzled.

"I got held up getting to Goodwood," he explained, "and didn't have time for a sweat, so I left the boots off to make the weight. That's all it was and I think a mountain's been made out of a molehill."

The weight Sanders wanted to make and succeeded in making was 9st 5lb. As riding boots weigh between 7ozs and 10 ozs, the contribution made by their absence was small.

During the previous quarter of a century Sanders had experienced considerable success. He had ridden over 100 winners in each of ten seasons and in 2007, when he was joint champion jockey with Jamie Spencer, he rode 213 winners.

Seb Sanders rides Langley Vale bootless at Goodwood in 2015.

His career was dotted with Group 1 successes, including the 1997 July Cup, 2004 Irish 2000 Guineas and Nunthorpe Stakes, 2008 Oaks and Golden Jubilee Stakes, and the 2010 Cheveley Park Stakes.

In 2004 he had succeeded George Duffield as Sir Mark Prescott's stable jockey, a significant feather in a jockey's cap, and rode over 400 winners for the yard, including at Group 1 level on Albanova, Confidential Lady and Hooray. But in 2008 there were setbacks.

On 10 August, Sanders was at Jagersro racecourse in Malmo, Sweden, to ride two of Prescott's horses. He failed the strict breath test in force on Swedish racetracks, was given a two week ban, and was replaced on Sourire by Fredrik Johansson. Sourire won his race.

More seriously, at Chester on 30 August Sanders was brought down on Speed Gifted, broke a leg and was sidelined for eight months. Towards the end of 2009, he had a further operation to remove the metal plates in his leg. Subsequently, Sanders struggled to keep his weight down, was less successful and in 2012 his retainer with Prescott ended.

2015 was Sanders' final year and his bootless ride a final, curious entry in the record books.

CHRISTOPHER DOES WHAT HE SHOULDN'T

Racehorses set off covered in tack. There are four horseshoes, one per foot, a saddle, to keep the rider in place, and a girth, to keep the saddle in place. There are weight cloths and number cloths. There are reins, a bridle and a bit, and nosebands, to help the jockey control the horse's speed and direction. Sometimes there are sheepskin nosebands, to help the horse's owner work out which one is his. There are tongue ties, to help the horse breathe, and blinkers, visors, hoods and cheekpieces, to try to persuade their wearer to concentrate on winning. When the horse reaches the winning post, if it does, not every item is always in the same place as the horse.

Shoes come off, bits slip, saddles slip, weight cloths fall to the ground and, one way and another, jockeys, trainers, owners, racegoers and punters are given another reason to believe that the Lord, in his infinite malice, has singled them out for another dose of misfortune and misery.

And so it was that on 23 January 1975, at Huntingdon, Mr Christopher Thomson-Jones set off on Even Sail to tackle the three mile Wyton Handicap Chase. The task the promising amateur rider faced was seemingly straightforward. Even Sail had won two of his three most recent races, the latest on Boxing Day over the same course and distance. When he was beaten, it was by the useful Even Dawn. Even Sail was in top form.

To make things easy for him, he faced just three opponents. Beau By boasted a record as bad as his odds of 33-1 implied. Avondhu was a 12-year-old in clear decline while the six-year-old Pava's Boy had bits and pieces of form but, at Leicester in mid-December, had finished a long way behind Even Sail. A 9lb pull in the weights was unlikely to bridge the gap. So bookmakers, ever fearful of being tricked, thought they smelt a possible rat in the emerging patterns of betting.

Managers at William Hill shops in York and Tadcaster reported big cash bets on Avondhu and Pava's Boy in singles and reverse forecasts. Hill passed its suspicions on to Ladbrokes, Coral and Mecca. Coral already had suspicions of their own. A spokesman said, "There was too much interest in horses that seemed unlikely to beat the favourite. We advised our betting shops and racecourse representatives to be extra cautious."

Nowadays, bookmakers offer 'early prices,' enabling customers to take the odds on offer hours before betting at the racecourse begins. In 1975, early prices weren't available and bets were settled at the official Starting Price – the price generally on offer in the racecourse betting ring when the race started.

Ladbrokes got on the phone to 'blow' money back to the racecourse, to shorten the odds on Avondhu and Pava's Boy. While Even Sail drifted from 7-4 on to 5-4 against, Avondhu's price shrank from 5-2 to 11-8 and Pava's Boy's from 6-1 to 3-1. It was a way of reducing off-course bookmakers' liabilities on particular horses.

The quartet set off towards the first fence but Even Sail failed to reach it. Thomson-Jones pulled the horse up, leaving Avondhu to stroll home, a distance clear of Pava's Boy.

When the local stewards asked Thomson-Jones what had happened, he told them that, while adjusting his stirrup leathers at the start, he had inadvertently unfastened a buckle on his saddle. When they galloped off, the saddle slipped. The stewards drew Thomson-Jones's attention to his responsibility for seeing that the tack was in a fit condition for racing, and cautioned him.

Those who had bet that Even Sail would be defeated at Huntingdon did not all receive their winnings. "Thousands of pounds are believed to have been paid out," *The Times* later reported, "but the larger bookmaking firms refused to settle the bigger sums until an investigation into the race had been carried out."

The police were called in, by which time Thomson-Jones had departed for South Carolina, where he worked as a work rider. "We would very much like to see Mr Chris Thomson-Jones," said Detective Chief Inspector Strickland Carter, "and I feel sure he is aware of this but so far he has not contacted us."

The wheels of justice turned slowly round until, on 8 September 1976, the Jockey Club held an inquiry into the race. Interest in the outcome was increased by Thomson-Jones's family connections. His father, Harry Thomson-Jones, always known as Tom Jones, was a well known and successful jumps trainer in Newmarket, who later concentrated on the Flat, while his older half-brother Tim was a multiple champion amateur jockey.

Christopher, then aged 22, did not attend the inquiry but submitted a statement in which "he admitted deliberately preventing a horse he rode at Huntingdon last year from winning." He was banned for seven years.

Two years later, he returned to Britain but did not stay. He lived, and in 2018 was still living, in South Carolina.

12 FRANKIE CHEWS GUM

Frankie Dettori, the most celebrated and successful jockey of his generation, thrived on the international stage but not every raceday was a triumph for the charismatic Italian.

On 4 January 1992 Dettori was riding at Sha Tin racecourse, in Hong Kong. He had three rides that day, none of which managed better than fourth place.

Although Dettori failed to catch the judge's eye, he caught those of the stewards of the Hong Kong Jockey Club, well known for expecting high standards. Something about the effervescent 21-year-old's behaviour troubled them and they summoned Dettori and cautioned him as to his future conduct. In future, they told the rising star, he was not to chew gum when riding in Hong Kong. Dettori revealed, "They told me it was not a fast food store."

Chewing chewing gum was not actually illegal in Hong Kong but perhaps the stewards were mindful of a regulation that had come into force in Singapore the previous day. Under the authoritarian direction of Lee Kuan Yew, the Prohibition of Imports (Chewing Gum) Order 1992 banned the manufacture, import and sale of chewing gum, although not the act of chewing it.

Dettori took it in his stride but the Wrigley Company was less sanguine. In 2003, when the USA and Singapore were negotiating a Free Trade Agreement, chewing gum was one of the sticking points. The chewing gum manufacturer lobbied hard for the Agreement to address the matter. Wrigley was partially

Frankie Dettori, chewing gum chewer.

successful. When the Agreement came into force in 2004, the sale of medicinal chewing gum by dentists and pharmacists was allowed.

That was too late for Dettori. When he won the Singapore Plate on Timahs in 2000 and, two years later, the Singapore Gold Cup on Kutub and Singapore Airlines International Cup on Grandera, he still needed to be careful on the chewing gum front.

13. FRED'S LIFE ENDS SADLY

On the afternoon of Monday 8 November 1886 Fred Archer, the idol of his age, killed himself, aged 29.

Two years earlier his wife Nellie had died in childbirth, not a rare fate in those days when the maternal mortality rate was about 40 per 1,000 births; today, it is less than one per 10,000. In Victorian England, having children was a dangerous business, for mother and child. The Archers' previous child had died shortly after birth.

His wife's death was not the only trigger for Archer's suicide but it played a part in producing the state of mind that led him to get out of his sick bed, pick up his revolver and shoot himself.

For all his unmatched triumphs, Archer carried the seeds of self-destruction. In Britain in the 1870s, the average height of men at the age of 21 was 5ft 5ins, compared with 5ft 9 ins today. The average height of Flat jockeys was less. Archer was 5ft 9ins tall and in adulthood waged debilitating war with his body to ride at less than 9st. Even as a precociously talented child, he had sometimes struggled to make weights that generally required poverty and deprivation to achieve.

In 1862, the minimum riding weight was raised from 4st 7lb to 5st 7lb. Six years later, aged 11, Archer was apprenticed to leading trainer Mat Dawson, had his first ride at the age of 12 and rode his first winner in 1870, aged 13. In 1872, he was given the ride on Salvanos in the Cesarewitch and won, carrying the minimum 5st 7lb.

The relentless battle with his weight was combined with another ultimately fatal ingredient, Archer's unbending determination to succeed. The records he set and the dominance he achieved owed much to his driven personality. Quiet out of his bespoke 1lb saddle, Archer was fearsome in it.

A different jockey with the same body could never have amassed Archer's record of 13 successive championships (1874 to 1886), 21 Classic successes, and a career total of 2,748 winners from 8,084 starts, an extraordinary strike rate of 34 per cent. In 1885 he rode 246 winners, a record that stood until 1933, when Gordon Richards, with the benefit of better transport, rode 259.

Fred Archer as seen by Spy in Vanity Fair, 1881.

Archer never relented nor bowed to the toll it took on his physical and mental health. Like other jockeys, he put on weight during the winter, then resorted to extreme measures to lose it again in time for the start of the Flat season. In Archer's case, the extremes were more extreme. Up to a more natural 11st during the off-season, he used a frightening purgative combined with Turkish baths to get down to around 8st 7lb.

On 1 May 1880, when he was 23, Archer was savaged by a horse on the gallops and his arm badly injured. Determined not to miss his Derby ride on Bend Or on 26 May, he lost 13lb in four days. He must have looked even more haunted than usual. Archer rode with his injured arm strapped to an iron rod. It was so painful that when he went to use his whip, he dropped it. He still drove Bend Or to a narrow victory.

In 1883, Archer married Mat Dawson's niece, Helen, known as Nellie, and finally moved out of his lodgings at Heath House, where Dawson trained, to the newly built Falmouth House. Lord Falmouth was Dawson's principal owner who retained Archer as his jockey and supplied him with many of his best rides.

Distraught at Nellie's death, Archer was persuaded to take a break and go on a tour of America. He returned and resumed the same draining regime and record-breaking results, including winning the Triple Crown on Ormonde in Archer's final season, 1886.

That October, he agreed to ride St Mirin in the Cambridgeshire at 8st 6lb. By the day of the race, 26 October, drastic action had forced his riding weight down to 8st 7lb. Riding, according to *The Sporting Life* (27 October 1886), "with a lack of his ordinary dash and vigour," Archer was narrowly beaten by The Sailor Prince.

On Thursday 4 November, after riding Lucretius and Tommy Tittlemouse at Lewes, both beaten favourites, he said that he felt unwell and was taken back to Newmarket. The next day a local doctor, Dr Wright, was summoned. He asked Dr Latham, from Cambridge, to attend. On Saturday, as Archer's condition deteriorated, the doctors penned a bulletin that read, "Falmouth House, 6 November, 1886, 6 p.m. Mr F. Archer has returned home suffering from the effects of a serious chill, followed by a high fever. Signed, P.W. Latham and J.R. Wright."

On Monday morning, there was mixed news. Shortly after 9am another bulletin read, "November 8, 1886. Mr Fred Archer is suffering from an attack of typhoid fever. There is an improvement in his symptoms today. Signed, J.R. Wright."

Emily Coleman, Archer's sister, who lived with him at Falmouth House, testified at his inquest, held the next day, that "He came home from Lewes unwell on Thursday last but I did not think he was very bad as he did not go to bed until about his usual time, 11.30, but when he was unable to get up on Friday morning I sent for Dr. Wright.

"He wandered a little during his illness and seemed to forget things. He appeared better yesterday morning, but during a long conversation I had with him he occasionally forgot the subject and frequently expressed himself anxious about his recovery.

"At his bidding, a little after two, the nurse was sent out of the room, deceased saying he wished to speak to me alone. I noticed nothing unusual about the circumstance, as he had done so several times before. When the nurse went out I was looking out of the window and deceased said 'are they coming?'

"Almost immediately after I heard a noise, and looking round saw that my brother was out of bed and had something in his hand. I ran to him and when

I saw it was a revolver tried to push it away. The revolver was in his left hand, and I had my hand in, trying to push it. He then threw his right arm around my neck and fired the revolver with his left hand. I saw him doing it but could not stop him, he seemed awfully strong. He then fell flat on his back close to a chair. I was screaming, but he never spoke."

Coleman added, "I had no idea there was a revolver in the room; it was in a pedestal by the side of the bed."

The six-chambered revolver bore the inscription, 'Presented to Thomas Roughton, on his winning the Liverpool Cup with Sterling.' That was in 1873 and Roughton, Sterling's owner, gave it to the winning jockey as a gift. Only Archer and his valet, Harry Sargent, knew that the revolver was in his room.

Sargent's evidence was that, "About a month ago, when the burglars broke into Mr Jewitt's house, my master sent me with the revolver to get it repaired and ordered me to always place it in the pedestal in his room when he was at home, but to take it into my own bedroom when he was away. I did not expect my master home last Thursday, but heard he had telegraphed to say he should be. I therefore put the revolver into the pedestal according to my orders. There was no lock on it."

Unfortunately, Sargent did not tell either Archer's sister or the doctors that there was a revolver in the pedestal.

Archer was fevered and delirious but his sister also linked his suicide to the struggle to get his weight down to ride St Mirin in the Cambridgeshire. She said, "I thought he did too much to ride St. Mirin. He seemed very anxious, he has seldom ridden so light as 8st 7lbs lately."

The coroner told the jury that there was no doubt that Archer had shot himself while in a state of unsound mind, his weak condition and fever having disordered his brain to the extent that he was insane at the time of his death.

Accordingly, the jury unanimously returned a verdict that "Frederick James Archer, while in a state of temporary insanity, induced by typhoid fever, did kill himself by then and there shooting himself with a revolver in the mouth and severing the spinal cord."

The offending weapon is now kept at the National Horse Racing Museum in Newmarket.

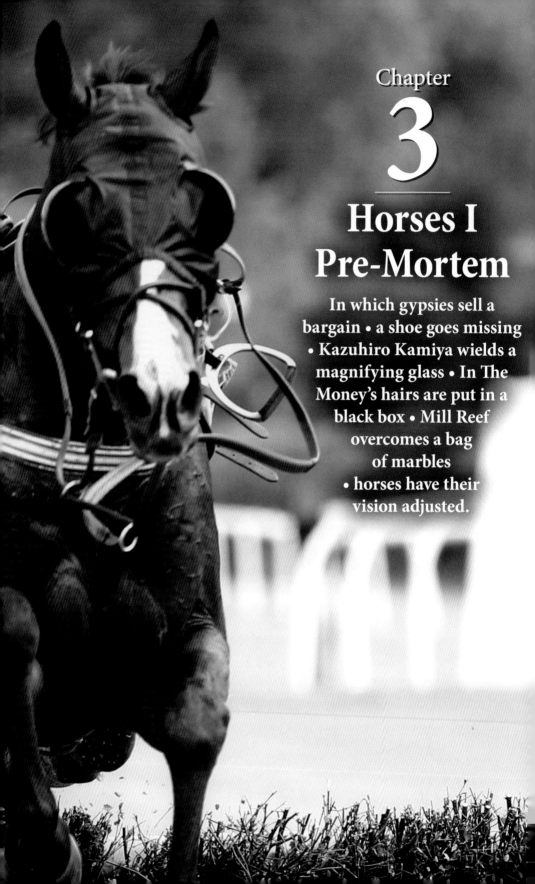

Chapter

3

Horses I Pre-Mortem

In which gypsies sell a bargain • a shoe goes missing • Kazuhiro Kamiya wields a magnifying glass • In The Money's hairs are put in a black box • Mill Reef overcomes a bag of marbles • horses have their vision adjusted.

14 GYPSIES SELL A BARGAIN

Henry Radford had a patch over one eye and a liking for Scotch whisky. He owned a mare called Lily Pond, who was barely a racehorse, and mated her with Master Stephen, who was better, but not much.

Lily Pond once won a point-to-point race, but only once. That was a maiden race at Cattistock, in Dorset, in 1960. She was unplaced in all her other 10 point-to-points and amassed a record of 0-26 over hurdles.

Master Stephen was better, winning twice on the Flat and twice over hurdles in the mid-1960s but he was a modest performer and unlikely stallion.

In 1972, when Lily Pond was 17, their unpromising union produced Master Smudge. He was the only winner Lily Pond ever foaled.

Radford was to be seen at Taunton market and so was John Tarr, a local pig farmer. Tarr thought the ill-bred creature might suit him for hunting so he arranged to buy him. He asked Radford if it would be all right to leave the horse with him for a week but when he went to collect it, Radford had sold the horse to some gypsies from a nearby camp for a crate of whisky.

So Tarr went to the gypsy camp, where the colt was tied to a fence, surrounded by children. He bought the gypsies' horse for the price of the crate of whisky, about £50, plus another £25. As his acquisition was an unbroken two-year-old, hunting him was a long way off, so Master Smudge was for sale at the right price.

Arthur Barrow was a Somerset farmer and livestock transporter who, with his father, Ken, trained a few point-to-pointers at Over Stowey, near Bridgwater. He regularly collected pigs from Tarr's farm. As he arrived one day, a horse came cantering across a field towards him. "He was the ugliest two-year-old you can imagine," Barrow told me. "If you had ten horses to choose from, he'd be your ninth choice but he moved so nicely, as if floating on air. And it was as if he was watching me."

When the pigs were loaded and Barrow drove off, the horse cantered lightly along beside the lorry. "It seemed as if he was telling me to buy him." Barrow tried to get the horse out of his mind but Master Smudge stayed resolutely in it.

So Barrow bought the ugly colt and his horse collar for luck, for £312. It was £312 wonderfully well spent for, as Barrow remarked, "looks don't win races." Luck sometimes does and it was lucky that in 1976, when Barrow went to enter Master Smudge for a selling hurdle at Taunton, he discovered that Tarr had not registered the horse with Weatherbys and that Barrow couldn't enter him until he was registered. "That was lucky," Barrow said, "because if he'd run, we'd have lost him."

His owner-trainer kept the name Tarr told him he'd given the colt; Master from the sire, Master Stephen, and Smudge from the white smudge he had on the side of his nose.

Over the winter of 1976/77, Master Smudge won two hurdle races and had good placed form against some of the best novice hurdlers, including The Dealer. He was entitled to a place in the inevitably competitive field for the Cheltenham Festival's Sun Alliance Hurdle.

The Dealer was favourite and Master Smudge, ridden by amateur Mr Richard Hoare, 33-1. The permit-trained outsider finished in front of The Dealer, beaten only by Irish raider Counsel Cottage.

Barrow, his wife Pauline and father Ken were elated, and Barrow believed that his £312 purchase would prove better over fences. In 1978, Master Smudge graduated to chasing. It was not a smooth transition although that autumn he won a novice chase at Newton Abbot and the following February won a handicap chase at Stratford. Just over two weeks later Barrow, optimistically, sent Master Smudge back to Cheltenham for the Sun Alliance Chase.

Silver Buck, from Tony Dickinson's powerful northern yard, had shown himself to be a high class chaser, a justified favourite likely to be too good for Master Smudge. But Master Smudge was a lucky horse; the weather was bad and the going heavy, perfect for Master Smudge, not for Silver Buck.

The horse once sold for a crate of whisky was equipped with endless stamina, willingness, head-down determination and a rare ability to relish the rain-softened ground of an era unfamiliar with modern drainage systems. At 16-1, Master Smudge outslogged his rivals.

"He had big feet and loved soft ground," Barrow said. "He wasn't the biggest but he never knew when he was beaten; he would gallop until he dropped."

The following month Master Smudge finished a creditable runner-up to Diamond Edge in the prestigious Whitbread Gold Cup at Sandown.

When the new 1979/80 season started, Barrow's champion collected plenty of prize money and recognition by finishing fifth in the Hennessy Gold Cup, fourth in the Welsh National and runner-up, eight days later, in the Mandarin Chase at Newbury.

Yet he was not considered to have the class to win a Cheltenham Gold Cup and, despite the blessing, for him, of testing conditions, Master Smudge started at 14-1. Three fences from home, with horses pulling up behind him, Richard Hoare's mount was way adrift. Two fences from home, pretty much the same. As the exciting, front-running Tied Cottage, ridden beautifully by Tommy Carberry, galloped on to an easy eight length victory, Master Smudge made up an unlikely amount of ground to finish second. His finishing effort would prove even more important than it seemed at the time.

Tied Cottage was found to have traces of the banned substance theobromine in his post-race sample, from contaminated feed, and was automatically disqualified. When Barrow was told, he said, "I can't believe it. Are you sure it isn't a hoax?"

For Tied Cottage's connections it was an appallingly cruel outcome. The previous year, Tied Cottage had fallen at the final fence when disputing the lead with Alverton. When the 1980 Gold Cup was run, Tied Cottage's trainer, Dan Moore, was too ill to be there and Anthony Robinson, the horse's owner, who had ridden his horse to victory in the 1979 Irish Grand National, was also terminally ill. Moore died in June and Robinson in August having, two months earlier, gone to Warwick races to hand Arthur Barrow the cherished Gold Cup.

"Anthony Robinson was the most lovely man you could ever wish to meet," Barrow remembers. "He took it on the chin and was genuinely pleased for us. I can't praise him enough."

Master Smudge en route to victory in the 1979 Sun Alliance Chase, proving himself well worth the price of a crate of whisky.

Three weeks later, Barrow invited the whole village of Over Stowey to a party in the village hall. It was a celebration of one of the fairy tale stories that give heart and soul to the sport of horseracing.

When unromantic analysts cast their eyes over the 1980 Gold Cup, they were less taken with Master Smudge's performance. John Randall's cold gaze viewed Master Smudge as "the worst Gold Cup winner in the race's history." He had won it due to Tied Cottage's unfortunate disqualification and "by virtue of having plodded his way past 15-year-old Mac Vidi," who had finished third. (*Racing Post*, 4 March 2010).

Arthur Barrow's champion did not have the virtue of outstanding class but he had other virtues and they gave his owner-trainer, jockey Richard Hoare and those close to them an unmatched thrill to savour for a lifetime – and a lot of prize-money.

Master Smudge's Sun Alliance Chase success was worth £12,832, the Gold Cup another £35,997 (about £155,500 today). In 1981, when ridden by Richard Linley, he won the Mandarin Chase, worth £4,552, and then the Golden Miller Chase at Cheltenham along with £13,403. Then there was all the place money. It was remarkable for a horse once bought for a few bottles of whisky.

Master Smudge was retired at the age of 13 and stayed with Barrow for the rest of his life, sometimes being taken hunting by 'Bonk' Walwyn, trainer Peter Walwyn's wife. One day, when he was 25, Master Smudge lay down in his field and died peacefully.

Eventually, in 2015, Arthur Barrow told his and Master Smudge's remarkable story in a privately published work, *From Traveller's Camp to Gold*.

15 A SHOE GOES MISSING

At the end of 1993, Sheikh Mohammed and his brothers met and decided to call his vision of making Dubai the base for a global horseracing enterprise, Godolphin. Together with the Byerley Turk and Darley Arabian, the Godolphin Arabian was the forefather of all today's thoroughbreds.

The bold initiative demanded bold colours. In April 1994 the royal blue colours bought from trainer Alan Bailey for £26,000 (see curiosity 59) were registered with Weatherbys. The same month, a small team of horses that had wintered in Dubai were flown to Britain and on 28 April, at Newmarket, Seismograph became the first horse to win a race in Godolphin's silks.

Initially, not every Godolphin runner carried the royal blue colours. When Balanchine ran, and was beaten by Las Meninas by a thin hair in that year's 1000 Guineas, jockey Frankie Dettori wore joint-owner Sheikh Maktoum's familiar blue and white silks.

Lammtarra winning the 1995 Derby, minus a shoe.

When she won the Oaks, to give Sheikh Mohammed's enterprise its first Classic success, Balanchine did wear the Godolphin blue, and again when winning the Irish Derby. Godolphin had arrived.

That August, a two-year-old colt called Lammtarra, trained by Alex Scott and owned by Saeed Maktoum Al Maktoum, Sheikh Maktoum's son, made a winning debut in a Listed race at Newbury. Lammtarra boasted a rare pedigree, being by a Derby winner, Nijinsky, out of an Oaks winner, Snow Bride. Scott thought highly enough of the debutant to back him with Ladbrokes, £1,000 at 33-1 for the 1995 Derby.

The following month Scott was murdered by a disaffected employee. Lammtarra didn't race again that year and was sent to winter in Dubai. He entered the New Year with a fever lasting several weeks and on 1 February was admitted to the still unfinished Equine Hospital.

On 12 February he returned to Godolphin's stables at Al Quoz; on 18 February he was ridden for the first time since becoming ill; on 6 March he started trotting and on 16 March had his first canter. On 11 April, two months before the Derby, he did his first piece of serious work.

By the time he flew back to England on 2 May, to join Saeed bin Suroor, Godolphin's new trainer, at Moulton Paddocks in Newmarket, Lammtarra had done just three short pieces of work.

On 14 May the select team's well-being was apparent when, on that day, Vettori, Flagbird and Heart Lake won Group 1 races in France, Italy and Japan. On 2 June, eight days before the Derby, Lammtarra showed that he was also in top form when outworking Vettori over a mile. Walter Swinburn came back and told Godolphin's Jeremy Noseda, "He'll win the Derby."

On 9 June, the day before the Derby, Godolphin won the Oaks with Moonshell. It still didn't seem likely that Lammtarra would win the Derby. The only horse in the twentieth century to have won the race on its seasonal reappearance was Grand Parade, in 1919. Only two horses, Bois Roussel in 1938 and Morston in 1973 had won it with just a single racecourse appearance to their names. Lammtarra was sixth in the betting, at 14-1.

Sheikh Mohammed gave Swinburn his instructions, which were to give Lammtarra a positive ride and take up a handy position early on. Swinburn, who had won the Derby twice, on Shergar and Shahrastani, and was mindful of nine time Derby winning jockey Lester Piggott's approach to riding the course, wanted to nurse Lammtarra up the opening hill.

Early on in the race, Lammtarra was fairly handy but then got squeezed and dropped back. As they descended Tattenham Hill, he was 12th of the 15 runners.

Coming into the straight, Swinburn made ground but two furlongs out Lammtarra still appeared to have no chance of winning. He was sixth, well behind the leaders. Then, a furlong from the finish, Lammtarra flew. It was a most unlikely but exciting victory, one that broke the course record.

"From being under pressure and not going anywhere much," said Swinburn, "he ran like a knife through butter. He just put his head down. He was like a lion."

Sheikh Mohammed might have been expected to have been disappointed because Tamure, wearing his own maroon and white silks, had looked set to win until Lammtarra's late swoop. The favourite, Pennekamp, also wearing Sheikh Mohammed's colours, had run disappointingly.

Yet Sheikh Mohammed was delighted and it was he who led in the winner. Lammtarra was carrying Sheikh Mohammed's nephew's green and white colours but he was part of the Godolphin team. "To win the Derby with a horse from Dubai has given me as much pleasure," said Dubai's new Crown Prince, "as winning four Derbys."

It was a memorable and remarkable success, for one more reason. Back at the starting stalls, a stalls handler was holding a horseshoe, the shoe that Lammtarra shed when leaving the stalls. He won the Derby on three shoes.

Alex Scott's death meant that Ladbrokes were not obliged to pay out on his ante-post bet but they sent a cheque to his widow Julia for £33,000.

Sheikh Mohammed was thrilled with the result but less impressed by Swinburn's execution of his instructions. When Lammtarra went on to win the King George VI and Queen Elizabeth Diamond Stakes and Prix de l'Arc de Triomphe, completing a treble only previously achieved by Mill Reef, Frankie Dettori was on board.

They were hard fought successes and, at home, Lammtarra had become difficult, sometimes refusing to work. It was decided to retire him to stud. As a stallion, he was a disappointment and at the end of 1996, Lammtarra was sold to Japan for $33 million. Ten years later he returned to spend his retirement at Dalham Hall Stud, where he died in 2014, aged 22.

I wonder where that horseshoe is?

16 KAZUHIRO KAMIYA WIELDS A MAGNIFYING GLASS

The thing about T.M.Opera O's heart was that it was unusually big, as was the number of yen won by the heart's owner.

Between 1998 and 2001 T.M.Opera O won 1,835 million yen, helped by 14 wins from 26 races, including 6 successes in domestic Group 1 events and one – the 2000 Japan Cup – in an international Group 1. At the time, 1,835 million yen translated into a less spectacular sounding but still satisfying US$16.2 million or about £11 million. At that time, T.M.Opera O was the world's all-time leading prize money winner. Later, Arrogate arrived and, in 2016 and 2017, earned US$17.4 million (£13.6 million) by winning seven of his 11 races, including the 2016 Breeders' Cup Classic and 2017 Pegasus World Cup International and Dubai World Cup.

But back to T.M.Opera O's heart. In 2001 a team of researchers led by Kazuhiro Kamiya took a sophisticated magnifying glass to the great horse's still beating heart and made some striking discoveries, reported two years later in 'Heart Size and Heart Rate Variability of the Top Earning Racehorse in Japan, T.M.Opera O' (*Journal of Equine Science. Vol.14 No.3*).

Kamiya and his colleagues also studied 15 other racehorses. The mean average weight of their hearts' left ventricular mass was 3.4kg compared to T.M.Opera O's 4.6kg (29 per cent heavier). The latter's resting heart rate of 25 beats per minute was significantly lower than the average of 30.3 beats per minute (17.5 per cent lower).

Then there was the horses' low frequency power and high frequency power to consider, as determined by heart rate variability. In both cases, T.M.Opera O's was "considerably higher than those of the other racehorses."

"These results," the researchers concluded, "suggest that a large heart, formed by genetic factors and training, markedly enhanced the parasympathetic nervous activity and reduced the resting heart rate of T.M.Opera O." Quite so.

The same had been suspected in 1789, when an autopsy carried out on the great Eclipse (see curiosity 20) revealed that his heart weighed 6.35kg or, as it was in those days, 14lb. Phar Lap, Australia's equine hero during the Great Depression (see curiosity 23), had a heart of the same weight, compared to the average of 3.5kg to 4.0kg.

Then there was the mighty Secretariat, who won the US Triple Crown in 1973, establishing records for the fastest times in each of the Kentucky Derby, Preakness Stakes and Belmont Stakes, which he won by a staggering 31 lengths. One of the all-time greats, Secretariat boasted a heart estimated to weigh up to 21lb, alias 9.5kg, more than twice the average.

After carrying out an autopsy on Secretariat, Dr Thomas Swerczek said, "We were all shocked. I've seen and done thousands of autopsies on horses and nothing I'd ever seen compared to it. The heart of the average horse weighs about 9lb. This was almost twice the average size, and a third larger than any equine heart I'd ever seen. I think it told us why he was able to do what he did."

During the 1970s, electrocardiographic studies led researchers to conclude that horses with large hearts were capable of greater athletic performances than those with smaller hearts. The use of ultrasound scans made it easier to evaluate heart size. Using ultrasound technology, Lesley Young, at the Animal Health Trust in Newmarket, measured the heart sizes of 400 racehorses and compared them with the horses' official handicap ratings.

Presenting her findings in 2002, Young concluded that "A good horse nearly always has an above average heart size," although the relationship applied to jump horses over longer distances rather than to Flat horses.

Six years later, an article by Rikke Buhl titled, 'A Review of Structural Features of the Equine Athlete's Heart. Is a Large Heart an Advantage for Racing Success?' appeared in the *Proceedings of the American Association of Equine Practitioners* (Vol.54, 2008).

Buhl concluded that "there is a significant correlation between left ventricle size and performance of the horse measured by average prize money per start and official rating for thoroughbreds."

A large heart enabled a horse to maximise the uptake of oxygen. Like Young, Buhl found that the benefits were seen most strongly in National Hunt horses.

Other studies reached similar conclusions but also pointed out limitations to the application of these findings. There was, firstly, the problem of accessing information about particular horses' heart size and function. Other factors needed to be taken into account. A large heart was of little benefit if the horse's conformation created problems, or if its training regime was sub-optimal. Secretariat was admired for his physique and movement well before his exceptionally large heart was revealed. If his legs had been wonky his wonderful heart would have availed him nothing.

It's interesting (well, you've got this far) but for punters seeking paradise, the search continues.

The big hearted TM Opera O winning the 2001 Tenno Sho at Kyoto, Japan.

IN THE MONEY'S HAIRS ARE PUT IN A BLACK BOX

In The Money often was. When he won a small race at Wolverhampton in March 1995, it was the six-year-old's fourth success. By then he had also been second eight times and third eight times.

He wasn't a headline-making horse, like his owner John Bigg's Oxo, who won the 1959 Grand National, but he paid his way at Reg Hollinshead's Staffordshire yard and was popular there, an attractive looking horse, with a nice temperament.

Then something went wrong. In The Money's form went downhill and after he finished a distant last at Wolverhampton in early May 1995, Hollinshead decided to give him a break. It didn't do the trick because when In The Money reappeared at Chester in July, he finished tailed off last.

Another five months off still didn't help. On his return at Lingfield just before Christmas, In The Money was beaten almost 20 lengths. It wasn't like him because In The Money was a trier.

Sarah Hollinshead, Reg's daughter, remembers, "He had hives and was off-colour. The vets treated him and we tried everything to get him right. We changed his feed, changed his bedding, moved stables but nothing worked."

Hives are bumps on the skin caused by an allergic reaction to all sorts of things but as Berys Connop, who worked at the yard, put it, "In The Money's illness was a mystery to all." He was given another break.

One day Sarah and Berys went to an antiques fair in nearby Stafford. Berys was looking for some "horsey jewellery" for her niece and the two of them got talking with a lady running a jewellery stall.

Sarah remembers, "She showed us some crystals and said they were for healing and she was a healer. I asked, 'Do you heal animals?' She said, 'Yes, but not for monetary gain. Have you got an ill dog?' 'No, a horse.' She asked me to take some hair from the horse's chest and put it in an envelope for her."

So they did. Berys took the envelope back to the jeweller, who had told them that she would be sending the hairs to someone with a black box.

Whatever the healer did with In The Money's chest hairs, two weeks later Sarah said to Berys, "God, it's worked. The hives are gone."

On his second run back, In The Money was beaten a neck and then, on 2 April 1996, won at Wolverhampton and won again there a month later. He was back on track.

When In The Money ran for the final time from Hollinshead's yard, in 1997, his career record was 91 runs, 12 wins, 10 seconds and 17 thirds. Not many horses achieve that but then, not many horses have the help of a crystal healer.

18 MILL REEF OVERCOMES A BAG OF MARBLES

No racing follower from that era forgets Mill Reef. What he achieved on the racecourse was extraordinary but there was something else about Paul Mellon's champion, the way he was, that grew his following.

Julian Wilson, the BBC TV's long-time presenter, not an obvious romantic, wrote that "to know him was to love him," which is what his trainer Ian Balding and groom John Hallum did.

Mellon bred Mill Reef at his Rokeby Farm in Virginia and named him after an exclusive club next to his winter home in Antigua. A committed Anglophile, the inheritor of a banking fortune and one of the richest men in America, Mellon chose to send Mill Reef to Balding's Kingsclere yard, near Newbury.

The new arrival was on the small side but neat, compact perfection, with a strikingly easy, athletic action and an endearing temperament. It did not take long for those close to Mill Reef to be in awe of him.

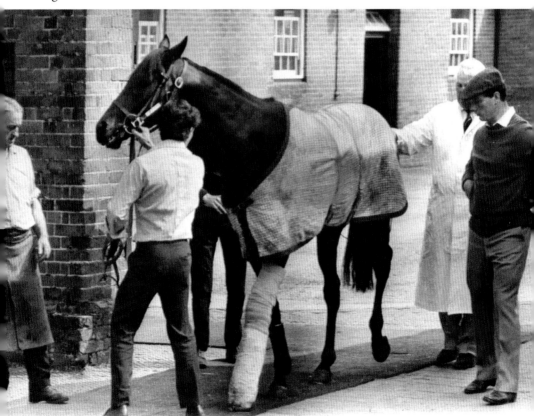

Trainer Ian Balding (in cap) stares at the sorry state of Mill Reef's leg.

For the two-year-old's first piece of work, in February 1970, Balding told Hallum to lead his group of four colts and then go a half-stride faster. When Mill Reef drew effortlessly clear of his hard pressed companions, Balding assumed that Hallum had gone too fast and told him his instructions were to just canter. "Guv'nor, I *was* only cantering."

Another piece of work before Mill Reef's debut at Salisbury in May produced another astonishing display. Yet impressive work at home is not always repeated on the racecourse; it was by Mill Reef.

At Salisbury he brushed aside Fireside Chat, the 9-2 on favourite, who had recently won impressively at Newmarket. Mill Reef then won the Coventry Stakes at Royal Ascot by eight lengths. Uneasy about running him in the Gimcrack Stakes at York on heavy ground, Balding was persuaded by Mellon to run, and Mill Reef sauntered to a 10 length victory.

He rounded off his juvenile season by winning the Dewhurst Stakes impressively, by four lengths. Those were not ordinary victories. Mill Reef, readily identifiable in Mellon's familiar black colours with a gold cross, and wearing a sheepskin noseband, made mincemeat (see curiosity 2) of his rivals and merited adoration from his fans.

Balding believed that Mill Reef was "an out-and-out two-year-old performer," rather than one likely to flourish as he matured. There were plenty of examples of top class two-year-olds overtaken by less precocious horses but Mill Reef was a regular surprise.

The 1971 2000 Guineas was billed as a duel between the good little one – Mill Reef – and the good big one, the unbeaten My Swallow, who had narrowly bettered Mill Reef in the previous year's Prix Robert Papin. At Newmarket, both were beaten by Brigadier Gerard.

My Swallow had a disappointing season but Mill Reef and Brigadier Gerard proved themselves outstanding champions. While Brigadier Gerard was dominant at up to 10 furlongs, Mill Reef dismissed doubts about his stamina by sweeping up the Derby, Eclipse Stakes, King George VI and Queen Elizabeth Stakes and Prix de l'Arc de Triomphe.

As Balding observed, "Horses that win races like he did as two-year-olds don't go on to be one and a half mile horses, and win the Derby. That was the phenomenon. The further he went, the faster he went. It was quite extraordinary."

Mill Reef started 1972 by strolling away with the Prix Ganay but then struggled to beat Homeric in the Coronation Cup, after which he succumbed to a virus. After a number of minor setbacks Mill Reef started his preparation for the Arc when, on 30 August, disaster struck.

In Balding's autobiography, *Making The Running: A Racing Life* (2004), he recalled the sad episode and its aftermath. As Mill Reef came to the end of a fine piece of work, he was suddenly to be seen standing on three legs, with Hallum beside him. When Balding reached them, Hallum said, "Guv'nor, I am sure he has broken his leg – I heard a terrible crack."

It got worse. When vet Barry Williams examined the near fore leg, he told Balding, "It feels like a bag of marbles."

Mellon, a likeable, modest and thoughtful man, according to Balding "the best owner any trainer could ever have," reacted to the news by asking how Hallum was.

A room at Balding's yard was converted into an operating theatre and Jim Roberts, assisted by Tony Ward, carried out a seven hour operation. Mill Reef's afflicted leg was put in a full length plaster cast, with iron splints made by farrier Tom Reilly. Fortunately, Mill Reef was an amenable patient.

The room would be his residence for several months, adorned by cards from well wishers, until he was eventually moved to the National Stud. There Mill Reef became an outstanding stallion, his offspring including Derby winners Shirley Heights (1978) and Reference Point (1987). Mill Reef died in 1986, aged 17.

HORSES HAVE THEIR VISION ADJUSTED

Devoid of devices, many racehorses would fail to match their riders' determination to reach the winning post first.

Without reins, they would be free to display a complete lack of the desired (by the jockey) direction. Reins, therefore, are de rigueur. Some horses, more than others, are liable to have other things on their mind than finishing first. They may, for instance (see curiosity 71), be happy for a rival to remain in front of them, even if, with a little more effort, they could pass it and make their rider, trainer, owner and backers, happy.

In order to encourage greater focus on winning, various devices have been resorted to, with varying degrees of success. The first and most prevalent resort is to a pair of blinkers, their invention so long ago that the date is lost in the proverbial mists of time.

Centuries later, in 1913, Aboyeur won the Derby when wearing blinkers. Admittedly, he didn't actually win but was awarded the race when the winner, Craganour, was disqualified. As Craganour was the 6-4 favourite and Aboyeur 100-1, the decision was not universally popular, although bookmakers were rather pleased. To make matters worse, in the same race the militant suffragette Emily Davison stood in front of King Edward VII's horse, Anmer, and was killed. It was a trying time; a year later, the First World War arrived.

Aboyeur might have been expected to be rewarded with a life of ease but instead was sold to Russia at the end of 1913 and disappeared during or after the Bolshevik Revolution. Perhaps that is why blinkers are rarely worn in the Epsom Derby, and Aboyeur remains the most recent winner to have worn them.

It is different in the Kentucky Derby, where blinkers and winners have often gone together. Even the mighty Secretariat, winner of the 1973 Triple Crown (Kentucky Derby, Preakness Stakes, Belmont Stakes) wore them. In fact, he wore blinkers in all his races.

Horse vision is different from human vision. Whereas our eyes are on the front of our heads and face forwards, horses' eyes are on the side of their heads and face sideways.

We are good at looking forward but our peripheral vision is very limited. We can see in an arc of about 45 degrees on either side of our noses, for a total of about 90 degrees. This is pathetic in comparison with horses and exposes us to the constant risk of someone sneaking up behind us and breaking an egg on our head.

Horses' forward vision is less good but their range of vision is almost four times greater than ours, extending to 350 degrees. If you stand directly behind a horse you can succeed in occupying its blind spot and being rewarded with a kick from the unsettled creature. This is why it is advisable not to stand directly behind a horse.

Blinkers prevent a horse from looking sideways or rearwards, with the intention of increasing its concentration on going forwards. It sometimes works.

If blinkers prove disappointing, visors offer an alternative. They are like blinkers but with a slit on each side, to allow the horse to see what is to its left and right during a race – other horses, mainly.

When that fails, or as an alternative, cheekpieces can be used. They are strips of sheepskin attached to each side of a horse's bridle. They are easier to fit than either blinkers or a visor, and restrict a horse's vision less severely than either.

If the problem is nervousness or too much keenness rather than too little, the hood is waiting in the tool bag. This covers the head and, in particular, the ears, reducing any unsettling external noises. Another option, particularly for horses that tend to hold their heads up, is a noseband. By affecting the horse's forward vision, this encourages it to lower its head.

For horses blind in one eye, the eye-shield awaits, to prevent material flying up into its blind or missing eye.

A horse wearing blinkers, in the hope that it will help.

As desperation sets in, the tongue-tie may be applied. It is a large elastic band or nylon stocking, wrapped around a horse's tongue, then tied around the lower jaw to prevent a horse's tongue from getting over the bit and consequently restricting breathing.

They are not universally approved of, are banned in Germany and opposed by the RSPCA in Australia although not in Britain. Mark Johnston, a leading trainer and qualified vet, is one of a minority of trainers who don't use them. "I just find that too many horses dislike them," he said. I'm not surprised.

If none of the above work, it may be worth giving the horse a good talking to, although if you've tried stuffing cotton wool into its ears to calm it down, it may not hear you.

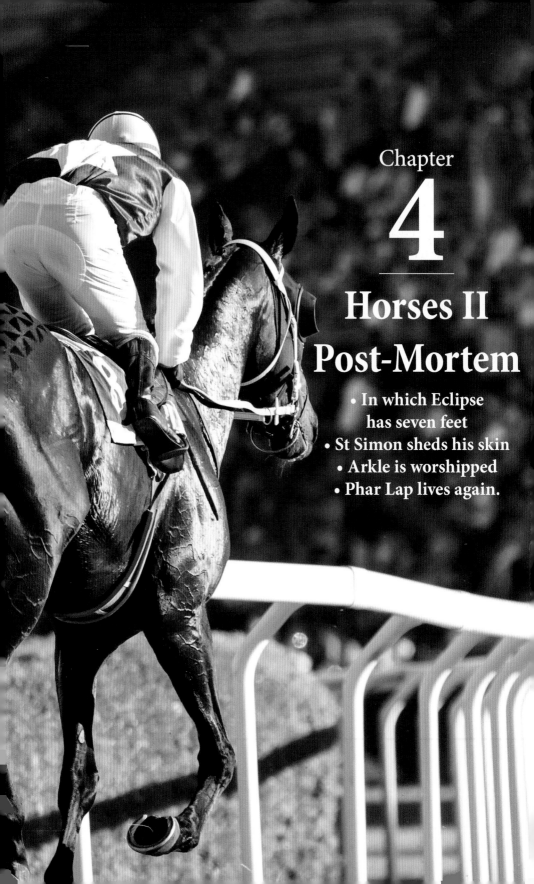

Chapter
4

Horses II
Post-Mortem

- In which Eclipse has seven feet
- St Simon sheds his skin
- Arkle is worshipped
- Phar Lap lives again.

20 ECLIPSE HAS SEVEN FEET

Great racehorses, like saints, tend to have bodies containing many more parts than an ordinary horse, or person.

Centuries before horseracing became an established sport, saints' bones were highly prized and their supply increased to meet demand. As I expect you know, in 1543, during the Protestant Reformation, John Calvin wielded his caustic pen in a Tract mocking the worship of holy relics. He wrote, "The great majority of the relics are spurious. It could be shown by comparison that every apostle has more than four bodies and every saint two or three."

Later, champion racehorses also attracted worshippers, with skeletons, hair and feet prominent in the market for posthumous parts. Eclipse's cult status among thoroughbreds made his body a desirable commodity.

Theodore Cook, in *Eclipse and O'Kelly* (1907), related, "Six 'undoubted' skeletons of Eclipse claimed my bewildered attention. No less than nine 'authentic' feet were apparently possessed by this extraordinary animal."

Eclipse engaged attention not just because of his outstanding racing and breeding performances but also due to the human company he kept. He was bred by the Duke of Cumberland, whose nickname 'The Butcher of Culloden,' was earned by leading the ruthless slaughter of Jacobite rebels at and after the battle of Culloden in 1746.

In 1765, as a yearling, Eclipse was sold to William Wildman, a meat dealer, before moving into the ownership of Dennis O'Kelly and his partner Charlotte Hayes, a brothel keeper who O'Kelly had met in the Fleet debtors' prison.

On their release, in 1761, Hayes ran a brothel in Soho before setting up a more celebrated establishment in King's Place, in sight of St James's Palace and convenient for the gentlemen of White's and Boodle's Clubs.

The 'nuns' were considered among the most desirable in their profession, with fees commensurately high. When the Duke of York, King George III's brother, paid Kitty Fisher only £50 rather than her usual fee of £100, she showed her contempt by placing the banknotes between two slices of bread, and eating them.

O'Kelly, an Irish rapscallion who, according to his contemporary John Lawrence, was "not overladen and depressed in his career by scruples," spent his days at coffee houses and racecourses, gambling on horses, boxing and dice. Eclipse, unbeaten in his entire career of 18 races during 1769 and 1770, was a uniquely safe, if invariably short-priced, betting medium.

At Epsom in May 1769, in the second heat of the Noblemen and Gentlemen's Plate, Eclipse was long odds-on to beat his four rivals, Gower, Chance, Trial and Plume. In search of better odds, O'Kelly persuaded three layers to offer prices of evens, 5-4 and 6-4 against his prediction of "Eclipse first, the rest nowhere." Eclipse won by a distance and O'Kelly's prediction became one of the sport's most famous sayings.

Eight of Eclipse's successes were walkovers because, as *The Farrier and Naturalist* recalled, in 1828, "No horse could be found to call forth his extreme pace." Eclipse was never seriously challenged.

Retired to stud in 1771, his success as a stallion ultimately resulted in approximately 95 per cent of today's thoroughbreds having Eclipse as an ancestor. His longevity – Eclipse died in 1789, aged 25 – helped fund O'Kelly's and Hayes's lavish lifestyle but failed to persuade the Jockey Club, particularly the influential and hostile Sir Charles Bunbury, that O'Kelly was a suitable candidate for membership.

O'Kelly pre-deceased Eclipse, dying of "luxury and hard living" in 1787. He left Charlotte Hayes an annuity of £400, a share in Eclipse and various other possessions, including a parrot called Polley.

One of Eclipse's feet after conversion into an ornament.

When Polley died, in 1802, the *Gentleman's Magazine* was moved to publish an obituary, an unusual accolade for a parrot. It read, "Died, at the house of Colonel O'Kelly, in Half-Moon Street, Piccadilly, his wonderful parrot, who had been in his family 30 years, having been purchased at Bristol out of a West India ship. It sang with the greatest clearness and precision, the 114th Psalm, 'The Banks of the Dee,' 'God Save the King!' and other favourite songs. One hundred guineas had been refused for it in London."

By then the profligate Hayes, her days as a madam behind her, had suffered another spell in the Fleet debtors' prison, emerging to live on into her 80s, dying in about 1813.

Meanwhile, Eclipse's demise had set the stage for relic seekers to descend on his corpse. Theodore Cook remarked, "The 'genuine' hair out of his tail would have generously filled the largest armchair in the Jockey Club." It is to be hoped that the the hair attached to the Newmarket Challenge Whip (see curiosity 55) was, as tradition has it, genuinely that of Eclipse.

Hair, bones and feet were freshly created long after Eclipse's death. His putative skeleton spent its early years being transported up and down the country, packed into boxes and reassembled for display. It ended its tortuous journey in the National Horseracing Museum in Newmarket and in 1991 was donated to the Royal Veterinary College, finally leaving Newmarket for the Eclipse Building at the College's Hawkshead Campus in Hertfordshire in 2003. But is it the real thing?

In 2012, an article titled *Truth in the Bones. Resolving the Identity of the Founding Elite Thoroughbred Racehorses* appeared in the journal *Archaeometry*. It reported the findings of a study carried out by a multi-disciplinary team led by Dr Mim Bower of Cambridge University.

The researchers used sophisticated DNA analysis of a tooth, humerus, metacarpus and tibia from Eclipse's skeleton, together with measurements of the skeleton compared with those taken during an autopsy in 1789, plus isotope, morphometric and pedigree analysis to establish whether or not the skeleton was that of Eclipse. Happily, they concluded "that the putative skeleton of Eclipse is the authentic skeleton."

It was a relief for the Royal Veterinary College and for anyone planning to visit Eclipse's skeleton.

There was then the question of Eclipse's feet. Although remarkable in many ways, including having a large heart weighing 14lbs, it was only posthumously that Eclipse appeared to boast more than four feet. Dr Mim Bower and her team noted that "at least seven purported hooves are currently in existence."

A particularly conspicuous specimen resides in the Jockey Club Rooms in Newmarket. The gold mounted foot stands on a silver gilt dish, along with the inscription, "This piece of plate with the hoof of Eclipse was presented by His Most Gracious Majesty William the Fourth to the Jockey Club May 1832."

It was one of two of Eclipse's feet owned by the King, the fate of the other foot still unknown. The gift was to be used as a trophy for a new race at Ascot confined to horses owned by members of the Jockey Club, together with £200 donated by the King. The prospect of displaying Eclipse's foot on the winning owner's mantelpiece proved insufficient to lure more than two runners to the inaugural running of the race, in June 1832. The fact that the Ascot Gold Cup, over the same distance of two and a half miles, was run on the same day didn't help.

Lord Chesterfield won the Foot with Priam, the 1830 Derby winner, but after the first three runnings of the race had attracted a grand total of only six runners, the King decided to withhold the £200, with the result that the 1835 race was a walkover. Eclipse's foot was then retired to the Jockey Club Rooms where it was used as a snuff box.

It was not alone. The Rooms contain the mounted feet of numerous famous horses, among them Hermit and Persimmon. They are not an uplifting spectacle, there being something macabre verging on repellent about amputated feet, even Eclipse's.

21 ST SIMON SHEDS HIS SKIN

Like Eclipse, St Simon's distinction as a racehorse and sire resulted in his body parts being separated from each other and displayed in different locations. It was a strange form of posthumous respect. Perhaps, one day, his skeleton, feet and skin will be reunited, although it is probably too late to stick them together.

Prince Gustavus Batthyany had the good fortune to breed St Simon but the misfortune to die two years later, in 1883, without having enjoyed St Simon's success. When the late Prince's bloodstock was sold, Newmarket trainer Mat Dawson advised the young 6th Duke of Portland to buy the unraced two-year-old for a modest 1,600 guineas. It was a fabulously fruitful purchase.

St Simon had been entered for only one of the following year's Classics, the 2000 Guineas, and that entry died along with Prince Batthyany. Yet St Simon's dominance of the prestigious races he was able to contest made him the champion of his generation.

Irritable and inclined to sweat, St Simon needed firm but patient handling. When Fred Archer applied the spurs to him on the gallops, his mount bolted, leaving the champion jockey to declare, "He is not a horse, he's a blooming steam engine."

He steamrollered his majestic way to an unbeaten and unextended nine career successes, including, as a three-year-old, the Epsom Gold Cup, Ascot Gold Cup, Newcastle Gold Cup and Goodwood Cup. Dawson trained six Derby winners but reflected, "I only trained one good horse, St Simon. He exuded electricity."

Retired to the Duke of Portland's stud at Welbeck Abbey, in Nottinghamshire, St Simon was a spectacularly successful stallion. Champion sire nine times, he sired the winners of 571 races, including 10 winners of 17 Classics, as well as three Ascot Gold Cup winners.

When St Simon died, aged 27, in 1908, he was buried at Welbeck Abbey but did not remain there.

In 1914, the Duke of Portland offered St Simon's skeleton to the Natural History Museum in London. The Museum accepted the offer, although even before the skeleton was collected from Welbeck, there was said to be a lack of exhibition space for the new acquisition.

Later, a pair of St Simon's feet found their way to the Jockey Club Rooms in Newmarket with the remaining pair ending up at York's racing museum. Meanwhile, St Simon's skin was displayed in a wood and glass case in the entrance hall of Welbeck Abbey.

When the 7th Duke of Portland died, in 1977, his enormous collection of land, property and possessions passed into the hands of his daughter, Lady Anne Bentinck. A strong and forthright character, "famously pompous to the point of rudeness," Lady Anne's wealth made her a desirable marriage partner but she was not available.

In 1937 an attempt to marry her to the future Prince Charles of Belgium was thwarted when Lady Anne declined to get out of bed to meet her suitor. Her own marriage ambitions were focused on the Duke of Leeds and when her parents refused to allow it she vowed never to marry, and never did.

Instead, she spent a lot of time hunting side-saddle in Nottinghamshire, stalking deer in Caithness, and doing good works, although her people skills were limited. When an expert on trees was introduced to her, with a view to providing advice on tree planting at Welbeck, Lady Anne told him, "I don't like trees."

In 2000, aged 83, she visited Queen Elizabeth the Queen Mother, aged 100, to whom she was related. The Queen Mother reported, "I've known her since she was a little girl. She was gruff then and she's gruff now."

Immersed in horses, Lady Anne employed a string of private trainers, namely Jeremy Glover, Owen Brennan and John Quinn. In the 1990s, Strath Royal won 20 races for her, notably the 1997 Rowland Meyrick Chase and 1998 Charlie Hall Chase, while Speaker Weatherill won the latter year's Great Yorkshire Chase.

Her affection did not extend to St Simon's skin, which she banished from the entrance hall. Sir Mark Prescott, the long standing occupant of Heath House, where Mat Dawson had trained St Simon, recalled, "I heard about the skins and said, 'I'll have them. I like things that are macabre.'"

In 1995 the skins arrived at Heath House, prompting Lady Anne to write to Mrs Scott Bolton, as follows, "Thank you for finding a home for the skins, which I still find very disgusting, and I'm astonished that someone like Sir Mark Prescott should be delighted with them. Still, each to their own."

To Sir Mark's continued delight, St Simon's skin now occupies a horizontal glass case at the entrance to Heath House's covered ride.

Helped, perhaps, by abstinence from both betting and alcohol, and surviving her devotion to cigarettes, Lady Anne Bentinck lived until 2008, by which time she was 92. By then, she was ready to go. Appalled that the tradition of dinner starting promptly at 8.00pm was no longer observed, she declared, "Well, I think I've outlived my time."

22 ARKLE IS WORSHIPPED

Skeletons are strange-looking objects and Arkle's skeleton is no exception. It stands, looking strange, on display at the Irish National Stud's Horse Museum at Tully, Kildare.

In company with other equine skeletons, Arkle's displays very thin leg bones, making it hard to believe that he could have jumped fences, let alone be skeletally equipped to be the best chaser of all time. Yet he was.

Named after a mountain on his owner Anne, Duchess of Westminster's Scottish estate, trained in Ireland by Tom Dreaper and usually ridden by Pat Taaffe, Arkle was held in unmatched admiration and affection.

His record embraced three successive victories in the Cheltenham Gold Cup (1964 to 1966), two Hennessy Gold Cups (1964, 1965), an Irish Grand National (1964), a Whitbread Gold Cup (1965), King George VI Chase (1965) and 19 other successes.

Arkle won races when giving enormous amounts of weight to talented rivals. He carried 12st 7lb to victory in the 1964 and 1965 Hennessy Gold Cup and only failed to repeat the feat in 1966 because he could not quite give 35lb to Stalbridge Colonist who, a few months later, after Arkle had retired, was narrowly beaten in the Cheltenham Gold Cup.

Ireland worshipped him. He was known simply as 'Himself' and letters reached Dreaper's yard addressed merely, "Arkle, Ireland."

Injury forced Arkle's retirement to his owner's farm at Bryanstown, Kildare, and when he died, afflicted with arthritis, in 1970, he was buried

Arkle past his best.

in a field at the farm. Some, including Taaffe, would have preferred the national treasure to have remained there, his grave marked simply, Arkle 1957 – 1970, but in 1976 his body was exhumed. When the museum at the Irish National Stud was opened, the following year, Arkle's skeleton took pride of place.

Thirty six years later, when Arkle's skeleton was still standing on the same spot, Sean Magee, author of the splendid *Arkle. The Life and Legacy of 'Himself'* (2005), organised a pilgrimage to visit all things Arkle.

Unlike pilgrimages to Mecca (1,426 killed in a stampede in 1990) there were no deaths and it was a marvellous trip. With Nick O'Toole to guide us and wonderful welcomes and hospitality from everyone linked to Arkle and still alive (those no longer alive would have been equally helpful if they could have been), it was a memorable experience.

We saw the stable where Arkle was born, the fields where he spent his childhood, the box where he lived when in training and his grave.

We met Paddy Woods, Arkle's work rider and one-time jockey; Johnny Lumley, Arkle's groom and TP Burns, then 89, who was the only jockey to have won a Flat race on Arkle, because it was the only Flat race (bumpers excepted) Arkle contested. There were some lovely black and white photographs on the walls, and a scrapbook on the table.

Then, of course, we saw his skeleton.

23 PHAR LAP LIVES AGAIN

After Lenin's death in 1924, his body was embalmed and put on public display in a mausoleum in Moscow's Red Square. It is still there but the display of dead people, however famous, has never caught on. Name anyone both famous and dead, and you can be pretty certain that they haven't visited a taxidermist.

As the cases of Arkle, Eclipse and St Simon testify, the same is not true of famous racehorses. Parts of them can still be seen, usually in glass cases, preserving life, of a kind, after death.

Phar Lap made his own posthumous mark by being preserved in two different countries after his death, separated by the Tasman Sea. Like the American equine heroes, Seabiscuit and Secretariat, Phar Lap also had a film made about him.

Tales of rags to riches have an enduring appeal and Phar Lap – adapted from farlap, Thai for lightning – started his racing life as a cheap ugly duckling (equine variety) and ended it the idol of a nation (Australia).

After Phar Lap's death in 1932, Joseph Lyons, Australia's Prime Minister, while celebrating an important legal victory, declared, "What is the use of winning a High Court decision and losing Phar Lap? The death of this wonderful horse is a great sporting tragedy."

It was a politically wise tribute but Lyons could have been excused for abstaining from the nation's outpourings of grief because Phar Lap's memorable victory in the 1930 Melbourne Cup must have brought back unwelcome memories of the 1887 version of the race.

It was in that year that Lyons' father, Michael, had a dream. In his dream, a horse called Tranter won the Melbourne Cup. Despite having failed as a hotelkeeper, farmer, butcher and baker, and with a large family to support, Michael decided that it was a good idea to follow his dream. In for a penny, in for a house, he sold the family home in Tasmania, travelled to Melbourne and put the house on Tranter.

The journey back must have been depressing, as Joseph's father should have dreamt about Dunlop, who won easily, while Tranter came nowhere.

In 1928, Phar Lap was sold at the Trentham Yearling Sales in New Zealand for 160 guineas. He was bought by Hugh Telford on behalf of his brother Harry, a low ranking trainer in Australia. Short of money, horses and owners, Harry hoped to persuade David Davis, a hard-nosed Sydney businessman, to buy Phar Lap.

When Davis was introduced to the gangly yearling, he told the anxious trainer, "Harry, I don't like the horse." He eventually agreed to buy him, with Telford leasing the horse and bearing the training costs while Davis got one third of any winnings.

At first, there didn't seem likely to be any. In 1929, as a two-year-old, Phar Lap was unplaced five times before winning a maiden race at Rosehill, Sydney. The following season began with four more unplaced runs but by the end of that 1929-30 season, Phar Lap had won another 13 times, including two Derbys and two St Legers, finished third in the 1929 Melbourne Cup and taken his career earnings to £(Aus)26,976.

Already deep into an economic depression that would reach its nadir in 1932, when unemployment in Australia reached 32 per cent, Phar Lap's rise captured the public's imagination and gave people pleasure and anticipation when both were in short supply.

On 1 November 1930, warming up for the Melbourne Cup three days later, Phar Lap easily won the Melbourne Stakes at Flemington but his victory was overshadowed by what *The Age* headlined as 'Dastardly Attempt To Maim Cup Favourite,' and went on to call "One of the greatest sensations in the history of the Australian turf." (3 November 1930).

The sensational Phar Lap at Flemington racecourse in 1930, with Jim Pike perched on top. The pair won that year's Melbourne Cup.

Tommy Woodcock, Phar Lap's devoted groom, had received threats that persuaded him to alter the time and route he took with Phar Lap to Caulfield racecourse for the horse's early morning exercise. On the way back to his nearby stable, Woodcock led Phar Lap while riding a pony.

Woodcock later reported seeing a sedan car with two men in it parked on the roadside. He became suspicious when they raised newspapers to cover their faces. When he turned into Etna Road, the car followed and the sound of its engine caused Phar Lap to rear and plunge.

Woodcock bravely positioned the pony he was riding between the passing car and Phar Lap.

He then saw a double-barrelled shotgun pushed through the back window. Woodcock spurred the pony on, with Phar Lap jumping forward as the shotgun was fired. The pellets whistled harmlessly past.

When Phar Lap set off for Flemington later that day, he had a police escort and, after the race, was moved to a secret hiding place at St Albans, near Geelong, almost 50 miles from Melbourne.

Having survived the attack, Phar Lap, ridden by Jim Pike, became the only horse to be odds-on to win the Melbourne Cup, and win it. His victory, by an easy three lengths, was the front page headline in *The Herald*'s raceday evening edition. "It was apparent two furlongs from home," the Melbourne paper's correspondent reported, "that he had the race in his keeping. Tremendous cheers broke out as Phar Lap increased his lead," winning "with ridiculous ease." The crowd "went mad. No Melbourne Cup could have been won in more stylish or more effortless manner. It was the crowning triumph of Phar Lap's remarkable career."

Two days later Phar Lap was brought out again, to win the Linlithgow Stakes, and two days after that, the Fisher Plate, both at Flemington.

Telford worked his horses hard, off and on the racetrack. Phar Lap needed to be tough. That season, he won 14 of his 16 races and, the season after, won eight of nine. The 160 guineas yearling had won Davis and Telford a grand total of over £(Aus)56,000.

There was to be a final, sad drama. In March 1932 Phar Lap was shipped to America and taken across the border into Mexico to contest the Agua Caliente Handicap at Tijuana, billed as the world's richest race, worth US$50,000. Ridden by Billy Elliott, Phar Lap came from last to first to win in record time.

Phar Lap was an intercontinental star but on 5 April, at Menlo Park in California, a distraught Tommy Woodcock found the five-year-old in acute suffering, and soon dead.

Speculation was rife as to the cause of his sudden death, including claims of Mafia involvement. There were suggestions that Phar Lap had been poisoned deliberately, for which the autopsy provided scant evidence, or poisoned accidentally, from something he had ingested. Veterinarians tended towards explanations based on acute digestive disease but at that time their knowledge of such diseases was less advanced than today.

In 2000, Geoff Armstrong and Peter Thompson, authors of *Phar Lap* (2nd edition, 2003), recruited Dr John Van Veenendal to review the post-mortem evidence. Van Veenendal had worked for several major racing stables in Australia, and had also treated horses trained by Woodcock. His conversations with Woodcock led him to the initial view, "that Phar Lap had died of an acute enteric disease."

After studying the post-mortem reports, he concluded that the most probable cause of death was uninnentional poisoning with a toxin that caused enteritis or jejunitis. The chief suspect, a particular form of jejunitis, had not yet been discovered in 1932 and, seventy years later, still killed 70 per cent of horses contracting it.

Van Veenendal reported that the arsenic found in Phar Lap's organs would not have been unusual at that time, when many thoroughbreds were given tonics containing it. It was not arsenic that killed him.

Dr Ivan Kempson of the University of South Australia and Dermot Henry of Museum Victoria disagreed. In 2006, using a synchrotron, they analysed several hairs and a sliver of hide from Phar Lap's preserved body. As well as arsenic from chemicals used to preserve the skin, they found a different form of arsenic.

In a broadcast on the Australian Broadcasting Corporation's *Catalyst* programme in 2008, Henry stated, "We were able to demonstrate that Phar Lap had ingested arsenic within probably the last 48 hours of his life and probably quite a large dose."

When the researchers studied Harry Telford's personal recipe book they discovered that the general tonic he gave his horses contained 12 ounces of arsenic. They concluded that "the most plausible theory is that he had an overdose of an arsenic based tonic."

The tricky bit was explaining why Phar Lap, or stablemates, hadn't been affected before? The researchers suggested that, following his demanding journey to America, Telford may have increased the dose of his tonic. Uncertainty remains and is likely to persist.

Reaction to Phar Lap's death included a lengthy poem by 'Dryblower' in the *Sunday Times* (Perth) of 10 April 1932, part of which read:

> *Phar Lap's dead and can't be deader;*
> *Phar Lap's gone beyond recall;*
> *Taken one great equine header*
> *To the grave that covers all.*
> *Said we grave? If so excuse us;*

Bones and hide will come back here.
To instruct and to enthuse us,
Lest we do not shed a tear.
Here he'll stand within a stable,
Where we'll bow a reverent head,
And upon a marble table
That last cable,
Phar Lap's dead.
O, the woe and lamentation
O, the grief that followed free!
O, the sobs that bind one nation
To another o'er the sea!

That year, Joseph Luke Fleury produced a remarkable painting titled *Phar Lap Before the Chariot of the Sun*. It depicted Phar Lap at the head of Apollo's chariot, surrounded by angels and the nine muses, with Dame Nellie Melba playing a harp, and the horses galloping on a bed of clouds, above Australia and New Zealand. The painting is on display in the Museum Victoria, Melbourne.

Dryblower was right about the bones and hide returning to Australia, along with Phar Lap's heart. He was a big horse, over 17 hands tall, with a large heart, weighing 14lb, compared with the average of 9lb to 10lb.

His heart was mounted in preserving fluid and sent via Sydney to the Australian Institute of Anatomy in Canberra, which later formed part of the National Museum of Australia. In 2011 it was given its own showcase in the new Landmarks gallery, where it is the most requested object.

Phar Lap's skin was sent to Jonas Brothers of New York, taxidermists, to be mounted for display. In September 1932, the work completed, the resurrected horse was paraded around New York's Empire City and Belmont Park racetracks before returning to Australia. There, it was put on display at the Museum Victoria in Melbourne. In 1980, on the 50th anniversary of Phar Lap's Melbourne Cup victory, it was paraded around Flemington racecourse. At the Museum, like the champion's heart in Canberra, the mounted hide is the most popular object.

Making up the Holy Trinity of heart, skin and skeleton, objects of pilgrimage and reverence, Phar Lap's bones were initially also sent to Museum Victoria but were then given to the New Zealand government, meaning a return to Phar Lap's birthplace.

For several years they were kept, unmounted, at the National Museum and Art Gallery in Wellington, finally in 1938 being put on display in the new Dominion Museum Building. The skeleton, reassembled in 2011, is now in the Museum of New Zealand, Te Papa Tongarewa.

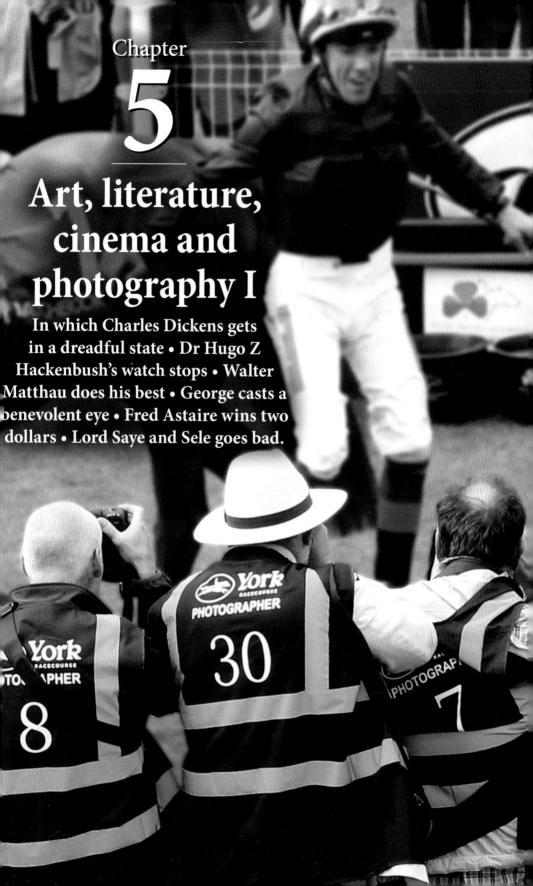

Chapter

5

Art, literature, cinema and photography I

In which Charles Dickens gets in a dreadful state • Dr Hugo Z Hackenbush's watch stops • Walter Matthau does his best • George casts a benevolent eye • Fred Astaire wins two dollars • Lord Saye and Sele goes bad.

CHARLES DICKENS GETS IN A DREADFUL STATE

When Charles Dickens spotted "a pair of little lilac gloves and a little bonnet" he confessed that the sight threw him into "a dreadful state." That was because they were worn by Ellen Ternan.

It was St Leger day, Wednesday 16 September 1857, and Dickens was at Doncaster racecourse, not as a passionate follower of racing but as a passionate pursuer of the young actress. Ternan was 18 and Dickens, already the celebrated author of *The Pickwick Papers, Oliver Twist, Nicholas Nickleby, David Copperfield* and *Bleak House*, was 45 and married.

A few months earlier Dickens had seen Ternan for the first time and quickly became infatuated. He and Wilkie Collins, who had not yet written the first of his successful novels, *The Woman in White*, had recently produced a successful play together, *The Frozen Deep*. In August, when the play moved to Manchester, Ellen, known as Nelly, was in the cast. Now she was due to appear in *The Pet of the Petticoats* at Doncaster's Theatre Royal, and Dickens was determined to be there.

Two days before the St Leger, Dickens and Collins arrived at Doncaster by train and made their way to the Angel Hotel, where they had already booked rooms. The four day meeting began the following day.

Dickens was complimentary about "pretty and pleasant Doncaster" but not about its occupants, "the mob-lunatics crowding the road, particularly crowding the outside of the betting rooms, whooping and shouting loudly after all passing vehicles. All degrees of men, from peers to paupers, betting incessantly."

The evening brought no respite. "Town lighted up," Dickens recorded, "more lunatics out than ever; a complete choke and stoppage of the thoroughfare outside the betting rooms. A vague echoing roar of 't'horses' and 't'races' always rising in the air, until midnight, at about which period it dies away in occasional drunken songs and straggling yells."

The next morning, at daybreak, "A sudden rising, as it were out of the earth, of all the obscene creatures who sell 'correct cards of the races.'" When Dickens looked out of his hotel window, he saw "the lunatics, horse-mad, betting-mad, drunken-mad, vice-mad."

They had come for four days of racing and revelry, Dickens for the theatre and the chance to see Nelly Ternan. On Monday evening, Dickens and Collins watched a performance of Edward Bulwer-Lytton's *Money*, which ended with a dance by girls dressed as jockeys, with whips in their mouths. Dickens had hoped his visit would go unnoticed but the *Doncaster, Nottingham, and Lincoln Gazette* reported, "The distinguished author of the Pickwick Papers – his greatest work – was evidently the lion of the evening."

Charles Dickens went to the St Leger at Doncaster in 1857, where the sight of Ellen Ternan threw him into "a dreadful state."

The following evening he returned to the Theatre Royal to see Nelly and her sister Maria in *The Pet of the Petticoats*.

On St Leger Day Dickens went racing, probably in the company of Nelly and her family. The *Gazette* reported that, at the racecourse, "The attendance was immense, never on any former occasion so great. As for the grandstand and enclosure, they were literally 'crammed to suffocation'. The demand for admission exceeded all anticipation, not a single ticket was left."

The *Gazette* put this down partly to the attraction of Blink Bonny, who had already won both the Derby and Oaks, and was favourite to add the St Leger. "So famous had Blink Bonny become in the minds of the racing community that the deepest interest was manifested in all parts of the country, as well as in Ireland, Scotland and elsewhere, even to get a look at so extraordinary an animal."

Despite the crowds, Dickens found the racecourse "a most beautiful sight, with its agreeable prospect, its quaint Red House, its green grass and fresh heath." He backed three winners but also fell into a "dreadful state concerning a pair of little lilac gloves and a little bonnet" worn by Nelly Ternan.

Blink Bonny, the 5-4 favourite, finished a disappointing fourth behind Imperieuse. Despite being trained by the celebrated John Scott, winning the St Leger for the fourteenth time, Imperieuse's victory was greeted, according to the *Gazette*, by "a funereal stillness."

Blink Bonny's jockey, John Charlton, was believed to have been paid to lose and, two days later, when Blink Bonny won the Park Hill Stakes, the *Gazette* reported that "an attempt was made to mob Mr I'Anson [the owner] and Charlton, on account of the time being less for this race than for the St Leger."

Dickens was there and wrote that there was "a violent scuffling, and a rushing at the jockey, and an emergence of the said jockey from a swaying and menacing crowd, protected by friends, and looking the worse for wear."

On the Sunday, Dickens took Nelly on a trip into the country and visited the ruins of Roche Abbey. The next day, Dickens and Collins left Doncaster on the 11.00am train to London but Nelly Ternan would continue to be an important but secret part of Dickens' life until his death in 1870.

25 DR HUGO Z HACKENBUSH'S WATCH STOPS

The trouble with films involving horse races is that the races rarely look real. That was true of the Marx Brothers' classic *A Day at the Races* (1937) but it didn't matter because it was the Marx Brothers and the climactic staged race didn't aspire to look believable.

Most of the film takes place away from the racetrack. Judy Standish (Maureen O'Sullivan) runs the struggling Standish Sanatorium but won't be running it much longer if she can't raise enough money to stave off the scheming attentions of the baddies, Morgan and Whitmore.

Standish is hoping for help from her wealthy, overbearing, hypochondriac client, Mrs Emily Upjohn, played magnificently by Margaret Dumont. Upjohn threatens to leave the Sanitorium unless it puts her in the care of Dr Hugo Z Hackenbush (Groucho Marx), of whom she has heard great things, although they don't include the fact that the sanitorium he runs is for small animals and horses.

"I have high blood pressure on my right side and low blood pressure on my left side," Mrs Upjohn insists, while Dr Steinberg, recruited by Morgan to expose Hackenbush as a fraud, believes that Hackenbush lacks medical qualifications and that Mrs Upjohn lacks illness.

Meanwhile, Gil Stewart (Allan Jones), Judy Standish's suitor, has bought a racehorse called Hi-Hat for $1500 in the hope that it will win enough money to save the Standish Sanitorium. Judy is not impressed and Gil has no money left to feed Hi-Hat.

The Sheriff, for reasons that I've forgotten, is forever trying to seize the horse and arrest Gil's helpers, Tony (Chico Marx), an ice cream salesman and tipster, and Stuffy (Harpo Marx), a jockey.

They first encounter Dr Hackenbush at the Sparkling Springs Racetrack, where Tony sells Hackenbush an envelope containing a tip for the next race. When Hackenbush opens the envelope, the tip is a jumble of letters. To decode them, Tony tells him, he will need to buy the code book, which he does, only to be told that the contents only make sense if he buys the master code book and, after that, the breeders' guide. By the time Hackenbush has finally discovered the name of the horse, the race is over.

Later, in his guise as a doctor, Hackenbush takes Stuffy's pulse, prompting one of the film's *Dictionary of Quotations* entries when Dr Hackenbush declares, "Either he's dead or my watch has stopped."

Gil is a singer at a casino and there is a wonderful period set-piece of singing and showgirl dancing at the Gala Water Carnival, rounded off by Chico and Harpo showing off their piano and harp skills.

The action eventually moves on to Hi-Hat and the vital race. Along the frenetic way, Stuffy slashes the bed mattress in Dr Hackenbush's room at the Sanatorium, in order to get the straw stuffing for Hi-Hat to eat; the horse being in the bedroom closet.

A scene in a barn establishes that the horse hates Morgan and has a hitherto hidden talent for jumping, evidenced by him leaping over the barn doors to escape, and then jumping over a car.

The big raceday arrives, the day of the $50,000 Grand Steeplechase at Sparkling Springs, a race for three-year-olds and upwards over two miles.

Dr Hugo Z Hackenbush, alias Groucho Marx, with Chico and Harpo in A Day at the Races (1937).

They raced jumpers young at Sparkling Springs.

With the Sheriff, Morgan and Whitmore in pursuit, getting Hi-Hat to the track in time for the race proves difficult, especially after the ruse of sneaking him there in an ambulance is rumbled. To delay the start of the race, the Marx brothers move a running rail and then divert traffic onto the track.

Racing pedants might point out that an awful lot of ground is covered for a two mile race, with plenty of other liberties taken with conventional rules and practices but it doesn't matter, neither does the fact that Hi-Hat finishes second. It soon turns out that mud has obscured the numbers carried by the first two home. Hi-Hat, who ran faster every time he heard Morgan's voice, was the winner after all.

As the closing victory procession moves gloriously on, Dr Hackenbush turns to Mrs Upjohn and says, "Emily, I have a little confession to make. I really am a horse doctor but marry me and I'll never look at any other horse."

It's wonderful! Now you don't need to actually watch it.

26 WALTER MATTHAU DOES HIS BEST

If *A Day at the Races* was a classic in horseracing filmography, *Casey's Shadow* (1978) wasn't. On the other hand, anything with Walter Matthau in it is worth watching. That's why it's here.

Matthau, best known for his screen partnership with Jack Lemmon, notably in *The Odd Couple* (1968), was a compulsive gambler so he may have been broke when he agreed to take the part of Lloyd Bourdelle, the impoverished trainer of *Casey's Shadow*.

Both the trainer and the horse were based on real creatures, Bourdelle on the well-known trainer Lloyd Romero and Casey's Shadow on Rocket's Magic.

Rocket's Magic was born in 1973 to a mare bought in foal for just $1800. He became an unlikely star of quarter horseracing. On his debut, at Delta Downs, Louisiana, in March 1975, he broke the track record for 330 yards, then won his next five starts, including the Old South Futurity and Florida Futurity.

In his qualifying race for the richest race in America, the $1 million All-America Futurity over 440 yards at Ruidoso Downs in New Mexico, Rocket's Magic recorded the fastest qualifying time. Then, after a fast breeze-up in preparation for the big race, Romero's champion returned with a sore leg. The trainer decided to run him anyway but after a slow start, Rocket's Magic was beaten into third place.

By then, a team from Columbia Pictures had already spent time, effort and money on a planned film based on Rocket's Magic. With Romero's cooperation,

The wonderful Walter Matthau, star of the rather less wonderful
Casey's Shadow (1978).

they decided to go ahead. Not everything in the film was true, particularly the bit where Casey's Shadow wins the $1 million All-America Futurity.

Randy Romero, Lloyd's son and the rider of Rocket's Magic, had mixed feelings about the movie. He and his family and friends enjoyed watching it, "we laughed like hell," but it irked Randy that he hadn't been interviewed or consulted. "Nobody talked to me about it," he complained. "Some parts of the movie weren't true. We were poor but not that poor. They didn't do a good job. In a way, it wasn't the real deal."

The financial arrangements didn't improve Randy's opinion. "My daddy never charged them. They didn't give us anything, not a penny." On the other hand, *Casey's Shadow* did have Walter Matthau in it, along with the line, "When we win this race, and we're rich, we're goin' ta Tahiti, where the women don't wear no top."

31 years later, after Mine That Bird won the 2009 Kentucky Derby at 50-1, top trainer Bob Baffert recalled the movie – "It was like Casey's Shadow."

In more ways than one. In the film, Dr Leonard Blach, Ruidoso Downs' veterinarian, appears in a scene where he and another vet examine Casey's Shadow's foreleg. Blach was the part-owner of Mine That Bird.

27 GEORGE CASTS A BENEVOLENT EYE

Men and Horses I Have Known (1924) is widely regarded as one of the best books ever written about horseracing. It's quite heavy, although only to lift, not to read.

George Lambton (1860-1945) wrote about a society whose attitudes and practices were generations removed from today's and he did it in an engaging, endearing way.

A son of Lord Durham, Eton then Cambridge but mainly hunting, shooting, fishing and gambling, Lambton trained successfully for successive Earls of Derby and, latterly, as a public trainer. Between 1896 and 1933 he trained the winners of a dozen English Classics. Eight of those successes were achieved before the book's publication yet it is far from being merely an account of Lambton's riding and training career.

There are interesting insights into changing methods of training and race-riding but, most strikingly, Lambton writes with a benevolent eye about the many characters he encountered along the way, at different positions in racing society.

Lambton had a talent for friendship and a tendency to think well of all but the most disagreeable figures. He even had a forgiving word for Horatio Bottomley, periodically a racehorse owner but mainly a charlatan and fraudster whose exploits ultimately led to him being sent to prison for seven years and expelled from the House of Commons. "Poor Bottomley," Lambton wrote, "I could not help being sorry for him when the crash came. Anyhow, I shall always think well of him for one thing, his patriotism, which I am convinced was real and genuine."

During the First World War, as editor of *John Bull*, Bottomley "always did his best to cheer people and keep them from being despondent," although Lambton conceded that "he was very vain, loved flattery and the applause of the mob." A less kindly observer might have added that some of the income from Bottomley's wartime Victory Bond scheme was converted into racehorses rather than Victory Bonds.

Times were, of course, very different, as evidenced by Lambton's praise for his brother Freddy, who "could kill a fox as well as any man," and for Lord Chaplin, 'The Squire,' who, in the days before the RSPCA, defied his own weight of between 18st and 20st to go hunting. "The Squire's pluck was marvellous," wrote Lambton, "for it was with the greatest difficulty that he could be got on or off his horse, but once in the saddle he was as happy as a sand-boy." The horse was probably less ecstatic.

Chaplin was also "a most dashing bettor," while Lord Jersey, who became the Jockey Club's senior steward, "as a young man had been a very fine gambler." Gambling runs like a rocky thread through the racing experiences of Lambton, his friends and acquaintances, some of them jockeys.

When 'Ted' Wilson, "perhaps the best steeplechase rider of my days" won the 1884 Grand National on Voluptuary, who had never run in a steeplechase before, Wilson confided that he had "won enough money to pay all his debts and start afresh." After repeating the feat on Roquefort the following year, "Wilson set himself up for life."

Fred Archer, "the greatest of all jockeys" and a friend of Lambton's, also bet heavily sometimes, although Lambton remarked, "I have known him ride some wonderful races against his own money." For Archer, who was only 17 when he won the 2000 Guineas on Atlantic in 1874, the winning of races was "the one object of his life." When he died, Lord Marcus Beresford said, "Backers have lost the best friend they have ever had."

Lambton's observations about the most celebrated and successful jockey of his generation are well worth reading but it's disappointing to discover that Archer didn't shoot himself in the Rutland Arms Hotel on Newmarket High Street but at home. I prefer Jeffrey Bernard's surmise, that, "knowing the place pretty well, I suspect he was trying to attract the attention of the staff in the Rutland Hotel."

Life was then much harder for jockeys, stable staff and horses. In his riding days, Lambton admired the prolific winner Durham, "a grand horse up to 14st" and later praised Archer's performances on Peter in 1881. After finishing second in the Manchester Cup then running out in the following week's Gold Vase at Ascot when ridden by Charles Wood, Peter, a fractious individual, won the next day's Hunt Cup with Archer aboard and came out again two days later to win the Hardwicke Stakes.

Hard to imagine today, as also the practice resorted to by Lambton himself of conquering a rogue named Pan, who finished second in the 1890 Grand National, by starving him and keeping him short of water.

The 'American invasion' of owners, trainers and jockeys in the 1890s taught Lambton and some other trainers valuable lessons, including on stable management. "Open doors and windows were unknown at that period and horses were heavily rugged up when at exercise. The Americans taught us that open doors and cool stables were far better than the hot-house atmosphere usually to be found in English stables."

Their racing plates were also "far better made and lighter than ours." And, of course, there was the phenomenon of 'Tod' Sloan, "a genius on a horse; off one, erratic and foolish."

There is a lot more to entertain and inform in Lambton's book so I suggest you get a copy. In the meantime, I leave *Men and Horses I Have Known* with two memorable images. The first, of Tom Cannon, winning at his leisure, "looking at his boots to see how well they were polished."

The second, of a jockey with an unsavoury reputation who had been beaten on a hot favourite. Riding back to the paddock, he kept looking down at the horse's legs, as if thinking that it might be lame. Fellow jockey Henry Huxtable, also returning to the paddock, shouted out, "Don't look at his legs, I think his jaw is broken."

28 FRED ASTAIRE WINS TWO DOLLARS

Jack Leach wrote, "*Men and Horses I Have Known* is the best book I have ever read on racing." Its author George Lambton's opinion of Leach's book, *Sods I Have Cut On The Turf,* is not known, as Lambton died in 1945 and *Sods I Have Cut On The Turf* was published in 1961. I'm sure Lambton would have enjoyed it, as many people consider Leach's book to be the best they have ever read on racing.

It has a striking title and Leach gets off to a cracking start, with the surprising revelation that he is not a horse lover. "I have loved only one horse in my life," he wrote, in the first paragraph, "an old hunter called Gamecock. The reason I loved Gamecock was that if I pulled the reins over his head onto the ground in front of him he would stay there while I went off and picked mushrooms for breakfast."

Apart from Gamecock – a terrible name for a horse – Leach admitted to "a certain fondness for a number of horses," including Nothing Venture, who Leach liked because "he hated his opponents."

As a jockey, Leach must surely have had a soft spot for Diomedes, a prolific winner who he partnered to win the July Cup and Nunthorpe Stakes in 1925 and the July Cup again in 1926. The following year Leach won the 2000 Guineas on Adam's Apple, so I expect he quite liked him, too.

When he got fatter, Leach followed his father's example and became a trainer, in which capacity he must have liked Figaro, who he owned and trained to win the 1934 Stewards Cup and Ayr Gold Cup.

Readers only have to make it to the second page to reach the observation, "Of course racing is necessary to improve the breed of horses, but it is also necessary to relieve people of a lot of money they would otherwise spend foolishly, and to help bookmakers make both ends meet." This bodes well for all the pages still to come, as does another early observation, that "racing people seem to have more than their fair share of fun." Leach certainly did and he supplied readers with plenty of it, second-hand.

By the third page (presented as page 17 but that's because Gordon Richards and Lord Oaksey take up space complimenting the author), Leach is relating a story told to him by Tommy Reece, who evidently played billiards. I wonder if Reece knew my Maths teacher, Mr Ansell, who also played billiards? Probably not.

Fred Astaire (second left), dancer, gambler and best man at jockey Jack Leach's wedding in 1928.

Anyway, a friend of Reece, Melbourne Inman, bought a horse that had just finished nowhere in particular in a selling race. Inman knew less about racing than Reece, so asked for his advice on the next step as an owner.

Tommy told him, "Go and find the boy who was looking after it, give him a couple of quid and ask if your horse has got any special peculiarities or faults."

Inman did as he was told and asked if the horse had any faults. "Well," said the boy, "it's got two. One is that if you turn it out in a field it will take you a long time to catch it again."

That didn't seem too bad, so Inman moved on, "What's the other one?" "The other one is that when you've caught it, it's no bloody good."

The pace slackens but Leach keeps up a decent gallop, both entertaining and informative. In the 1920s he met and formed a lifetime friendship with Fred Astaire, who was brilliant at dancing but less good at picking winners. On the other hand, when Leach told him that Call Boy was a certainty for the 1927 2000 Guineas, Astaire still backed Leach's mount, Adam's Apple, which was just as well, as Adam's Apple beat Call Boy by a short-head.

Astaire was prone to falling victim to betting systems. In 1938, as he watched the 18 runners parade before the prestigious Santa Anita Handicap, Astaire realised that his current system had led him to back every horse in the race, apart from Stagehand. Yet Stagehand was Astaire's pick of the paddock, so he backed him as well.

When Stagehand beat Seabiscuit, the hot favourite, it was a happy but not notably lucrative outcome for Astaire. Leach recalled, "Luckily for Astaire it paid a long price and so he won two dollars on the race."

There are plenty of interesting opinions on jockeys, race-reading, racecourses and betting, and Leach gave helpful advice to novice racegoers and punters. Good jockeys, Leach maintained, were made, not born. Apart from the blessing of 'good hands', it was all practice and experience.

When watching a race, many racegoers search out a particular horse, usually the one they have backed, but Leach wrote, "knowing the jockeys is the most important thing to me in the reading of a race. I know all the well known jockeys by the way they sit on a horse, or by little movements or mannerisms they all have," which made me think of Luke Morris.

Leach added, "this is an easier method for me than trying to sort out some almost unknown set of colours when the runners are all bunched up in a big field a long way from home."

He was not an admirer of hard luck stories, which tended to result in losing even more money when the unlucky horse ran again. "One way and another," Leach wrote, "excuses can cost a stable a small fortune and excuses for an ungenerous horse are the worst of the lot." Trying blinkers and a change of tactics and jockey tend to leave the horse unconvinced. Leach's recommendation was, "give a horse two chances and then take no excuses; stop backing him before he breaks you."

It's sound advice, although it overlooks the dreaded possibility that, when you finally give up on the horse, it wins at 33-1. If you'd stuck with it one more time, you'd have almost made a profit.

Leach was not sanguine about the prospects of betting profitably, at least in the long term. As he put it, "In my time I have seen hundreds of 'lucky' punters go up like a rocket and come down like the stick."

They would have been better off buying a copy of Leach's book, although copies are currently priced at £75.20 upwards on Amazon, so while you are saving up I suggest you buy a copy of Alexander McCall Smith's *44 Scotland Street* (2005). It has nothing to do with horseracing but is a very engaging read and costs next to nothing.

29. LORD SAYE AND SELE GOES BAD

At Broughton Castle, up many flights of steps, unseen by the public, are 'The Barracks,' the attic rooms of this magnificent fortified manor house near Banbury.

'The Barracks' date back to 1642, when Sir William Fiennes raised a regiment to fight on the side of Parliament against King Charles I's troops at the battle of Edgehill. On the eve of the battle, Fiennes's soldiers slept in the attic.

Bats live there now, above the dry dust and relics of the past, together with an enormous, 10ft by 8ft painting of Placida, carrying the colours of John Fiennes, the 17th Lord Saye and Sele. In 1877, Placida won the Oaks, the highlight of Fiennes's ramshackle life.

There was cause to celebrate the horse but not his owner, condemned by the present, 21st Lord Saye and Sele, aged 100, as "a BAD man."

It was an era when the sons of wealthy aristocrats had a habit of squandering family fortunes but few achieved it with the recklessness and indifference of John Twistleton Wykeham Fiennes. You would not have wanted to be his father. Unfortunately for Frederick, the 16th Lord Saye and Sele, he was.

John Fiennes's mother, Emily Wingfield, died when he was seven, which spared her from the misery inflicted by John on her husband. Educated, or at least sent to Harrow then Oxford University, Fiennes quickly embraced the practice of spending as much as he liked, particularly on gambling, confident that his father would pay his debts and that, in due course, he would inherit a fortune.

In 1855, Fiennes's father rescued him from Oxford prison, where he was resident as the result of owing a moneylender £3,300 (about £265,000 today). Not all the money, or that supplied by lenders or his father, was spent on gambling; some was used to buy racehorses.

In 1856, Fiennes married Augusta Hay, the daughter of Lord Kinane. Within a year, Kinane was writing to Lord Saye and Sele to express concern about the newly weds' financial situation. Where, for instance, were they to live?

Not at Broughton Castle but at Trunkwell House, in Reading. As Augusta lacked her husband's enthusiasm for the Turf, Fiennes ran many of his horses under the pseudonym of Mr Pulteney and concealed his financial situation – usually dire, from his wife. Fortunately for their ten children, Lord Saye and Sele paid for their education.

In 1861, when a horse that Fiennes wanted to win but didn't left him owing £600, his father rescued him but extracted "his word to abandon the Turf." A fat chance.

In 1863, possibly seeking salvation from his eldest son but also from his other children, who were similarly inclined to write begging letters, Lord Saye and Sele became Archdeacon of Hereford Cathedral, a position he held until his death.

Lord Saye and Sele complained that Fiennes had not consulted him about his occupancy of Trunkwell House, which he left owing money, nor about the sale of 16 Queen's Gate Terrace, Kensington. That was a particularly upsetting transaction, as Lord Saye and Sele was its sole owner. Fiennes nevertheless managed to sell it for £7,000, £2,000 of which went to pay his debts and the remaining £5,000 towards the purchase of a house at Palace Gate, Kensington.

That was in 1876, the same year that the Legal and General Life Insurance Society advanced Fiennes £10,000, in consideration of which he committed himself to pay the Society an annuity of £1,640 for the rest of his life, to commence after the death of his father.

1877 was Fiennes's *annus mirabilis*, the year of Placida. Backed heavily into 2-1 favourite, Mr Pulteney's Placida attracted a variety of raceday opinions, including from two of *The Times*'s correspondents. One considered that, "always a nice mare, she has let down and furnished into a really splendid animal, of fine length and good at all points. We certainly never saw a better shaped or more perfectly trained animal strip for the Oaks." The other correspondent held a very different opinion, pronouncing Placida to be "light in the barrel and overdone," fidgety and sweating.

Whatever her appearance, facing eight opponents, Placida led from start to finish and "won in a canter by three-quarters of a length" from Belphoebe, a winning margin that could have been extended had Placida's jockey, Harry Jeffery, so desired. Fiennes doubtless won plenty of money and won more when, two weeks later, Placida won the Fern Hill Stakes at Ascot.

The relief was short-lived. Fiennes and money found it impossible to live together and at the end of 1878 he obtained two more loans from the Legal and General Life Insurance Society. The first, for £5,500, involved committing to another annuity, this time for £880, while the second, for £7,300, committed him to pay an annuity of £951 for the rest of his life, after his father's death.

At about this time, Williams and James, the family solicitors, informed Fiennes that they were "unable to borrow further moneys on expedient terms," with the result that Fiennes "went elsewhere." He may well have obtained the two later loans from Legal and General with the help of his new advisor.

All three loans were linked to insurance policies. By 1881, Fiennes had defaulted on the payments and by 1882 his father, unlikely to have been told the truth about his son's financial situation, was in a state of advanced despair.

In July, he wrote to his troublesome son, "It was the painfullest thing to me a few days ago to have had from Mr James (Archibald James, of Williams and James) a notification that, unless I come to your rescue, you would inevitably be put into the Bankruptcy Court, and that a thousand pound was needed to meet your difficulties; but that, and this is the bitterest intelligence of all, that Messrs Herries, Farquhar and Co (bankers) were unwilling to lend that sum unless I were willing to put my additional signature or signatures to various drafts, to which your own signatures are affixed, and running over a series of years, amounting to £5,500 which, without my privity and knowledge, but with a secrecy which they had preserved, you had taken up."

This had come to light partly because of the "untoward and offensive language used by you to [Messrs Herries, Farquhar and Co.], who you left for Messrs Blandy and whom you have left again for Messrs Coutts and Co."

Four months later, Lord Saye and Sele wrote again, to a friend, relating the sad tale of decades of financial help to Fiennes, with little thanks in return. "I have paid his debts at Oxford, at Reading, at London," he wrote. He had paid for John's eldest son Geoffrey's education at Eton and beyond, and was now giving Geoffrey an allowance of £350 a year.

As for John himself, Lord Saye and Sele complained of "his continuous system of writing letters home in place of coming to see me and talk over matters with his father, face to face; endeavouring to avoid an interview."

Throughout the long, trying years, Lord Saye and Sele had continued to give John an allowance and pay his debts, yet "I never remember his uttering a word of gratitude to me for this considerable benefit."

It was a sad story and by the time of his death, in 1887, the 16th Lord Saye and Sele had been brought to his knees. He died insolvent and towards the end of his life let Broughton Castle.

One of the first things the new Lady Saye and Sele did was to write to Mr James asking that the trustees of her marriage settlement pay the income from it into her own personal account and not that of the 17th Lord Saye and Sele.

In his reply, James explained, "the reason for this is that Lord Saye and Sele's financial position is so very grave that it is not safe for that money to which you are personally entitled, to go to his credit.

"The fact is this; that for a great number of years past, Lord Saye and Sele has been borrowing money upon securities which did not become effective until his father's death. The amount which he has borrowed is so very large that the whole of the rents of the properties which have devolved upon him by his father's death are insufficient to pay the interest premiums of insurance owing."

This was not entirely his Lordship's fault, as the agricultural depression meant that the Estate's rental income was "about 40 per cent less than 12 years ago."

For decades, John Fiennes had relied on his father's death to put him out of the red and into the black and he was "excessively angry" when James and his partners told the new Lord Saye and Sele, "we can't make any payments to him out of the late Lord's Estate."

The 16th Lord Saye and Sele's own creditors had to be paid first. Broughton Castle itself was mortgaged far beyond its value and when the next round of rent payments were received, "they will be much less than the interest on his debt. The catastrophe," James concluded, "is most dreadful."

"I myself do not know what Lord Saye and Sele is to do except break up the family" and Lord and Lady Saye and Sele "should go abroad and live at some small place in France or Germany on the interest of your Ladyship's own fortune."

James ended his letter, "It is perfectly astounding to me that your Ladyship has not been made aware of the state of affairs before this." No wonder the present Lord Saye and Sele described him as "a BAD man."

The 17th Lord Saye and Sele, owner of the winner of the 1877 Oaks, never did live at Broughton Castle, which was let to Lord and Lady Algernon Gordon-Lennox until returning to the Fiennes family in 1912, five years after the 17th Lord's death.

Today, it is in splendid shape and well worth visiting. Although you may not be able to see the painting in the attic, a smaller picture of Placida is on display, together with the faded silks Harry Jeffery wore at Epsom; white body, blue sleeves, orange cap.

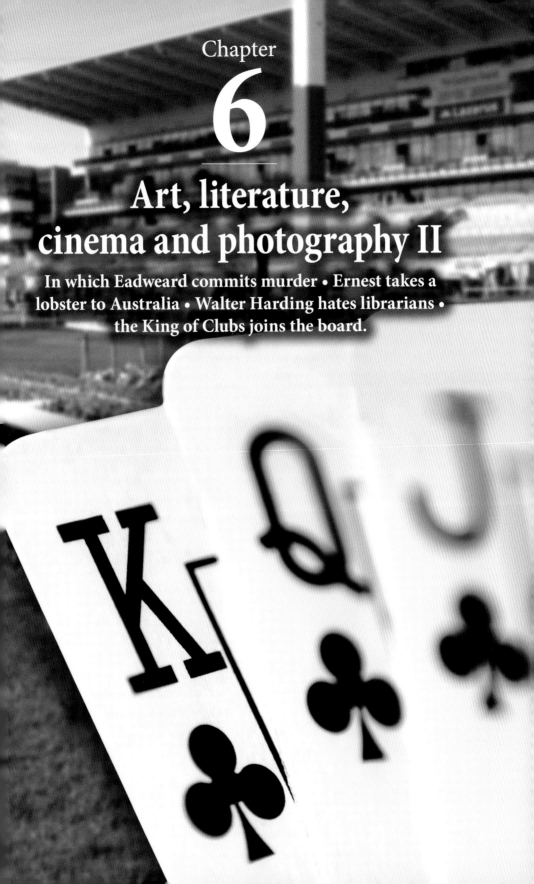

Chapter
6

Art, literature, cinema and photography II

In which Eadweard commits murder • Ernest takes a lobster to Australia • Walter Harding hates librarians • the King of Clubs joins the board.

EADWEARD COMMITS MURDER

It was a Smith & Wesson Model No. 2 Army revolver that Eadweard Muybridge carried with him on his journey to the Yellow Jacket Ranch, eight miles from Calistoga in the Napa Valley, California.

When he arrived, he knocked on the door and asked for Harry Larkyns. When Larkyns appeared, Muybridge said, "I am Muybridge and this is a message from my wife." Then he shot Larkyns dead.

The previous day, 16 October 1874, Muybridge had learnt that his wife, Flora, 20 years younger than him, was having an affair with Larkyns. Six months earlier, Flora had given birth to a son and Muybridge was shown a photograph of the boy with the name 'Harry' written on the back, in Flora's handwriting.

Susan Smith, the midwife who had shown Muybridge the photograph, later testified that Muybridge had "stamped on the floor and exhibited the wildest excitement. His appearance was that of a madman."

The murder was clearly premeditated and at the end of the three day trial, in February 1875, Judge William Wallace instructed the jury that they had four options, either 1) guilty with the death penalty, 2) guilty with life imprisonment, 3) not guilty or 4) not guilty by reason of insanity. He told the jury that knowledge of an adulterous relationship was not sufficient grounds for murdering your wife's lover nor, therefore, for returning a verdict of not guilty.

Muybridge's defence lawyers, Cameron King and Wirt Pendegast, had launched the defence by claiming a not guilty verdict "both on the ground of justifiable homicide and insanity."

In 1860, a stagecoach on which Muybridge was travelling to St Louis crashed. Muybridge was thrown out and hit his head on a rock or tree

Eadweard Muybridge, murderer and photographer.

stump, causing serious injuries. He returned to his native England for several years to recover and when he went back to the USA longstanding friends testified that his personality and behaviour had changed. Previously genial and pleasant he was now eccentric, irritable and prone to emotional outbursts.

Yet the all-male jury did not deem Muybridge to be insane. Encouraged by a rousing closing address by Pendergast, which the *San Francisco Chronicle* reported, "carried the audience away, and at the close they broke into a storm of applause," the jury "acquitted the defendant on the ground that he was justified in killing Larkyns for seducing his wife. This was directly contrary to the charge of the judge but the jury say that if their verdict was not in accord with the law of the books, it is with the law of human nature."

The jury's perverse verdict would soon have important consequences for the development of photographic techniques and understanding of the motion of horses and other animals, including homo sapiens. If Muybridge had not shot Harry Larkyns he may not have gone on, famously, to shoot horses, nor Edgar Degas to have painted them quite as he did.

When he returned from Britain, Muybridge took up photography in a serious way. In 1867 exhibitions of his large photographs of the Yosemite Valley made him a well known name and five years later Leland Stanford, a former governor of California, President of the Central Pacific Railroad Company and future founder of Stanford University, hired Muybridge.

Stanford wanted to establish whether or not, when galloping, horses had all four feet off the ground simultaneously.

Over the next few years Muybridge developed equipment and techniques that led, on 19 June 1878, to a filming session that produced a series of images of lasting fame.

The demonstration took place at Stanford's Palo Alto estate, the future site of Stanford University. A former racehorse, Sallie Gardner, was chosen for the task, ridden by Gilbert Domm, who worked at Stanford's farm. Sallie Gardner, a six-year-old, had raced in Kentucky, Tennessee and Texas, where, in 1875, she had once won six races in the space of four days.

Muybridge set up 12 cameras along the track, each with an electromagnetic shutter with a speed of $1/1000^{th}$ per second. The shutters were held cocked by a thread strung across the track. When Sallie Gardner galloped past, the threads were broken and the shutters tripped.

The sequence of photographs proved that, at one point in the horse's movement, all four legs were off the ground at the same time.

The photographs were widely reproduced and Muybridge subsequently increased the number of cameras to 24 and began to apply his method to other animals. In 1881 he published the photographs taken at Stanford's farm in a book titled *The Attitudes of Animals in Motion*.

The work had widespread influence, including on artists' portrayal of racehorses. Degas may have attended a lecture that Muybridge gave in Paris and certainly made drawings from Muybridge's famous photographs.

Muybridge's stop-motion technique also made its mark on the evolution of the movie industry, with his invention of the zoopraxiscope, a motion picture projector.

Having toured Europe with displays of his work, he returned to the USA where, supported by the University of Pennsylvania, he continued his work, taking over 20,000 photographs between 1884 and 1887, when he selected 781 of them for inclusion in his book *Animal Locomotion*.

Eventually Muybridge returned to Britain, spending the last 10 years of his life in his birthplace, Kingston upon Thames. When he died, in 1904, Muybridge left his equipment and prints to Kingston Museum, where the collection remains.

31 ERNEST TAKES A LOBSTER TO AUSTRALIA

It's a cracking picture and a very big one. In 1856, when William Powell Frith stood in front of the bare canvas, paintbrush in hand, he surely thought, "I'm never going to finish this." There were about 24 square feet to cover and his paintbrush wasn't very big.

Luckily, Frith viewed his art through the lens of his wallet and Jacob Bell had recently commissioned him to paint a large picture of Derby Day at Epsom for £1,500 (about £90,000 today).

Bell was a former MP and prominent pharmacist who had already commissioned one celebrated painting, Edwin Landseer's 1839 portrayal of two dogs, titled *Dignity and Impudence*. The dogs, a bloodhound called Grafton and West Highland terrier named Scratch, were owned by Bell.

He commissioned Frith after seeing an initial sketch based on the artist's first visit to Epsom. Frith went to great lengths to lay the foundations for the image he wanted to create, hiring models, as well as an acrobat and his son, and recruiting family and friends to pose for a place among the 88 figures identifiable towards the front of the Derby Day scene. A jockey called Bundy was persuaded to pose on a wooden horse and Frith later acknowledged that John Frederick Herring had helped his depiction of horses by providing drawings of two of them, one carrying a jockey.

At the 1857 Derby another celebrated figure, the photographer Robert Howlett, was employed to "photograph for him from the roof of a cab as many queer groups of figures as he could." Later that year, Howlett's lasting fame was ensured by his iconic photograph of Isambard Kingdom Brunel in front of the launching chains of the *Great Eastern* steamship.

Frith laboured for 15 months, further motivated by selling the engraving and exhibition rights of the picture to Ernest Gambart, a leading art dealer and publisher, for another £1,500.

Frith already had one considerable Royal Academy exhibition success to his name, his painting of *Ramsgate Sands* having attracted the approval of Queen Victoria when exhibited in 1854. Her Majesty subsequently bought the painting for £1,000 and in 1863 commissioned Frith to paint the *Marriage of the Prince of Wales with Princess Alexandra of Denmark*. Both paintings are now in the Royal Collection.

When *The Derby Day* was exhibited at the Royal Academy, in 1858, it attracted such large crowds that a policeman was employed to keep viewers in check, backed up by a railing in front of the painting. Queen Victoria and Prince Albert were among the viewers, although not required to queue.

The painting was enormously popular, although in the eyes of some staid critics, its popularity was a mark against it. A review in *The Art Journal* (1 June 1858), written while the author was simultaneously holding his nose and looking down it, remarked, "We have often had occasion to speak of the descending tone of subject-matter which characterises our exhibitions. This impression is this year more forcible in relation to the Royal Academy than we have ever before experienced it.

"The picture of the season is 'The Derby Day' by Frith; and when we remember that this work, directly and indirectly, picture and copyright, will return to the artist something like £3,000, we cannot regard 'The Derby Day' otherwise than as an accurate indication of public taste.

"It contains the material for twenty pictures, and has cost the painter an inconceivable sum for models. It will be advertised and exhibited in town and country, and will eventually return a rich premium to the print-publisher. Such is 'the picture' of the exhibition; the tone of the subject is essentially vulgar, and no supremacy of execution can redeem it. We cannot rejoice that this subject has been painted; we shall always regret that so great and accomplished a master in Art did not select a theme more worthy."

The critic, sitting on his high horse, concluded that Frith's work "will give much delight but no 'teaching' – at least, none of that teaching which is the highest aim and holiest duty of Art."

The painting is extraordinary and full of interest, which grows when examined through a magnifying glass. Men in top hats stand around a thimble-rigger's table, one, looking crestfallen, with his hands in pockets that have just been emptied; a woman begs the attention of a lady in a carriage, apparently with as much success as the girl offering ribbons or posies to the disdainful young man leaning against the same carriage.

In the centre of the picture an acrobat, on one knee, holds his arms out towards his small son, who is distracted by a display of food spread out on a tablecloth on the ground. A lobster catches the eye. To the far right, a horse and jockey are both almost identical to those in the sketch supplied to Frith by Herring.

In detail, the painting is full of activity yet the overall impression is rather static. That, at least in part, is because most of the prominent faces were of individuals who had posed in Frith's studio. On the canvas, although surrounded by others, many seem isolated and disengaged.

Nevertheless, *The Derby Day* is a magnificent work, a real tour de force, but its owner, Jacob Bell, did not enjoy it for long. Just over a year after the exhibition opened, Bell died.

He bequeathed the painting to the National Gallery but it would be six years before it appeared there. Gambart lost no time in exploiting his engraving and exhibition rights to the picture. He sent the masterpiece to Paris, to the engraver Auguste Blanchard, and in 1864, in a sign of *The*

William Powell Frith's The Derby Day (1858).

Derby Day's spreading fame, negotiated free passage to Australia for the painting, which was put into the hands of Gambart's agent, William Shield.

Taking in Melbourne, Sydney and Adelaide but also several smaller towns, the tour was a great success, not least commercially. Entrance charges to the exhibitions and the sale of prints were lucrative but in the Spring of 1865, Gambart's money-making initiative was interrupted by unwelcome questions about the whereabouts of Bell's bequest.

On 26 April 1865 a letter signed by 'Y' appeared in *The Times*, drawing attention to the fact that *The Derby Day*, "generously presented to the nation by the late Mr Jacob Bell, about six years ago, is not yet on the walls of the National Gallery. Where is it?

"'The Derby Day' was then in the possession of Mr. Gambart, who has the copyright of it. The original term allowed by Mr Bell for the retention of 'The Derby Day' by Mr. Gambart was four years and a half but Mr Bell extended the term to five years, for exhibition in any part of the United Kingdom during six calendar months, commencing from 18 April 1859. The agreement for this arrangement, signed by Mr Bell, is dated 16 April 1859.

"'The Derby Day' was exhibited at the Royal Academy in 1858, and at the close of the exhibition was delivered to Mr. Gambart. It is rumoured that this picture has been sent to Australia, but it need hardly be observed that such a rumour is too absurd to be credible. It would be desirable to receive from the trustees of the National Gallery a satisfactory explanation."

The following day's paper contained a response from Gambart, who wrote, regarding the agreement of 16 April 1859, "that I have no trace of any such document, and that the last time Mr. Jacob Bell and myself met to try and agree about a time of delivery of the picture, in the presence of Mr Edwin Field, of Lincoln's Inn Fields, who by mutual consent acted as friend to both parties, no agreement was arrived at, Mr Field pointing out to Mr Bell that I ought not to damage my position by binding myself to any definite epoch of delivery.

"It is, therefore, in perfect good faith, and with the conviction that it was my right to proceed with the further exhibition of Mr Bell's picture, that I have sent it to Australia, where it has already been exhibited at Melbourne, Ballarat, and Geelong. It is now going to Sydney, whence I expect it home next August."

Four days later the exchange of letters prompted a question in the House of Commons directed at Thomas Baring, MP for Huntingdon and a trustee of the National Gallery. He was asked, "whether a picture belonging to the nation has been sent to Australia, whether the person who sent that picture had a right to do so; and, if not, what steps the trustees of the National Gallery are about to take?"

Baring replied that, at the end of the term for which Bell had agreed that Gambart should be entitled to possess the painting, namely June 1864, the trustees "wrote to the executors of the late Mr Bell, asking them why the picture was not delivered and the reply was that Mr Gambart had said that he had a right to the picture for another year, and he had sent it to Australia but had promised it should return in August. About six weeks ago the whole circumstances of the case were sent to the Treasury and submitted to the Law Officers of the Crown to ascertain what proceedings, if any, should be adopted."

Gambert may have taken advantage of Bell's premature death to prolong his possession of the painting but when he learnt that the government was inquiring into the matter, he arranged for its return. He squeezed in a final display of the painting for a week in Sydney, followed by three days in Melbourne, ending on 2 September 1865. On 9 September, Shield and *The Derby Day* sailed for England.

Now, over 150 years later, it can be viewed at Tate Britain.

32 WALTER HARDING HATES LIBRARIANS

On 14 December 1973 officials from the Northern Trust Bank removed a number of boxes from 110 North Pine Avenue, on the unfashionable West Side of Chicago. There were enough books and documents to fill hundreds of boxes and the Bank, the executor of Walter Harding's estate, was moving a few of them to a safer place of storage.

The officials were watched by Dr Robert Shackleton, Head of the Bodleian Library in Oxford, who was there to keep an eye on what proved to be the biggest donation ever made to the Library, and to attend Harding's funeral.

Early the following year, 900 boxes weighing 22 tonnes were loaded onto two chartered aircraft and flown from Chicago to Oxford. They contained the biggest collection of songbooks, sheet music and musical miscellanea in the world, collected by a man who was not rich, bequeathed to a library he had never seen, in a country he had not set foot on since he was four years old. In one of the boxes was a songsheet from 1784. It was titled, *A New Song, Called SKEWBALL*.

Walter Newton Henry Harding was born in London in 1883, the son of an East End bricklayer who soon afterwards emigrated to America. Harding spent the rest of his life in Chicago, where he worked as a pianist in music

Walter Harding, donor of 900 boxes of musical miscellanea to the Bodleian Library.

halls and night spots, favouring the ragtime music of Scott Joplin. Later, he expanded his repertoire and began to play the organ in cinemas and churches.

Harding didn't have much spare money to indulge his passion for collecting musical material but he collected it at a time when there was little interest in popular songsheets or scores, which could be bought cheaply.

Later described as "the West Side hermit," Harding had no close relatives and lived a quiet life, devoted to his ever-growing collection. When Clarence Tracy, a Canadian academic, visited him in the 1950s he expected to meet an affluent Chicagoan but instead found Harding living in a poor working class district, in a gloomy house. From bedroom to basement was full of books and little else.

Reporting Harding's death, the *Chicago Tribune* (15 December 1973) ran a headline reading, 'Collector hated city librarians – Leaves $500,000 in music.' The hatred stemmed from an encounter with the head librarian at the Chicago Public Library 70 years earlier which alienated Harding and prompted him to consider leaving his beloved collection to a library elsewhere.

For 20 years before his death, he corresponded with the Bodleian Library and by 1970 had agreed to gift his collection to it. Although Harding had diligently indexed the collection, when it arrived it took years to process. It was a long time before the broadsheet with the song about Skewball was unearthed.

In 2012, when the British Museum staged a major exhibition called 'The Horse. From Arabia to Royal Ascot,' *A New Song, Called SKEWBALL* was among the exhibits.

Skewball was not a figment of the songwriter's imagination but a racehorse foaled in 1741, a son of the Godolphin Arabian. Having won races in England, Skewball won several more in Ireland.

When the match race celebrated in the song took place over four miles at the Curragh, Kildare, on 28 March 1752, Skewball was an 11-year-old. The song's circulation 30 years later was testimony to a lasting recollection of the event. It is the earliest known ballad about Skewball and went as follows, subject to a few indecipherable words:

> *Ye gentlemen sportsmen I pray listen all,*
> *And I'll sing you a song in praise of Skewball,*
> *And how he came over you shall understand,*
> *It was esquire Mirvin, a peer of our land.*
> *And of his late actions as I have heard before,*
> *And how he was challenged by one Sir Ralph Gore,*
> *For five hundred guineas on the plains of Kildar,*

To run with Miss Sportsly, that charming grey mare.
Skewball then he hearing the wager was laid,
He to his kind master said be not afraid,
For I on my side you thousands will hold,
I'll lay on your cattle a fine make of gold.
The time being come and the cattle led out,
The people came flocking from east, west and south,
To beat all the sportsmen I vow and declare,
They'd enter their money all on the grey mare.
Squire Mirvin he smiled and then he did say,
Come gentlemen sportsmen that's money to lay,
All you that's got hundreds I will hold you all,
For I will lay thousands on famous Skewball.
Squire Mirvin did smile, and thus he did say,
Ye gentlemen sportsmen tomorrow's the day.
Your horses and saddles and bridles prepare,
For we must away to the plains of Kildar.
The time being come and the cattle walked out,
Squire Mirvin he order'd his rider to mount,
With all the spectators to clear the way.
The time being come not a moment delay,
These cattle were mounted away they fly,
Skewball like an arrow past Miss Sportsly did fly.
And the people leapt up for to see them go round,
They swore in their hearts he ne'er touch the ground.
And as they were just in the midst of their sport,
Squire Mirvin to his rider began this discourse.
O loving kind rider come tell unto me,
How far is Miss Sportsly this moment from thee?
O loving kind master you bear a great style,
The Grey Mare is behind us a full English mile,
If the saddle maintains us I warrant you there,
We ne'er shall be beat on the plains of Kildar.
And as they were running past the distance chair,
The gentlemen cry'd Skewball never fear,
Although in this country thou wast never seen before,
Thou by beating Miss Sportsly has broke Sir Ralph Gore.

The relish shown at Miss Sportsly's defeat probably reflected Gore's unpopularity and hastened the break-up of his landed estate. Only 26 at the time of the famous match, the previous year the Curragh had been the scene of a contrastingly successful encounter, when Gore's Othello beat the Earl of March's Bajejet in a match for 1000 guineas. Although the match involving Skewball was for a smaller amount, 300 guineas, that would have been dwarfed by the owners' bets on the outcome.

In 'Belleisle and Its Owners' (*Clogher Record* Vol.16 No.2 1998), Anthony Malcomson wrote that "the dissipation of his inheritance had begun in 1752, with the sale for £6,500 of a lease" of a piece of land. Perhaps that was triggered by Miss Sportsly's defeat as well as by Gore's extravagant lifestyle. Two years later, Gore borrowed £9,000 and when he died, in 1802, he left debts of £14,000, despite having disposed of most of his extensive inherited property.

Skewball lingered in the background for almost 200 years until resurrected, usually under the name of Stewball, by a string of folk singers. There were several different versions, more than one sung by the folk movement's hero, Woody Guthrie, in the 1940s.

One of the versions sung by Guthrie, sharing the factual inaccuracy of all of them, went:

> *Way out in California, where Stewball was born,*
> *All the jockeys in the country said he blew there in a storm.*
> *You bet on Stewball, you might win, win, win. Bet on Stewball, you might win.*
> *It was a big day, in Dallas. Don't you wish you was there?*
> *You would have bet your last dollar on that iron grey mare.*
> *You bet on Stewball, you might win, win, win. Bet on Stewball, you might win.*
> *When the horses were saddled, and the word was given 'go', given 'go',*
> *All the horses, they shot out, like an arrow from a bow.*
> *You bet on Stewball, you might win, win, win. Bet on Stewball, you might win.*
> *When that big bell was a-ringing, and the horses was run,*
> *And that big bell was a-singing and the horses did run.*
> *You bet on Stewball, you might win, win, win. Bet on Stewball, you might win.*
> *The old folks, they hollered, the young folks did bawl.*
> *The children said look, look, at that noble Stewball.*
> *You bet on Stewball, you might win, win, win. Bet on Stewball, you might win.*

In the 1950s and 1960s, and beyond, Stewball became a staple on folk singers' menus. Among the popularisers were Peter, Paul and Mary, and Joan Baez. Their renditions, while reminiscent of one of the versions sung by Guthrie, were different again.

Peter, Paul and Mary (1963)

Oh Stewball was a racehorse, and I wish he were mine.
He never drank water, he always drank wine.
His bridle was silver, his mane it was gold.
And the worth of his saddle has never been told.
Oh the fairgrounds were crowded, and Stewball was there
But the betting was heavy on the bay and the mare.
And a-way up yonder, ahead of them all,
Came a-prancin' and a-dancin' my noble Stewball.
I bet on the grey mare, I bet on the bay
If I'd have bet on ol' Stewball, I'd be a free man today.
Oh the hoot owl, she hollers, and the turtle dove moans.
I'm a poor boy in trouble, I'm a long way from home.
Oh Stewball was a racehorse, and I wish he were mine.
He never drank water, he always drank wine.

Joan Baez (1964)

Stewball was a racehorse, he wore a high head,
And the mane on his foretop, was as fine as silk thread.
Yes his mane it was silver, and his bridle was gold,
And the worth of his saddle has never been told.
He was ridden in England, was ridden in Spain,
And he never did lose, boys, he always did gain.
So come all you gamblers, wherever you are,
And don't place your money on the little grey mare.
She's liable to stumble, she's likely to fall,
But you never will lose, boys, on my noble Stewball.

Ah, the fairgrounds were crowded, and Stewball was there,
But the betting was heavy on the little grey mare.
Ah, the hoot owl she hollered, and the turtle dove moaned,
I'm a poor boy in trouble, and a long ways from home.
Cause I bet on the grey mare, and some on the bay,
If I'd bet on old Stewball, I'd be a rich man today.

As they were a-riding, 'bout halfway around,
That grey mare she stumbled, and fell on the ground.
And way out yonder, ahead of them all,
Came a-prancing and dancing, my noble Stewball.

33 THE KING OF CLUBS JOINS THE BOARD

Totopoly wasn't Monopoly, I think we can all agree on that. Monopoly is an iconic board game, a worldwide big seller that John Waddington Ltd obtained the right to produce in 1935 and is still selling today, although not with Waddington's name on it. The company sold their games division to Hasbro in 1994.

But I digress. Although Totopoly wasn't Monopoly, it was a popular board game in which the ultimate object was to win the horserace that was the game's climax. The race followed on from earlier elements of the game, which involved the leasing and training of the dozen horses that eventually contested the race. That part of the game took place on one side of the board, featuring the Stevedon and Walroy stables, each housing six horses. The race itself was run on the other side of the board. It was all rather clever and quite complicated.

Waddington was based in Leeds and the Watsons, who owned and ran the company, decided to give the game's 12 horses the names of the winners of the

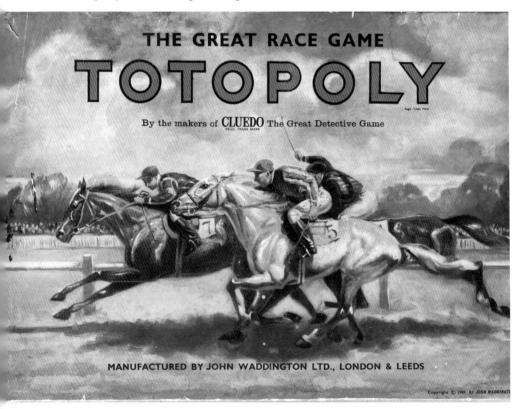

Totopoly, a bit like Monopoly but with fewer streets and more racehorses.

Lincolnshire Handicap in the years preceding Totopoly's launch in 1938. The first of these, the winner in 1926, was King of Clubs, who had won at 100-1, the same price as the 1929 winner, Elton.

In early editions of the game the horses were made of lead and hand-painted. Like the real thing, their legs were susceptible to injury, while the lead may also have been a health hazard, especially if swallowed. Later versions used plastic horses.

The box for the 1949 version, sitting on the table as I write, declares itself to be 'The Great Race Game. Totopoly. By the makers of Cluedo The Great Detective Game.' Cluedo was a new addition to the Waddington collection, with its memorable cast of suspects. Who could forget Miss Scarlet, Colonel Mustard or the Reverend Green? Or the cast of murder weapons, including a candlestick, dagger and rope? Cluedo was set in a mansion you would not have wanted to visit, for someone was always getting murdered in the conservatory, or library, or the billiard room. I think you'll find it was Mrs Peaccock who did it, with a lead pipe, in the Study.

But I digress (see above). The rules for Totopoly took some digesting, as indicated by the fact that they took up four pages, in small print. One curiosity was that, as the final rule stated, "The winner of the game shall be the winner of the race, irrespective of whether he has the most money at the end of the game, as a player without a horse in the first three may have had a heavy bet on the winner, and thereby finish the game with more money than the winner of the race."

This was changed in later versions of Totopoly, so that the winner was the player with the most money. It was jolly good fun, and could take hours. On the other hand, when Victor Watson, formerly managing director then chairman of Waddingtons, assembled *The Waddingtons Story* (2008), he managed to produce a book 210 pages long without once mentioning Totopoly.

Chapter

7

From start to finish

In which Captain Brown grapples with knicker elastic • an umbrella is found guilty of race-fixing • Jane feels ghastly • jockeys get their sums wrong • metres almost arrive • Kodiac loses weight.

CAPTAIN BROWN GRAPPLES WITH KNICKER ELASTIC

34

Just as legs are made for kicking footballs, flags are made for waving. In wartime, the losing side waves a white flag; in football, assistant referees wave coloured flags; in motor racing officials wave chequered flags and in horseracing Captain Keith Brown waved an unfurled red flag but only for the first of the 1993 Grand National's two false starts.

Curiously, just as old soldiers never die, so army officers, although long retired, never lose their military rank. So it was that Captain Brown, who had left the army 35 years previously, pulled the ancient lever that released the 60 metres long, sagging elastic tape, to start the 147th Grand National.

Unfortunately, some of the 39 waiting horses, delayed and agitated by an animal rights' demonstration, were standing too close to the starting tape. The Jockey Club's senior starter would have been well advised to insist on the contestants turning around and lining up again. Sadly, when the elastic went 'twang', the tape became entangled with several horses.

Captain Brown, resplendent in a bowler hat, waved his red flag vigorously to indicate a false start.

Waving a flag at the rapidly disappearing rumps of a cavalry charge is an optimistic method of communication but, flags being de rigeuer, a second flag was called upon. This flag was held by Mr Ken Evans, a part-time employee allotted the role of 'recall man.'

Mr Evans, standing between the start and the first fence, either did (according to Mr Evans) or did not (according to the subsequent inquiry) wave his flag to let the jockeys know that it was a false start. Whether he did or didn't wave his flag, the runners returned to the start to have another go.

Unfortunately the horses were restless and again inclined to nudge the starting tape. Time passed, exacerbating their restlessness without reducing their proximity to the tape. When Captain Brown finally activated the lever again, the elastic twanged and wrapped itself around jockey Richard Dunwoody's neck, while also interfering with several other horses and riders.

Briefly, Dunwoody seemed on his way to an entry in the record books under the heading, "Most Bizarre Deaths." Mercifully, he survived.

Meanwhile, on the starter's rostrum, Captain Brown waved but did not unfurl his flag. Mr Evans either did (according to Mr Evans) or did not (according to the subsequent inquiry) wave his recall flag.

Whatever, precisely, went wrong, the result was that 30 of the 39 runners set off in vain pursuit of glory. As they galloped on, various attempts were made to encourage them to stop. Although many did, many did not. When

Captain Keith Brown wishes that he'd stayed at home.

the winning post finally arrived, Esha Ness, at 50-1, led a group of seven who completed the course.

The race was declared void and was not re-run. The 1993 Grand National wasn't.

A lot of people were cross, including Jenny Pitman, the sometimes fiery trainer of Esha Ness. Pitman scathingly called the starting tapes "sixty yards of knicker elastic." After mature reflection, Sir Peter O'Sullevan, the distinguished journalist and commentator known as 'The Voice of Racing,' described the race as "the greatest disaster in the history of the Grand National."

An inquiry was set up under Sir Michael Connell, a High Court judge and Master of the Grafton Hunt. Various elements of the starting system were found wanting, including the equipment and procedures but Captain Brown escaped severe censure.

While it was concluded that he should not have allowed the horses to be so close to the starting tape, Mr Evans's sins were deemed more serious. "Despite his assertions to the contrary," the report asserted, "we conclude that Mr Evans did not wave his recall flag on either false start."

Evans might have felt that his treatment was similar to that of his namesake, but probably no relation, Timothy Evans. In 1950, Timothy was convicted of murdering his daughter and allegedly also his wife but it was later established that they had been killed by John Christie, a serial killer. Unfortunately, Evans had already been executed but, by way of consolation, in 1966 he was given a posthumous pardon. Ken Evans was not pardoned but on the plus side, neither was he executed.

A working party under Brigadier Andrew Parker Bowles considered what steps should be taken to avoid a recurrence of the 1993 fiasco. Various changes to the equipment and procedures were recommended but after pondering the merits of modern technology, such as horns and flashing lights, it was decided that where false starts were concerned, the future remained with flags, albeit more of them.

In the event of a false start, two flag men, in touch with the starter via radio, would wave fluorescent yellow flags. A third person, a 'stop man', would be there to sweep up any escapees, if necessary by driving after them. So far, it seems to have worked.

AN UMBRELLA IS FOUND GUILTY OF RACE-FIXING

Hamlet cigars were first introduced into the UK in 1964. A year later, they were followed by starting stalls, a line of connected boxes into which racehorses are placed immediately before a race is run.

In a bid to get the horses off to a level start, stalls are used for virtually all Flat races. It makes things more difficult for jockeys not wanting to break on equal terms, who face the awful possibility of finding themselves well placed to win a race unintentionally. For them, the old system was preferable.

Under that system, horses lined up behind a set of wires, which were released when the starter dropped his flag. Notoriously, and perhaps apocryphally, starters would shout, "Triers at the front, non-triers at the back."

In the USA, after various experiments, from 1929 starting stalls were used regularly at Hawthorne racecourse, Chicago. Their use spread rapidly, particularly after Clay Puett's electric starting gates were introduced at Exhibition Park in Vancouver in 1939. The following year, the Kentucky Derby was started with an electric starting gate.

Meanwhile, in England, the Jockey Club's intensely conservative rule ensured that electric starting stalls were not used for the Epsom Derby until

1967, having first appeared at Newmarket two years earlier. It was the same with McDonald's (USA 1955, UK 1974) and drive-through coffee shops (USA 1930s, UK 2008).

Occasionally, when the stalls open, one occupant remains perfectly still, as content and untroubled as his rider and those who have backed him are the opposite. In a celebrated 1980s advertisement for Hamlet cigars, a horse remains in the stalls while Jacques Loussier plays Bach's 'Air on the G String.' The resigned jockey lights up a cigar. "Happiness is a cigar called Hamlet," the caption read.

Loussier was wonderful and if anyone's got the LPs I used to have of The Jacques Loussier Trio, Play Bach Numbers 1, 2, 3, 4 and 5, can I please have them back? Thank you.

At some tracks, over certain distances, the horse's draw – the stall it is allocated – can be very important. Nowadays stalls are numbered from the inside running rail, so the horse drawn nearest to the rail is in stall 1. At Chester and Beverley, particularly in sprints, a low draw bestows a significant advantage. On the eve of races, horses drawn badly have a tendency to fall sick and be withdrawn with a vet's certificate. If they run, it is part of a jockey's expertise to exploit a good draw or overcome a bad one.

Sometimes, particularly when a horse is playing up, it can take a long time to load the stalls. On these occasions, it may be worth drawing the starter's attention to Race Manual (B) Schedule 5 of the Rules of Racing – Starting Procedures. Section 3.4.2 states that "a horse which refuses to go into the stalls on the first occasion may be blindfolded and tried again." Section 3.4.3 requires that "if the horse again refuses it will be sent to the rear and at the starter's discretion may be given one final chance after the other horses have been loaded." Starters often overlook this and offer the culprit further chances, to the detriment of other horses. I wish they wouldn't – and now they've changed the starting procedures so starters can carry on allowing what they shouldn't have been allowing before.

Occasionally the stalls open prematurely, occasionally some open and others don't, sometimes a horse manages to break out and gallop down the track and sometimes a horse jinks after exiting a stall and dumps the jockey on the turf. None of these incidents compare to the case of the umbrella.

In 2009 the stewards of the Selangor Turf Club in Malaysia disqualified assistant trainer Wee Mung Hua for a year for having allegedly arranged to have an umbrella waved at the stalls.

At about 5.15pm on 6 December 2008, just before the start of race 9, Azmi bin Senawi, acting on Wee Mung Hua's instructions, opened an umbrella in the direction of the starting stalls.

This was deemed to be a signal to a jockey or jockeys, "the effect of which may have prevented a horse or horses from winning or obtaining the best possible placing."

The stewards' report didn't say whether or not it was raining.

36 JANE FEELS GHASTLY

Eyes are vital for racecourse judges, given the heavy responsibility of deciding which horse has reached the winning post first. For centuries, judges lacked technological aids although, by way of compensation, it was difficult to prove that their judgement was faulty. Unfortunately for 'Calamity Jane' Stickels, by the time she was appointed as a judge, in 1993, photofinish cameras were able to supply evidence for the prosecution.

In the USA, by the early 1930s photofinish cameras were commonplace but 10 years later they were still absent from British racecourses. The Jockey Club did not believe in acting hastily nor, very often, at all.

In a rush of blood to the head, in 1947 the Jockey Club authorised the use of a photofinish camera at Epsom. The pioneering cameras were so successful that less than 20 years later, in 1966, it was announced that by the end of 1968 photofinish equipment would be operating at most courses. By 1983, they were in use everywhere.

In the meantime, judges' verdicts could be controversial. Famously and possibly factually, a judge, having announced an unexpected verdict, descended from his box to be confronted by an irate racegoer. Clinging to politeness, the racegoer asked, "Are you sure you got that right, sir? It must have been very close."

"Yes, it was," replied the judge, "damn close, and I don't mind telling you, it got my treble up."

Even when judges were unbiased, mistakes were not unusual. In 1967, in a four runner chase at Newcastle, the judge declared that Tant Pis had beaten Moidore's Token by a short-head. Later, he declared that it was the other way around.

Six years later, at Carlisle, Ian Johnson was convinced that he had won the apprentice race on Brass Farthing but the judge declared Brother Somers the winner, by a head. Driving home, Johnson heard on the radio that the judge had made a mistake and Brass Farthing was the winner. By then, it was too late. The next day, *The Sporting Life*'s headline read, "Not a Brass Farthing for winner backers."

In those days it could take several minutes for the film to be developed and studied and the judge to announce the result. During the wait, racecourse bookmakers continued to bet on the outcome. Professional gambler Alex Bird made a fortune by standing in line with the winning post, one eye closed, pretending to be a camera. He was reputed to have placed 500 successive winning bets on photofinishes.

Not all official judges were as good, even when armed with a photograph. 'Calamity Jane' Stickels survived a string of blunders between 1994 and 2006, when she committed a blunder too far.

In 1994, at Kempton, Stickels declared a dead-heat between Absalom's Lady and Large Action, before realising that Absalom's Lady was the winner. In 1997, at Goodwood, her decision not to declare a dead-heat but to announce that Midnight Line had beaten Alignment in the Prestige Stakes offended many observers.

Two years later, at Lingfield, the horse first past the post, Monacle, was disqualifed by the stewards and the race awarded to the runner-up, Gold Plate. Fourdaned, who finished fifth, should have been promoted to fourth but instead, 'Calamity Jane' moved the sixth placed horse, Statajack, into fourth place. Asked to explain why, Stickels said that the mistake was caused by "a slip of the pen."

It was particularly unfortunate because the race was a 16 runner handicap, which meant that, on bets for a horse to finish placed, bookmakers paid out on the first four horses home rather than the first three. To many punters, fourth place mattered.

Steven Simon claimed that Stickels' blunder had cost him about £20,000 because among his Tote Placepot bets was a £7 line that included Fourdaned, who started at 25-1, while Statajack was the 5-1 second favourite. Simon argued that the winning dividend of £434.30 would have been much bigger if the judge had got the placings right. He threatened to sue the Jockey Club and failing that, Stickels, but legal precedents suggested that such action was doomed to fail.

Less than a month after the Lingfield fiasco Stickels was in the soup again. In a five runner race at Newmarket she initially announced that Full Flow had beaten the favourite, Thady Quill, by a short-head. Soon afterwards, she realised her mistake and announced that Thady Quill was the short-head winner.

"I felt ghastly when I realised what had happened. I'm afraid I've made a few mistakes before," Stickels confessed. "There is a certain amount of pressure to give the result quickly and that can lead to mistakes."

The Jockey Club suspended Stickels, who underwent a period of retraining followed by several months of accompanied judging. By February 2000, 'Calamity Jane' had been let loose again. All went well until 2006 when Stickels called Welsh Dragon, the 9-4 favourite, the winner at Lingfield, when Miss Dagger, at 14-1, held a more compelling claim, having reached the winnng post first.

It was alleged that her blunder cost the betting industry over £2 million, although the betting industry was prone to exaggerate. The Jockey Club launched an internal inquiry at the end of which it was decided that Stickels should vacate the judge's box.

Since the development of digital technology, resulting in Scan-O-Vision scanning the winning line an enormous number of times per second, dead-heats have been in danger of extinction. It was a sad day for punters when, in 2008, a nose replaced a short-head as the smallest official winning margin. It was bad enough being beaten by a short-head but worse when the nose took over.

So credit to Dave Smith who, at Kempton in 2013, after 13 years as a racecourse judge, took just 50 seconds to boldly declare a dead-heat between Extra Noble and Fire Fighting. Unfortunately, the British Horseracing Authority felt obliged to ask Smith to reconsider his verdict, after which Extra Noble was declared the winner, by a nose.

Smith had a reputation as a fast decision maker which may have encouraged the BHA's decision to remove him permanently from the judge's box. Smith described himself as "gutted."

Mistakes continued to be made, notably by Felix Wheeler. In March 2018, at Kempton, Wheeler deemed Bird For Life, at 8-1, to have beaten Oregon Gift, the odds-on favourite, by a nose. Five days later, the result was reversed. Trainers, owners and favourite backers were not amused. Nor was

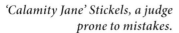

'Calamity Jane' Stickels, a judge prone to mistakes.

the BHA, which announced that, in future, judges' decisions would be subject to a second opinion prior to the official result being announced.

It was just as well because, four months later, at Sandown, the stewards' intervention prevented Wheeler from declaring Rio Ronaldo the winner from Vibrant Chords, rather than the other and correct way round.

Racecourse bookmakers often pay winning punters after a result is announced but before the 'weighed-in' signal that makes the result official. At Sandown in March 2019, Barry Dennis, a prominent bookmaker, was busy paying out backers of One For Rosie, the 12-1 winner of a valuable hurdle race, when it was announced that the initial announcement was mistaken and Third Wind, at 9-1, had won by a short-head. Dennis claimed that paying out on both horses cost him £20,000.

The argument for making full use of the latest technology to settle results is irresistible but the fact that it is rational does not necessarily make it welcome. Sherlock Holmes managed perfectly well with a magnifying glass. Indeed, who could forget its value when Holmes examined a hat in *The Adventure of the Blue Carbuncle*?

Judges, having embraced noses, seemingly will not be satisfied until they have provoked a suicide in every betting shop in Britain.

37 JOCKEYS GET THEIR SUMS WRONG

For an object of such vital importance, winning posts are often of inconsequential appearance. Generally a white stick, topped by a red circle, placed in the ground in what, for many observers, is the wrong place.

In order to baffle and bemuse generations of racegoers, Sandown Park has two winning posts on its jumps course. The first, for chases, stands 20 yards before the second, which is for hurdle races. The reason is that the chase and hurdle courses approach the winning line from different angles.

By 2019, various aids and safeguards were in place to spare racecourse judges the embarrassment of being tricked into calling a wrong result. Advanced digital technology produced images of great detail and precision. In 2018, with errors persisting, it was decided that judges' decisions would be scrutinised before the 'weighed-in' signal, which confirmed the official result.

It didn't provide a complete cure. At Sandown in March 2019 Race Tech, responsible for supplying photofinish prints to the judge, had one camera trained on the hurdle course finish and another on the chase finish. Both should have been focused on the hurdle course's winning post. Unfortunately, the photo studied by the judge was of the wrong winning post. As a result, (see curiosity 36), One For Rosie was initially announced as the winner rather than the actual winner, Third Wind.

Judges are not alone in mistaking the winning line. Jockeys occasionally forget how many circuits of a racecourse they are supposed to complete or have completed. The more circuits, the more likely a mistake when adding up.

Fakenham is a delightful, idiosyncratic jumps course in Norfolk, well worth a visit. If you do, you'll see that the track is only one mile around, which requires jockeys to be able to count – one time round, two times round, three times round?

In 2008, Denis O'Regan was banned for 14 days for riding a finish a circuit prematurely on Harringay, in a three mile chase. As Harringay was prominent in the betting and going well at the time, it was not surprising that a race report observed, "the crowd was understandably in uproar."

On these occasions, punters who have put their faith in the errant jockey tend to consider a temporary ban inadequate and, in the absence of a guillotine, feel that a lengthy prison sentence would be more appropriate.

A few months later Sam Thomas committed a similar crime at Fakenham on Oumeyade, who was the odds-on favourite in a two mile five furlong chase. Thomas was banned for 17 days.

Ten years later, Maxime Tissier, a promising conditional jockey, punched the air to celebrate passing Fakenham's winning post first on Iconic Sky. When Tissier looked up he noticed that those behind him had set out on another circuit. Tissier buried his face in his hands, which was better than the burial backers of Iconic Sky had in mind for him. He was banned for 14 days.

Various suggestions were made to reduce the chance of Fakenham's racegoers being incensed and jockeys banned but there was no easy solution. It was the jockeys' responsibility to familiarise themselves with the course.

Lucy Wadham, Iconic Sky's disappointed trainer, remarked, "Some people have suggested having a bell for the final circuit, like they do in athletics, but that would just shift the responsibility on to someone else to do the counting."

On the Flat, Wolverhampton has been the scene of similar embarrassments. In 2012, the Italian jockey Mirco Demuro's promising spell in Britain was interrupted by a 12 day suspension caused by riding a finish a circuit too soon on The Bells O Peover. Five years later, Rob Hornby copied his example on Almutamarred and was also banned for 12 days.

In September 2020, the promising apprentice George Rooke was given 14 days off for committing a similar offence on the aptly named Sophar Sogood.

It could have been worse and at Tramore on New Year's Eve 2007, it was. Fourteen horses, each with a jockey, set out on the two mile five furlong journey around the one mile track. According to the *Racing Post*'s reporter, "Several of the riders rode a finish a circuit early and every other rider in the race pulled up after passing the post, thinking the race was over or wondering whether it was. It was only quite quick thinking by the riders of the first two staying on the track that prevented the race being voided, rather than the utter calamity which it turned out to be. Take your pick which was preferable."

Eventually, five runners completed the race, headed, fortunately for public order, by the favourite, Mr Aussie.

38 METRES ALMOST ARRIVE

Furlong poles are an important part of the racing experience and each race's final furlong pole has profound implications. It heralds the appearance, 220 yards further on, of the winning post and with it joy or sorrow, elation or despair.

When the race commentator announces that the leader has entered the final furlong, tension rises, concentration intensifies and racegoers are prone to leap up and down and shout a lot. It's pointless, because neither the horses nor the jockeys can hear what is being shouted and, even if they could, they wouldn't take any notice. Still, it has to be done.

Few things in life compare with the sight of a horse you want to win moving smoothly forward inside the final furlong, the furlong post behind it, the winning post ahead, victory a formality. Admittedly, few things in life compare with the disheartening realisation that the final furlong will not be a furlong to savour.

Traditionally, horseracing has been notoriously insular and resistant to change, particularly when ruled by the Jockey Club. It was therefore a shock when, in March 1974, the Club announced that a Metrical Committee was being set up under the chairmanship of Brigadier Sidney Kent, the inspector of racecourses, to consider the conversion of race distances from furlongs to metres.

Under the headline, 'Last of the Flat As We Know It!' the *Sunday Mirror* warned readers to "Stand by for the biggest revolution that has ever hit racing in this country – metrication. On Thursday, 'They're Off' for the last ever Flat season, English style. From March 20 next year, the start of the 1975 Flat season, you can forget about miles, furlongs and yards. Instead races will be measured in terms of metres."

Last of the Flat AS WE KNOW IT!

STAND BY for the biggest revolution that has ever hit racing in this country—metrication.

On Thursday "They're Off" for the last ever Flat season, English style.

From March 20 next year, the start of the 1975 Flat season, you can forget about miles, furlongs and yards. Instead races will be measured in terms of metres (one metre equals 1·094 yards).

Forget about jockeys' weights in terms of stones and pounds. Instead think of kilogrammes and half kilogrammes (one kilo equals 2·2lb.).

That's the way it is on the Continent. And that's the way it is going to be here.

The Jockey Club may not make their announcement with full details until January 1 next year. But it will come.

I can reveal that the Jockey Club's inspectors of courses are carrying out a detailed programme of re-measuring every course in the country, ready for the conversion.

They started their measurements last year, with some alarming results.

They found that many distances on the race-cards were inaccurate by 30 to 40 yards. An that's a lot of short-heads. The discrepancies had been caused over the years by racecourse staff shifting starting barriers.

The effect of racing 1975 style on betting shop pundits and the most precise students of form will not be sufficient to cause a surge in the suicide rate. The metric conversions are fairly simple.

The minimum racing distance of five furlongs will be 1,000 metres. Six furlongs will become 1,200 metres. Seven furlongs will be 1,400 metres. A mile (eight furlongs) will be 1,600 metres. The mile-and-a-quarter will be 2,000 metres. And the mile- and -a-half will become 2,400 metres.

The Derby and the Oaks will become 2,400 metre races with the horses

By RACING EDITOR MONTY COURT

carrying 58 kilogrammes, instead of 9st.

Handicap weights will be in units of half-kilos, instead of pounds, so that from 45 kilos (7st. 1lb.) to race weights will range to 63 kilos (10st.).

The whole switch to metrication is going to mean a hectic summer for the Wetherby's Computer IBM 360/30 at Welling-

borough, which is used for all the Jockey Club handicap, entry and acceptance work.

The switch to metric of the National Hunt races will come at the start of their season in August, next year.

If next season is going to mean a strange and possibly alarming time for the punters and students of form, then this coming season is guaranteed to provide a king-size shock for unscrupulous trainers. The Jockey Club is alarmed at the use of anabolic steroids. "bulk bombs," in the preparation

of horses. A whole team of veterinary scientists is working on a clear line which is going to "nail" a trainer using these drugs.

The Jockey Club "detectives" have been given a running start in their research by the team of doctors from Guy's Hospital who have developed a system of detecting the drugs in athletes. The world knows the freak effects the drug has had on athletes' performances.

The Sports Council announced the results of

the Guy's team's research.

The Jockey Club will give no such warning. No announcement of any kind will be made.

The first the racing world will know of the breakthrough will be when a trainer is invited to the Jockey Club to explain how traces of steroid were found in tests on a winner.

The first case will be a sensation which will explode on the race scene with a violence that will send a shudder through the ranks of unscrupulous men.

Furlongs out, metres in! Almost.

Weights as well as distances would be transformed. "Forget about jockeys' weights in terms of stones and pounds," the *Sunday Mirror* continued. "Instead, think of kilogrammes and half kilogrammes. That's the way it is on the Continent. And that's the way it is going to be here."

It was reported to be "almost certain" that the 1975 Derby would be run, not over one and a half miles but 2400 metres. Furlong poles would presumably become 200 metre poles.

The Metrical Committee met for the first time on 17 April 1974. It included Phil Bull, the founder and head of Timeform, Tony Fairbairn of the Racing Information Bureau, and Major Val Gorton, described as the chief adviser to the Jockey Club on the metric system.

Fairbairn remarked, "The metric system has been introduced throughout the country in industry, why should it not come into racing?"

The new look would see five furlong races converted to 1000 metres, six furlongs to 1200 metres and, dramatically, the Derby's one and a half miles to 2400 metres.

It was a Bognor Regis moment for the Sport of Kings, reminiscent of the time when Harold Steptoe, in *Steptoe and Son*, suggested that he and Albert, his curmudgeonly father, abandon their annual holiday in Bognor in favour of a trip abroad. Albert, aggrieved, whines, "But we always go to Bognor. What about Mrs Clifford, she's expecting us?"

Since the birth of modern racing, in the 17th century, races had been measured in furlongs, a measure dating back to Anglo-Saxon times, being the length of a furrow in one acre of a ploughed field. The term was derived from the Old English 'furh' (furrow) and 'lang' (long). A furrow was 220 yards, one eighth of a mile, equal to just over 200 metres. Now the long reign of furlongs and furlong poles was to end.

Monty Court, the *Sunday Mirror*'s racing editor, wrote, "It will come. I can reveal that the Jockey Club's inspector of courses are carrying out a detailed programme of remeasuring every course in the country, ready for the conversion."

Court was sanguine about the impact of the change. He assured readers, "The effect of racing 1975 style on betting shop pundits and the most precise students of form will not be sufficient to cause a surge in the suicide rate. The metric conversions are fairly simple."

The weights carried by horses would be expressed in units of half-kilos instead of pounds, so that 10st would become 63kilos.

The same metrication system would be applied to National Hunt as well as Flat racing, starting with the beginning of the jumps season in August 1975.

From apparent inevitability to the waste paper bin happened rapidly and with barely a murmur. It was, after all, an unlikely initiative for such a conservative sport. In August 1974 the *Daily Mirror* complained that racecourses had spent £20,000 on acquiring metric scales which would not be needed as the Jockey Club had decided to defer metrication indefinitely.

Metrication disappeared from racing debates for 38 years until, in 2012, Racing For Change put it back on the proverbial table.

Racing for Change was set up in 2009 with the aim of making British racing more accessible, particularly for new, younger customers. The existing audience had a tendency to be old and male while the education system tended to teach young people a lot about kilometres and kilograms and very little about furlongs and stones.

With Rod Street as project director, Racing For Change developed a string of initiatives, including a fresh look at the case for metrication. Describing the use of furlongs as "archaic," Street observed that, "Imperial measures don't mean a great deal to kids and tourists, so it makes sense to trial the use of metric information."

The trial was launched at a mid-week evening meeting at Sandown Park in July 2012. Metric markers were displayed alongside furlong poles and racecards included jockeys' weights in kilograms as well as stones and pounds. "It was not a case of replacing traditional measurements," said Street, "but explaining them."

The experiment failed to prompt the debate the Racing for Change team had hoped for and neither the racing media nor racefans displayed an appetite for metres and kilograms. The issue simply faded away. Street later reflected, "Racing's language is part of its appeal as well as its heritage and I firmly believe that it is about explanation not replacement. To this day people ask me what a furlong is and when I tell them it's about 200m, they say, 'Oh, okay'"

In another 38 years time, perhaps.

39 KODIAC LOSES WEIGHT

In Norway, Kaia Ingolfsland was a champion, a former champion amateur jockey and champion Scandinavian apprentice jockey. She rode in Dubai and New Zealand and in 2020 wrote to Sir Mark Prescott, in Newmarket, asking if there was a vacancy. He replied that she could come for a week.

Kodiac Pride and Kaia Ingolfsland pass the winning post first but spot the weight cloth on the ground.

After that week, Prescott arranged for Ingolfsland to come back and be apprenticed to him. It wouldn't be easy in Britain's highly competitive racing scene, especially as Kaia had ridden over 50 winners and therefore could only claim a 3lb allowance.

Her third ride, at Salisbury on 9 August 2020, was on Kodiac Pride. Five days earlier Kodiac Pride had won a handicap easily at Lingfield. Prescott is an acknowledged master at planning and placing his horses and Kodiac Pride was able to run at Salisbury before the handicapper's reassessment, carrying just a 5lb penalty for his Lingfield win.

It was an apprentice race and Kodiac Pride was the 11/8 favourite. Ingolfsland made all the running in the seven furlong contest and, a furlong from the finish, going strongly, had the race won. Then the weight cloth slipped off. With it, Kodiac Pride would still have won but without it, disqualification was inevitable.

It was horribly bad luck and when the season ended, Ingolfsland, after 16 rides, was still without a winner.

Kodiac Pride and Pinehurst Park (see curiosity 53) were merely two on a list of unlucky losers so long that only a flavour can be supplied here. In 1978, Jellaby was about to win the prestigious Lockinge Stakes at Newbury when he put his foot in a hole and unseated Brian Taylor. In a hurdle race in 1986, at what was then called Devon and Exeter racecourse, Amantiss carried Tony Charlton to within a couple of feet of the winning post, where he jinked and deposited Charlton on the ground. At Royal Ascot in 1988, Ile De Chypre performed a similar unwelcome service for Greville Starkey (see curiosity 83).

Then there was Adecco. In a chase at Towcester in 2007, jockey Eamon Dehdashti experienced a different manifestation of cruel bad luck. Six lengths clear on the run-in, racing against the stands rail, he was suddenly confronted by a loose horse running in the wrong direction, straight in front of him. Adecco was stopped in his tracks. By the time Dehdashti got him going again, Golden Oak had galloped past.

Not forgetting – the Queen Mother wouldn't have done – Devon Loch's bizarre demonstration of the art of snatching defeat from the jaws of victory. Famously, in the 1956 Grand National, as the winning post loomed, Dick Francis's mount jumped where there was no jump, sprawled and came to a halt.

Owned by the Queen Mother and fourth joint-favourite, Devon Loch's inexplicable action lost a great many punters a great deal of money. Yet there was an individual unluckier than any of the backers of Kodiac Pride or Jellaby, Adecco or Devon Loch, because a fortune was involved. If you think you've been unlucky, read curiosity 76 and change your mind.

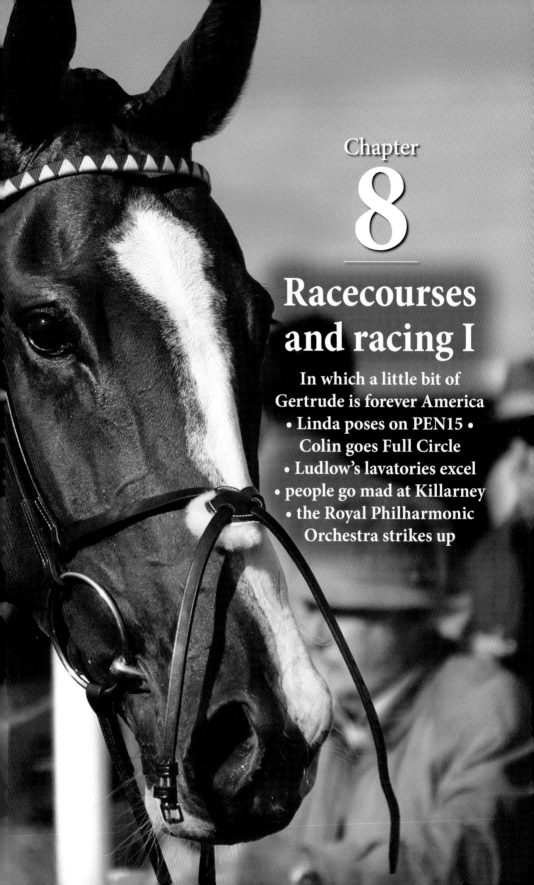

Chapter

8

Racecourses and racing I

In which a little bit of
Gertrude is forever America
• Linda poses on PEN15 •
Colin goes Full Circle
• Ludlow's lavatories excel
• people go mad at Killarney
• the Royal Philharmonic
Orchestra strikes up

40 A LITTLE BIT OF GERTRUDE IS FOREVER AMERICA

In 1966, when David Shilling was 12 years old, he made a hat for his mother, Gertrude. David had "a passionate relationship with white," which may have influenced his decision to make a black and white hat, three feet wide. Gertrude, then 56, managed to wear it to Royal Ascot, marking the start of 30 years of extraordinary headware, designed by David and displayed by Gertrude.

Gertrude's Ascot appearance may easily have been her last for shortly after the Royal meeting she was diagnosed with breast cancer, went to Monte Carlo for a second honeymoon with her husband Ronald, then had a mastectomy. Although unwelcome, it gave Gertrude the chance to be a pioneer not only in hats but also breast implants.

In 1967 a 'Tru Life' breast form was transported from its place of manufacture in Michigan to Mrs Shilling's chest, prompting her to remark that there was "a little bit of me that is forever America."

She was the first woman in Britain to have a breast implant although it was not without complications. Shortly after recovering from the operation she barged into the surgeon's office to complain, "One side I am me and the other side I am Jane Russell."

A 'Tru Life' breast form once owned by Mrs Shilling is now held by the Science Museum in Kensington.

Having survived cancer, Mrs Shilling gave annual millinery displays at Royal Ascot. Many of her hats were not suitable for perambulation but Gertrude was adept at finding spots likely to attract cameras and then standing still.

In 1969 she appeared in an enormous apricot extravagance and two years later in a giraffe hat 5 feet high. The slightest breeze threatened to knock the giraffe over.

In 1973 her choice was a Common Market hat in the form of a huge disc with the member states' names circling it. On other occasions her head was adorned with a tall black top hat with a rabbit emerging from it, a picnic hamper containing strawberries and champagne flutes, William Tell's famous apple impaled by a 4 foot arrow, a snooker cue, frame and balls, and a television set complete with aerial. Gertrude's face was peering out of it.

Appropriately, in the year of the television set, 1983, Mrs Shilling appeared as Mrs Sopwith in 'The Luncheon,' an episode of the popular television series *Tales of the Unexpected*. Her acting career failed to match the dizzy heights of her hats and in 1984 cancer of the colon almost prevented her from appearing at Royal Ascot, but didn't.

Gertrude Shilling determined to be noticed.

By then Mrs Shilling, nicknamed 'The Ascot Mascot', was in her mid-70s and rather old hat. Younger models attracted the attention of cameramen but Gertrude remained enthusiastic and an easily recognised, established feature of the Royal meeting.

David's hats and Gertude's head helped to promote his millinery business which reached a record-breaking peak in 2007 when, at a show in Monaco, several of David's jewelled hats were offered for sale for £1 million each. Perhaps they were big ones.

Doubtless Gertude would have liked to wear one but in 1999 cancer had finally killed her, aged 89.

41 LINDA POSES ON PEN15

As the crowds arrived for the opening day of Royal Ascot in 1974, a white Rolls-Royce Silver Cloud joined them. It was eye-catching in two respects; it bore the registration number PEN15 and Linda Lovelace was inside.

Linda Lovelace was newly infamous, the star of the surprise hit film of 1972, *Deep Throat*. A surprise because *Deep Throat* was pornographic, with a story based on the notion that Lovelace's clitoris was situated in her throat.

Despite being banned in many US states as well as in the UK, the film was a multi-million dollar box office success, although Lovelace received a paltry $1,250.

The censor prevented British cinemas from showing *Deep Throat* but Royal Ascot racegoers were able to see Linda Lovelace in the flesh. When she stepped out of the Rolls Royce, there was quite a lot of flesh on display.

Three years earlier the crusty Duke of Norfolk, the Queen's representative, had banned hot pants from Royal Ascot and he was not going to allow a scantily-clad porn star through the hallowed gates. A gentleman in a bowler hat refused to admit her, leaving Lovelace to pose for photographers on the bonnet of the Rolls. The shots made the national press, which was what Lovelace and her manager wanted.

A policeman finds Linda Lovelace arresting.

42 COLIN GOES FULL CIRCLE

Foot Patrol, Lotus Island, Flyway, Arum Lily, Ghadbbaan, Corn Lily, Rawaan, and many other horses owned by Full Circle Thoroughbreds won races wearing white bridles and reins.

It was unusual but so was Full Circle Thoroughbreds and so was Full Circle's creator, Colin Tinkler.

One of racing's great characters, in 1980 Tinkler had given up training and passed the reins to his son Nigel. A restless individual, still only in his mid-fifties, Colin pondered the idea of making racehorse ownership accessible to more people through shared ownership.

Shared ownership already existed but its scope was limited by rules that restricted the number of members of partnerships to four and the number of members of syndicates to a dozen. More were allowed if the owners were shareholders in a public company, a situation that Tinkler intended to exploit to gain access to a much bigger market.

Having obtained the Jockey Club's approval, in 1984 Tinkler set up Full Circle Thoroughbreds Limited, soon to be Full Circle Thoroughbreds PLC. He advertised in *The Sporting Life* and sent out brochures to the many who responded. At the time, this was a novelty.

In its first year, Full Circle recruited 360 shareholders at £450 a share, sending £162,000 in Tinkler's direction. The plan was to buy and race horses, to be trained by Nigel, then dissolve the company each year, distribute its assets and set up a new company with a different suffix, with the first year's operation called Full Circle Thoroughbreds A.

In June 1984 Tinkler bid 5,250 guineas to buy Octolan after the two-year-old had won a selling race at Warwick. Two months later, wearing Full Circle's colours of blue with red seams and cap, Octolan gave the venture its first success when winning a selling race at Catterick.

Tinkler was a big gambler and one of the features of Full Circle was the betting that regularly accompanied their horses to the post. He had a bet of £3,500 to £2,000 on Octolan and when Rainbow Vision gave Full Circle their second winner, at Ayr, Tinkler had £7,000 to £2,000.

Meningi then won three hurdle races for Full Circle before finishing a creditable fifth in the Supreme Novices' Hurdle at the Cheltenham Festival. Tinkler recalled, "I managed to win a great deal of money backing him."

Year one had been promising and year two was better, with more than twice as many shareholders and 15 winners; year three better still, with more shareholders and 25 winners, including The Ellier's victory in the Kim Muir Challenge Cup at the Cheltenham Festival.

The upward trajectory continued under Full Circle Thoroughbreds D and E, with the former attracting over 2,000 shareholders, funding 24 horses and winning 38 races, and the latter over 2,500 shareholders, nearly 40 horses and 50 winners.

As no one was to own more than one share in the company there were no dominant figures, apart from Colin Tinkler himself. A showman, habitually adorned with dark glasses, a noticeable hat and trainers, Tinkler made his presence felt in the winner's circle, especially after a Full Circle horse had won a selling race and therefore faced the possibility of being bought at the subsequent auction by someone other than Tinkler.

Full Circle's horses ran in a lot of selling races and when one won, Tinkler tended to make a conspicuous show of removing the bandages from the winner's legs, the implication being that they would probably have collapsed without support.

In those days it was widely considered bad form to buy a horse out of a selling race unless the current owner was happy to see it go. Tinkler, sometimes holding a large wad of banknotes and sometimes wearing a hand puppet to bid – Mr Frog was his favourite – displayed a deterrent determination to see off all but the most dedicated rival bidders. They were liable to face the disapproval not only of Tinkler but also of the many Full Circle members who were at the racecourse celebrating their winner.

Full Circle had quickly made a big impact, its colours a common sight, and in 1987 Tinkler launched a premium rate telephone service, characterised by his tendency to lucratively, if often amusingly, extend the length of his monologue before reaching the vital ingredient of his tips.

In its first two years, the telephone service attracted over a million calls. Tinkler claimed not to have had a losing year and to have backed 90 per cent of his own selections, including Norton's Coin, the 100-1 winner of the 1990 Cheltenham Gold Cup.

Then, Full Circle fell as quickly as it had risen. The number of shareholders collapsed and with them the number of horses and winners. In 1989/90 Full Circle Thoroughbreds F amassed 26 winners, the next year only nine, followed by three. In 1995 Full Circle came to an end, having won 176 races, 69 on the Flat and 107 over jumps, many of them with the winners sporting white bridles and reins.

Tinkler expressed puzzlement as well as disappointment. He concluded that "the main bone of contention, existing amongst the majority of the shareholders, was that they considered, though wrongly, the whole enterprise to be a Tinkler benefit; that the horses were solely for me to punt on, Nigel to train and his wife, Kim, to ride." He added, curiously, "I'm sure that most shareholders had become spoilt, with too many runners and too many winners.

Colin Tinkler, trainer, gambler and showman.

It was just like a child having too many toys to play with, it becomes quickly bored with them all."

Amazingly, 54 of Full Circle's 176 wins, almost a third, started odds-on. This was partly because a lot of the winners ran in races, particularly selling races, which their handicap marks entitled them to win. Tinkler was prepared to buy horses back at the subsequent auctions for sums that left little if any profit from the prize money but added to the tally of Full Circle successes and provided an often attractive betting opportunity for Tinkler and others.

It was rather a sad end to an imaginative venture that gave a lot of pleasure to a lot of people, especially Tinkler. A teetotal non-smoker and vegetarian, in his autobiography, *A Furlong to go ...* (2001), Tinkler wrote, "We're only here for about 75 years on average, though I'll live longer, so we might as well enjoy ourselves." He was right, dying in 2015, aged 89.

43 LUDLOW'S LAVATORIES EXCEL

Ludlow is an idiosyncratic country racecourse in Shropshire, an exemplar of the wonderful variety of British racecourses. Even before a racegoer arrives its eccentricity becomes apparent as it is difficult to avoid noticing that the track is criss-crossed by roads, with seven road crossings in all.

After arriving, no visit would be complete without witnessing the toilets on the ground floor, underneath the Club Stand. It is a pity that they are not portable or they could be introduced to a wider audience on the BBC's *Antiques Roadshow.*

The urinals are of Edwardian vintage, made by Scull Bros of Shrewsbury, in leadless glaze. The toilet bowls are of the very old 'The New Kingston' variety.

Ludlow's urinals. Serving racegoers for over 100 years.

Next door, in the ladies cloakroom, the walls are covered in pre-1914 white glazed tiles; magnificent.

At the time when the racecourse urinals were installed, Scull Brothers described themselves as 'Sanitary & ventilating engineers, plumbers & gasfitters' but when the firm when into liquidation, in 1975, they were, less expansively, 'Heating and plumbing engineers.' Their lavatory days were over.

At racecourse toilets throughout Britain, Armitage Shanks reigns supreme, so vintage urinals are to be savoured. Doncaster's Clock Tower Stand, built in 1881, harbours the 'Adamant,' manufactured by 'Twyfords Ltd Cliffe Vale Potteries.'

The Cliffe Vale factory in Staffordshire, founded in 1887, was the creation of Thomas W. Twyford, whose sanitary ware was already popular. In 1893 a trade journal reported that 400 potters were employed at Cliffe Vale and that their products "are sold and in constant demand wherever civilisation holds sway."

The 'Adamant' trademark was introduced in 1899 and the 'Adamant' urinals highly thought of by connoisseurs. Today, specimens of this titan of urinals are on display at the Chiltern Open Air Museum in Buckinghamshire.

From a historical point of view, Market Rasen's toilets are undistinguished but when, between 2005 and 2007, I conducted a tour of every British and Irish racecourse, it was Market Rasen's toilets that won the award for the best toilets at a British racecourse.

This led to one of my proudest moments when, in 2007, some toilets at the racecourse were named after me and a plaque displayed – 'David Ashforth Toilets.' Sadly, they were later swept away in the name of improvements. Life's full of disappointments.

44 PEOPLE GO MAD AT KILLARNEY

It's important to have something to look forward to and if you haven't been to Killarney races, you have.

Once there, your eyes will be drawn to the mountains of MacGillycuddy's Reeks, with glimpses of Lough Leane and Ross Castle. The mountains were put there to make Killarney racecourse beautiful and have been a great success.

They were there in 1842, 20 years after racing was first staged at Killarney, when William Makepeace Thackeray – what a splendid name – visited the town and the racecourse.

It was several years before Thackerary made himself famous by writing *Vanity Fair* but he did write *The Irish Sketch Book* (1843) about his tour of Ireland.

Thackeray knew approximately nothing about horseracing but couldn't help noticing that Killarney races were a powerful magnet. "The town of Killarney was in a violent state of excitement," he wrote, "with a series of horse races, hurdle races, boat races and stag hunts by land and water which were taking place and attracted a vast crowd from all parts of the Kingdom. All the inns were full and lodgings cost five shillings a day, nay, more in some places."

Thackeray lodged with a Mrs Macgillicuddy, possibly named after the mountains. At dinner, "the conversation was of the horse. How Mr This had refused fifteen hundred guineas for a horse which he bought for a hundred; how Bacchus was the best horse in Ireland; which horses were to run at Something races; and how the Marquis of Waterford gave a plate or a purse.

"They are all mad for it. People walk for miles and miles round to the race. They come without a penny in their pockets often, trusting to chance and charity, and that some worthy gentleman may fling them a sixpence. A gentleman told me that he saw on the course persons from his part of the country who must have walked eighty miles for the sport."

When he ventured to the racecourse himself, Thackeray found it to be "one of the most beautiful spots that ever was seen; the lake and mountains lying along two sides of it and of course visible from all. They were busy putting up the hurdles when we arrived, stiff bars and poles, four feet from the ground, with furze bushes over them. The grandstand was already full; along the hedges sat thousands of people, sitting at their ease doing nothing, and happy as kings. I never saw a vast multitude of heads and attitudes so picturesque and lively. The sun lighted up the whole course and the lakes with amazing brightness."

The author's opinion of the races themselves was more ambiguous. "I won't pretend to say," Thackeray said, "that they were better or worse than other

"One of the most beautiful spots that ever was seen."   © Pat Healy
William Makepeace Thackeray's verdict on Killarney racecourse.

such amusements, or to quarrel with gentlemen who choose to risk their lives in manly exercise.

"In the first race there was a fall; one of the gentlemen was carried off the ground, and it was said he was dead. In the second race, a horse and man went over and over each other, and the fine young man (we had seen him five minutes before, full of life and triumph, clearing the hurdles on his grey horse, at the head of the race); in the second heat of the second race, the poor fellow missed his leap, was carried away stunned and dying, and the bay horse won."

Understandably upset by the high death rate, Thackeray continued, "I don't care to confess that the accident to the poor young gentleman so thoroughly disgusted my feelings as a man and a cockney, that I turned off the racecourse short, and hired a horse for sixpence to carry me back to Miss Macgillicuddy." The following day, he gave the races a miss and visited Mucross instead. It is fair to say that Thackeray did not leave Killarney a convert to horseracing.

Two venues were used for race meetings but after 1900, for 35 years, no venues were used as there were no race meetings. Eventually a team of local enthusiasts, led by Ted O'Leary, recruited enough subscribers to revive racing at the site the racecourse now occupies.

In 1937, in advance of Killarney's two day meeting on 5 and 6 July, *The Irish Times* ran an advertisement for the Killarney Racing Carnival – "The Ascot of Ireland." While the races may not have matched the quality of those at Ascot, the scenery was superior.

O'Leary's son-in-law, Finbarr Slattery, ran the racecourse from the late 1970s until 1991, when he rounded off his reign by tempting Lester Piggott, aged 55, to make his first appearance at Killarney.

A special souvenir racecard was printed for a meeting featuring the £8,000 Heineken Handicap. On the opening day of the four-day meeting, Monday 15 July, a record crowd watched Piggott ride three winners, all trained by Vincent O'Brien, including the feature race on News Headlines.

The Irish Times reported that the visiting hero was "cheered to the echo as he returned to the winner's enclosure. Piggott allowed himself one of his rare grins." It was not recorded whether or not Piggott also said something.

A contented Slattery later recalled, "It was undoubtedly my most exciting day in racing."

45 THE ROYAL PHILHARMONIC ORCHESTRA STRIKES UP

Racecourses have long staged music events when the racing is over but in 2009 Amy Starkey, Kempton Park's new managing director, decided to recruit the Royal Philharmonic Orchestra to play while a race was taking place.

Kempton's programme of summer evening fixtures had attracted disappointing crowds and Starkey thought that the idea might get welcome publicity. It did, with the result that a crowd of 2,793 turned up on Wednesday 8 July, compared with 1,023 the previous week and 1,285 the week after.

As the 11 runners for the third race, the digibet.com Handicap, set out on their one mile three furlongs journey, the brass section of the Royal Philharmonic launched itself at Gioachino Rossini's William Tell Overture.

The appropriately named Action Impact, ridden by Ryan Moore, won comfortably but the jockey's post-race reaction was not what Starkey had hoped for. An outstanding jockey, that year's champion, Moore was not a disciple of marketing and promotion; he complained that the music had caused his mount to jink.

He was not the only critic. Writing in the *Daily Mirror*, David Yates reported that after the race finished, "and the conductor put down his baton, the reaction to the event varied between unimpressed and vitriolic."

Yet Yates defended the initiative, pointing out that, "it was a publicity stunt and it got publicity" but it proved to be a one-off. The Royal Philharmonic was not invited back to have a crack at Tchaikovsky's 1812 Overture.

Oompah Oompah.

Chapter
9

Racecourses and racing II

In which John draws some maps • Harry
hands Chris an envelope • Camilla
meets her husband • Emily becomes a
martyr • racing goes all-weather.

46 JOHN DRAWS SOME MAPS

In 1766 or 1767, leading figures in Newmarket's racing society received a proposal from John Chapman, a land surveyor and engraver living at nearby Dalham.

The proposal was "for publishing by subscription, engraved from an actual survey, a map of Newmarket; with the Heath, the several courses, stands, roads and every thing remarkable on the said Heath.... The price to subscribers to be ten shillings; five to be paid at the time of subscribing, and the remainder on the delivery of the map." To encourage waverers, Chapman added, "When published the price will be raised."

Chapman's initiative was well timed for, as C.P. Lewis observed in his article 'John Chapman's Maps of Newmarket' (*Proceedings of the Cambridge Antiquarian Society* Vol. LXXX for 1991, published 1992), Newmarket was "the most aristocratic small town in England, crowded with titled and wealthy residents and visitors, a household name in the households of the horseracing classes. Probably nowhere else in England could a small town and its hinterland, easy to survey on grounds of size, yield so many potential sales."

Newmarket's Houghton and Craven meetings were not launched until 1770 and 1771 respectively but its July meeting was a regular fixture from 1765 and "a coterie of mostly young aristocrats and gentlemen intent on the pleasures of the Turf" provided a market for a racing-oriented map.

In 1768, or possibly late the previous year, Chapman produced two maps, a *Plan of Newmarket* and a *Map of Newmarket Heath*. The former contained the inscription "To the Right Honourable William Earl of March & Ruglen, Baron Douglas of Nidpath, Lymn & Maner, Vice Admiral of Scotland, one of the Lords of His Majesty's Bed Chamber, Knight of the Most Ancient & Noble Order of the Thistle &c. &c. This plan of Newmarket is humbly Inscribed by his Lordship's most humble & obedient servant J. Chapman."

The 3rd Earl of March (from 1778 the 4th Duke of Queensberry), one of the richest men in Britain and a racing enthusiast, was a subscriber, along with ten other noblemen and 14 gentlemen listed on the Plan.

The Earl of March was a notorious roisterer, gambler and lecher. In 1750, in his role as a gambler, he partnered the 10th Earl of Eglinton, also a subscriber, in a bet with Theobald Taaffe that a man could cover 19 miles on Newmarket Heath in less than an hour in a four wheeled carriage. The wager was for £1,000.

Taaffe, a friend of the Duke of Bedford and Lord Sandwich, enjoyed similar pursuits to the Earl of March. In 1751, Horace Walpole, describing Taaffe as "a gamester, usurer and adventurer," told a friend that "he is the hero who, having betted Mrs Woffington five guineas on as many performances in one night, and demanding the money which he won, received the famous reply, 'double or quits?'"

Taaffe's bet with March and Eglinton was settled on 29 August 1750, when a purpose-built lightweight carriage, pulled by four horses, appeared on the Heath, with "the greatest part of the sporting gentlemen in England present."

At 7am the challenge began, starting at the Six Mile House on Newmarket racecourse. The result was a comfortable success for the two noblemen, as the carriage completed the 19 miles in about 54 minutes.

When it came to the *Map of Newmarket Heath*, it was the turn of the Duke of Ancaster, another subscriber, to receive the sycophantic dedication, "To the high, puissant, and most noble prince, Peregrine, Duke of Ancaster and Kesteven, Marquis and Earl of Lindsey, Baron Willoughby of Eresby, Heriditary Lord Great Chamberlain of England, Master of the Horse, Lord Lieutenant and Custos Rotulorum of the county of Lincoln, &c. This map of Newmarket Heath, & the adjacent villages, is humbly inscribed, by His Grace's most humble & most obedient servant J. Chapman."

Five other noblemen and gentlemen with stables, namely the Duke of Bridgwater, Lord Grosvenor, Lord Farnham, Sir John Moore and Captain Shafto, were mentioned.

George III had been content to appoint the Duke of Ancaster as the Court's Master of the Horse in 1766 but Lord North, who was to become Prime Minister in 1770, had a low opinion of him. When it was suggested that Ancaster might be suitable for the post of Lord Lieutenant of Ireland, Lord North was reported to have exclaimed, "Good God, it is impossible to send into such a responsible station, such a very egregious blockhead, who is besides both mulish and intractable." On the other hand, he did subscribe to Chapman's maps.

Those maps helped to establish his reputation and a few years later Chapman was working on a map of Essex and subsequently on other significant projects. He died in 1778 and the plates of the Newmarket maps were later acquired by another map maker, William Faden. In 1787 he reissued the maps with updated lists of the owners of racing stables and an engraving of Eclipse, the champion of the age.

47 HARRY HANDS CHRIS AN ENVELOPE

In 1991 the racing journalist and author Chris Pitt was asked to interview a former bookmakers' clerk called Harry Green for *BOS Magazine*. Green was about to celebrate his 100th birthday and Pitt hoped that he might have some interesting tales to tell.

The imminent centenarian still had a lively mind and a remarkable memory, stretching back to his first visit to the races in 1905, when he saw Imari win the

Chester Cup. Clerking for bookmakers, Green was at Epsom and Liverpool for virtually every interwar Derby and Grand National, including the 1921 National, extraordinary even by Grand National standards.

Thirty-five runners set out but only one, Shaun Spadah, completed the course without falling. Green was standing by the second-last fence when The Bore, in second place, fell heavily, breaking jockey Harry Brown's collar bone. Someone stepped out from the crowd and gave Brown a leg-up, enabling him to finish a distant if painful second. The third and fourth placed horses, the only others to finish, had also fallen and been remounted.

For Green's 100th birthday, Pitt arranged a visit to Stratford races, where Green was entertained and introduced to the champion jumps jockey, Peter Scudamore. A year later, for his 101st birthday, Ladbrokes organised a trip to Wolverhampton, gave him £101 of free bets and arranged for Jack Berry (see curiosity 61) to present him with a clock.

At the time, Pitt was working in the area and every fortnight, on Friday evenings, he visited Green. There were more tales from the past until, one Friday, Harry said, "I've got something for you. I've been saving it for

Mementoes of Gordon Richards' record breaking days at Chepstow.

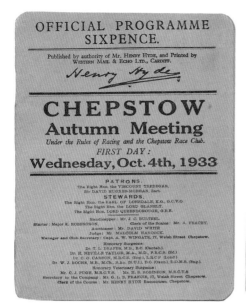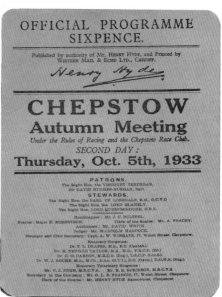

Mementoes of Gordon Richards' record breaking days at Chepstow.

someone but could never find anyone who I thought would appreciate it, but I think you will."

He handed Pitt an envelope. When he opened it, he found three racecards dating from 1933. The trio, in perfect condition, were for successive days' racing, from 3rd to 5th October, at Nottingham, Chepstow and Chepstow again. With them were two admission badges for the meetings at Chepstow, priced at six shillings each. Green had been there, clerking, on all three days.

Pitt's expression told Green what an exciting shock it was. "I thought you'd know what they were," he said. An enthusiastic and knowledgeable student of racing, Pitt knew immediately what the racecards' significance was. They were for the days when Gordon Richards had 12 consecutive winning rides, the first at Nottingham, six more when going through the card at Chepstow on 4 October, and another five at the same venue the following day.

It was a memorable achievement by the jockey who dominated British racing between the First and Second World Wars and in the early post-war years. Richards was champion jockey an unmatched 26 times between 1925 and 1953, failing to win the title only three times during that period.

In 1933 he was already widely admired, with a large following, and his latest feat prompted a celebratory song, *Well Done, Gordon!*

Well done, Gordon!
How you can ride!
Well done, Gordon!
How you have tried!
Beating every record in racing, that's true.
We have simply got to take our hats off to you.
Well done, Gordon, on every course,
You just win on any old horse.
Crowds shout 'Hooray!'
And the bookmakers pay.
Well done, Gordon! Well done!

Harry Green died in 1996, aged 104. The racecards and badges are still with Chris Pitt, safely stored in a box. He has no intention of parting with them.

48 CAMILLA MEETS HER HUSBAND

In 1961, the rotting Club Stand at Manchester Racecourse was replaced with an expensive new Members Stand, featuring the first executive boxes on a British racecourse. Unfortunately, the relevant word was 'expensive.' Two years later, financial problems forced the racecourse's closure.

The final meeting, held on 9 November 1963, was attended by a crowd estimated at 20,000 (some people love a funeral). Lester Piggott won the last race, The Goodbye Consolation Plate, on Fury Royal. It might come up in a quiz, you never know.

The racecourse's signature races were either moved elsewhere, the November Handicap to Doncaster, the Lancashire Oaks to Haydock Park or, in the case of the Manchester Gold Cup, consigned to history.

Every cloud is reputed to have a silver lining and ten years later the University of Salford bought most of the site, established the Castle Irwell Student Village with extensive accommodation and turned the Members Stand into an entertainment venue, run by the Students' Union. It was called The Pavilion, 'Pav' to successive generations of fun-seeking students.

While members of the Manchester Race Committee responsible for building the original Club Stand, opened in 1902, were spinning incredulous in their graves, students were spinning to disco music at the Pav. It was, according to the University's website, "a huge part of our identity and history" and "the catalyst for many student memories."

That became clear after the Pavilion was closed in 2010 and then devastated by a fire in 2016, when nostalgic former students fired off regretful tweets.

"What a shame," wrote Naomi, "so many happy memories of The Pav. What a terrible way to go." Melanie C "had some fab nights in that place!" while for Camilla Roughan it was "where I met my husband."

There had been spasmodic hopes of the racecourse's resurrection. In 2002, Peel Holdings unveiled plans for a development nearby that included a new racecourse. These were withdrawn and revised proposals submitted in 2004, for a £100 million development to include Salford Forest Park racecourse, complete with a revived Manchester Gold Cup.

When this proposal stalled, in 2007, the company submitted a freshly revised plan and, with a final decision by the local planning authorities delayed, appealed to John Denham, the Secretary of State for Communities and Local Government. In 2010 Denham rejected the appeal.

Eventually, in 2019, Salboy Limited bought the Castle Irwell site, which had outline planning consent for up to 500 houses, for a reported £15 million. In 2020, Salboy submitted a full planning application for residential and commercial development, and obtained permission to begin work on the first phase of 157 homes.

What remained of the racecourse was the entrance building housing the turnstiles. Salboy announced its intention of "Restoring the locally listed, historic Turnstile Building to become a key gateway to the development." The plan was for the building to eventually house retail outlets.

Salboy was a recently established company, founded in 2014, but it had an interesting link with the past. The company is owned by the Done family, with its patriarch Fred Done, the driving force behind Betfred, its guiding director.

Fred and his brother Peter's first betting shop, opened in 1967, was in Cromwell Road, just a short walk away from the old racecourse and the new Castle Irwell.

49 EMILY BECOMES A MARTYR

On 4 June 1913 Emily Davison called in at the new headquarters of the Women's Social and Political Union at Lincoln's Inn House, Kingsway, and borrowed two flags in the organisation's colours – purple, white and green. She then went on to Victoria Station, where she bought a return ticket to Epsom. The train would have been crowded, for it was Derby Day.

A few hours later, when Police Sergeant Frank Bunn emptied Davison's pockets, he found the return half of the ticket. By then, the 40-year-old militant suffragette was lying unconscious in Epsom Cottage Hospital, where she died four days later.

At the inquest, held on 10 June, the coroner recorded a verdict of death by misadventure, Davison having died from a "fracture of the base of the skull caused by being accidentally knocked down by a horse through wilfully rushing on to the racecourse at Epsom Downs."

The horse was King George V's horse, Anmer, and there was no doubt that Davison's death was the result of standing in Anmer's path as the field rounded Tattenham Corner, with predictably dire consequences.

Davison was a passionate campaigner for women's rights and an enthusiastic participant in direct action to try to force the Liberal Government to address the issue of women's suffrage. In 1909 she had abandoned her teaching career to devote herself to the cause and two years later refused to be counted in that year's Census, declaring, "As I am a woman and women do not count in the State, I refuse to be counted."

Later that year, she soaked a piece of cloth in paraffin, lit it, and pushed it into a pillar box, an initiative soon followed by other suffragettes. Sent to Holloway prison for six months, Davison threw herself down a stairwell in protest at the treatment of fellow prisoners, many of whom were repeatedly force fed.

In April 1913, the government passed an Act nicknamed 'The Cat and Mouse Act,' under which suffragettes who went on hunger strike were released from prison then, after recovering, rearrested, to complete their sentences and face more force feeding.

Davison felt a burning sense of injustice but although the WSPU's leaders shared her sentiments, they regarded her as dangerously independent and unpredictable. When she caught a train from Victoria to Epsom, it was without their knowledge or approval.

Newsreels were an exciting recent development but of the three operators with cameras at Epsom, only Gaumont Graphic produced footage useful as evidence of what actually happened. The pictures, held at the British Film Institute, are indistinct.

As the field of 15 rounded the turn, led by Aboyeur, the first nine horses were fairly well bunched, then there was a gap. Emily Davison stepped into the gap.

The first horse to reach her was Agadir. The newsreel shows that Davison deliberately avoided Agadir and also the following two horses, after which there was another gap to Anmer and two stragglers. Davison deliberately stood in front of Anmer.

It is impossible to be certain that she knew the horse's identity, although the King's colours, purple, scarlet and gold, were distinctive. After hearing conflicting evidence from eye-witnesses, Gilbert White, the coroner, expressed the opinion that she had not known. Whether she did or not, she snatched at the horse's reins and was violently bowled over.

Anmer crashed to the ground, his rider Herbert Jones suffering "abrasions of the left side of the face, over the left eye and shoulder, contusion of the left elbow joint and shock." He recovered sufficiently to be taken back to the grandstand in an ambulance and to return to Newmarket the next day.

Did Davison intend to commit suicide? Almost certainly not, but she knew that her plan to send a dramatic message to the King and his government put her in danger. She knew that she might die in the attempt and, if necessary, she was prepared to die.

The press showed no sympathy, depicting her as a mad woman and, in some cases, giving greater prominence to the controversial disqualification of the favourite, Craganour, and promotion of Aboyeur, at 100-1.

The Sporting Life was particularly callous. Its editorial complained, "If it were not enough to have the disqualification of the winner, we were not allowed to see anything to indicate the class of the King's horse, Anmer, for the reason that some wild woman broke from the crowd and stepped right in front of the royal representative." The royal representative, at 50-1, was already well beaten.

It was a very different story in *The Suffragette*, the WSPU's weekly paper. Its front page portrayed an angel, with the caption, 'In honour and in loving, reverent memory of Emily Wilding Davison. She died for women.'

Suffragettes march through central London alongside Emily Davison's coffin.

Christabel Pankhurst described Davison's action as "a tremendous imaginative and spiritual achievement! A wonderful act of faith! So greatly did she care for freedom that she died for it. So dearly did she love women that she offered her life as their ransom."

Davison was presented as a martyr in a noble cause, and the WSPU intended to make maximum political capital from her death. On Saturday 14 June, 6,000 suffragettes, some wearing black and carrying purple irises, others in white, watched by tens of thousands, accompanied Davison's coffin from Victoria station to St George's Church, Bloomsbury, and then on to King's Cross, en route to Newcastle and Morpeth, where she was to be buried.

The mourners included jockey Herbert Jones's wife. Another 30,000 attended the funeral at Morpeth, where Davison's gravestone, appropriately, bears the WSPU's motto, 'Deeds not words.'

It took the contribution women made during the First World War to persuade the government, in 1918, to give the vote to most women aged 30 and over. In 1928, the qualifying age was reduced to 21, the same as for men.

When Emmeline Pankhurst died that year, Herbert Jones attended the funeral, bringing a wreath bearing the forgiving inscription, 'To do honour to the memory of Mrs Pankhurst and Miss Emily Davison.'

50 RACING GOES ALL WEATHER

Martin Collins knelt down, picked up a handful of polymer-coated sand and let it run through his fingers. I'm guessing, but I bet it was something he did often because he had developed the material and in 1989, under the name Equitrack, it provided the surface for Britain's first all-weather racetrack, at Lingfield.

On 30 October, Niklas Angel became the answer to a popular quiz question by winning the first race on an all-weather track in Britain. Two days later, Zulu achieved a similar distinction by winning the first all-weather race over jumps, a novice hurdle on Southwell's Fibresand. Fibresand was a mixture of sand particles and fine polypropylene fibres, slower than Equitrack.

On 8 November, Southwell staged its first Flat meeting on Fibresand, with the opening race won by Frankie Dettori on Crystal Pool. Eight days later, to complete the set, Lingfield held its first jumps meeting on Equitrack, with Irish Ditty winning the opening novice hurdle

When the Jockey Club first considered the possibility of authorising the installation of all-weather surfaces, it was jumps racing it had in mind. A lot of jump meetings were being lost to winter weather – 72 days racing during the winter of 1984/85 – and all-weather tracks offered the prospect of plugging the expensive gap.

Some of jump racing's future stars won over hurdles on Southwell's and Lingfield's all-weather tracks. In 1989, Run For Free, later the winner of the Welsh and Scottish Nationals, won at Southwell. In 1991, at Lingfield, it was the turn of Viking Flagship, subsequently an outstanding chaser, dual winner of both the Queen Mother Champion Chase and Melling Chase, as well as the Tingle Creek Chase. Then, at Southwell in January 1994, Pridwell became one of the last horses to win over jumps on an all-weather track. While he later achieved considerable success, finally beating Istabraq, the triple Champion Hurdle winner, in the Martell Aintree Hurdle in 1998, those horses were very much the exceptions.

Most all-weather races were for low level horses unable to win anything better. They were watched in betting shops rather than at racecourses, the prize-money was low, the temptation to top it up by skulduggery relatively high and the surfaces in their infancy.

Jump racing was particularly problematic because of the demands made on a group of horses likely to harbour an above average number of physical problems. A spate of fatalities in January 1994 intensified questions about the safety of all-weather jumping. When War Beat was added to the list of deaths, at Lingfield on 24 February, the BHB brought the all-weather jumps season to a premature end and subsequently made the suspension permanent. The existing all-weather surfaces were deemed too unforgiving for jump racing.

Two months earlier, on 27 December 1993, a third all-weather track opened under floodlights at Wolverhampton, on Fibresand. By then, Betfair was impacting the betting market and offering punters a much easier way of backing horses to lose as well as to win.

The major bookmakers, their profit margins under threat, campaigned for exchange betting to be outlawed, citing its threat to racing's integrity. The attitude of the Jockey Club and other racing authorities was strongly influenced by the unprecedented access Betfair gave them to their customers' betting records. Identifying and dealing with cheats and crooks was easier than it had been when Jockey Club investigations were often hindered by bookmakers' reluctance to disclose information, pleading client confidentiality.

Betfair, well led and very professional, survived the onslaught and flourished but there were legitimate integrity concerns, particularly when Regional or Banded racing was introduced in 2004. It catered for horses rated 45 and below, the lowest of the low. Previously, such horses rarely won a race. Now there were 70 fixtures, mainly on all-weather tracks, exclusively for them. They were 'betting races,' intended to increase the levy yield from betting shops, with average prize money of only £2,000 a race.

The initiative may have pleased the owners, trainers and riders of the chosen band of horses but it was viewed with concern and contempt by those worried about racing's integrity, image, and the fate of punters.

Ron Cox, a respected tipster, considered that "no right minded backer should go near Banded racing" (*The Guardian*, 23 June 2005). At the end of 2006, the experiment was ended. In the *Mail Online* (2 January 2007), David Milnes approvingly referred to "The dreaded Banded meeting, binned by the BHB."

The all-weather surfaces, at least, had improved. In 2001, Lingfield replaced its Equitrack with Polytrack, a mixture of wax-coated sand, recycled synthetic fibres, rubber and PVC, developed by Martin Collins Enterprises. Three years later, Wolverhampton replaced its Fibresand surface with Polytrack.

In 2006, Kempton moved its turf Flat fixtures to a floodlit Polytrack. The following year, Ireland opened its first all-weather racecourse at Dundalk, again on Polytrack, and in 2008, the new racecourse at Great Leighs also opted for Polytrack.

The racing generally remained low grade but periodically rose above the mundane. In 1995, the first Listed race on an all-weather track took place at Wolverhampton with prize money of £50,000. In 1998 the first Winter Derby was staged at Lingfield, became a Listed race the following year and achieved Group 3 status in 2006.

Great Leighs went into administration in 2009 but was resurrected as Chelmsford racecourse in 2015, on Polytrack. Three years earlier, Lingfield installed a new Polytrack and the following year an All-Weather Championship was launched, climaxing with a £1 million Finals Day at Lingfield on Good Friday, 18 April 2014. It became a successful annual event.

The same year, a new all-weather surface made its debut at Wolverhampton. Tapeta was developed in the USA by Michael Dickinson, a former jump jockey and very successful trainer, famous for having trained the first five home, headed by Bregawn, in the 1983 Cheltenham Gold Cup.

First produced in 1997, at least 10 subsequent versions were developed, composed of silica sand, wax and fibres, designed to simulate the root structure of turf. In 2016, when Newcastle installed a floodlit all-weather track, it chose Tapeta. With a one mile straight and nearly two mile circuit, Newcastle was the largest all-weather track in the world.

It was also the first in Britain to stage a Group 1 race, won by Kameko in 2019, the same year that Southwell installed floodlights. In 2021, Southwell replaced its fibresand track with Tapeta.

All-weather racing has gone a long way since 1989, not least in its share of the fixture list. In 2019, 351 of the total of 915 Flat fixtures (38.4 per cent) were scheduled for Britain's six all-weather tracks, a proportion way beyond the intention and expectation of its initiators.

Chapter

10

Officialdom

In which Admiral Rous
condemns twaddle • a spade is
called something else
• Alec can't tell the time
• it's time for chips.

51 ADMIRAL ROUS CONDEMNS TWADDLE

Like Keith Brown (see curiosity 34), Henry John Rous retained his rank of Captain many years after finishing active military service. Yet while Brown remained forever Captain, Rous continued to rise, as it were posthumously, through the ranks.

The second son of the 1st Earl of Stradbroke, Rous completed his final naval voyage in 1836. He was still Captain when his slim, celebrated work on *The Laws and Practice of Horse Racing* was published in 1850 but by the time a third edition appeared in 1866, Rous had been promoted to Admiral, via the titles of Rear-Admiral (1852) and Vice Admiral (1858).

Brown was not lauded for his services to racing, having cocked up the start of the 1993 Grand National, but Rous is regarded as a great, reforming administrator and handicapper.

Elected to the Jockey Club in 1821, at the unusually young age of 26, Rous was appointed as a Steward of the Jockey Club in 1838. From 1841 to 1846 he was MP for Westminster but when Lord George Bentinck, the 'Dictator of the Turf,' died unexpectedly in 1848, Rous's reputation as an authority on horseracing made him the obvious successor.

The 1850 book, measuring just six and a half inches by four inches and only 128 pages long, addressed several significant issues at a time when there were plenty to address. Horseracing was a sport full, to the modern eye, of curiosities, and Rous, in the first and subsequent editions, supplied examples of several of them.

One was the habit some racecourses adopted of making the winner of certain races pay back part of the prize money. At Doncaster, the winner of the Great Yorkshire Stakes received £200, "winner to pay back £50," while the winner of the Doncaster Stakes received £100 but was required to pay back £20.

Rous railed against this practice. "What can be in worse taste," he asked, "than to advertise a £100 Plate, winner to pay back £20? Why not have the honesty to call it an £80 Plate?"

Then there were the races themselves, problematic from start to finish. "Nothing can be more disorderly than the system of starting on the provincial racecourses," Rous wrote. "The starters are respectable men but notoriously incapable. They have no control over the jockeys." What was needed was professional starters.

Another practice targeted by Rous was that of racing a horse several times on the same day, over long distances, when carrying 11st or more. Even the scheduled distance could not be relied upon. In 1813, at Ayr, Llewellyn and Tam-o'-Shanter contested a heat over four miles. "By mistake these horses went round the course once oftener than was necessary, the first heat making a distance of about five miles and a quarter, at the end of which Llewellyn was first but Tam-o'-Shanter having the lead at the end of four miles, the heat was adjudged to him."

The publication of *The Laws and Practice of Horse Racing* consolidated Rous's reputation and in 1855 he was appointed as the official Jockey Club handicapper. Under his long, benevolent dictatorship, two miles became the normal maximum race distance and weights were allotted by reference to the weight-for-age scale he had carefully devised.

It specified weight differentials according to the competing horses' age, sex, month in which the race was run and its distance. For example, the 1866 edition of *On the Laws and Practice of Horse Racing* stipulated that, in a conditions race run over one mile in July, a two-year-old would carry 5st 7lb, a three-year-old 7st 8lb, a four-year-old 8st 8lb and horses older than four, 8st 10lb. Luckily poverty, malnutrition and an early end to education ensured a satisfactory supply of lightweight jockeys, although in 1862 the minimum weight had been raised from 4st 7lb to 5st 7lb.

The basic elements of Rous's weight-for-age scale remained in force with only minor amendments until 2016, when further adjustments were made.

His reforms were not always popular. In the 1866 edition Admiral Rous, a straight talker and writer, recorded that "a very absurd crusade has been got up against light weights and short courses. Some writers condemn the system on the plea that it is a deterioration of the sport and an encouragement to gamble. This is genuine twaddle."

Rous asserted, "as far as light weights and short courses are concerned, the lighter the weight the less chance of breaking down the horse, and the shorter the course, the oftener you can run your horses without detriment."

Twaddle is an excellent word and it is disappointing to learn that it was not Rous's creation but first appeared in the late 18th century. Nevertheless, his use of it does him credit.

Although Rous regarded gambling as an inevitable concomitant of racing, he also considered "excessive gambling" to be "the enemy which threatens our extinction," a consequence of "the obnoxious tendencies which are transparent when large sums of money are dependent upon the issue of a race. Betting on a great scale frequently produces grievous results, and the wholesome excitement of a fine race, or the patriotic inducement of improving the breed of horses, become secondary considerations."

This encouraged Rous's conviction that "the first duty of the Jockey Club is to protect the horse-owners, who are the only pillars of the Turf – the interests of the betting gentlemen, a very secondary consideration." Unfortunately, the pillars of the Turf were often also betting gentlemen, which helps to explain the hostility of the Jockey Club Rules, as modified in 1857, towards anyone secretly watching horses in training.

The relevant Rule declared, "If any person shall be detected in watching a trial, or shall be proved to have employed any person to watch a trial, he shall be served with a notice to keep off the [Newmarket] Heath; and if in the employment of any Member of the Club or of any groom or rider employed by any Member of the Club, he shall be dismissed from his service and not again employed."

The tendency of an owner's betting book to take priority over "the wholesome excitement of a fine race," sometimes resulted in "the practice of a person starting two horses in a race and declaring to win with the worst if it suits his book."

In the 1840 St Leger, it suited Lord Westminster's book for Launcelot to finish in front of stablemate Maroon. Rous recalled, "Maroon was pulled up when he could have won by fifty yards." Maroon was pulled rather than pulled up, finishing runner-up to Launcelot.

The *Globe* reported, "it appeared evident to us that Maroon had the most speed left in him at the close of the race. but as his noble owner had declared to win with Launcelot it was not under the circumstances requisite to put his powers to the test. The backers of Maroon are not a little mortified, for that he was the best horse in the race seems to be the opinion of nine out of every ten who saw it."

Two years later *The New Sporting Magazine* had not forgotten. "The powerful manner in which [the jockey] held Maroon 'to orders' will always be remembered by those who unluckily forgot to back 'Scott's Lot' that time." Backing Scott's Lot meant betting that any one of trainer John Scott's runners would win, both Launcelot and Maroon being trained by him.

In 1838 the Jockey Club had resolved, "That it is the opinion of this Club that it is necessary to declare the extreme disapprobation of horses being started for races without the intention on the part of the owners of trying to win them." The same resolve has been expressed many times since but, like the poor, non-triers are always with us, to a greater (then) or lesser (now) extent and Lord Westminster was not deterred. In 1866 Admiral Rous was still bemoaning the practice exposed in the 1840 St Leger, and complaining that "this is not racing, it is an illegal conventional act to facilitate a gambling transaction."

Rous died in 1877 but his name lived on, including in the form of the Admiral Rous Inn at Galleywood Common near Chelmsford, where Rous oversaw Galleywood races from the Stand he had built there.

Things went awry at the Inn in 1899 when, abandoning respect for Admiral Rous, the violent and drunken publican, Samuel Crozier, killed his wife Cecilia, with the result that Crozier failed to reach Christmas that year, having been executed on 5 December.

52 A SPADE IS CALLED SOMETHING ELSE

A lot of praying is involved in horseracing, and quite a lot of it is to do with the ground. Most horses perform relatively better on one kind of going rather than another. Trainers, owners and punters therefore regularly pray that the going will be soft, although they equally regularly pray that it will not be soft. Meanwhile, other trainers, owners and punters pray for the opposite, with the danger that competing prayers will cancel each other out.

Traditionally, each racecourse's clerk of the course announces what the state of the going actually is, aided by their footwear and a stick. The heel of the footwear is dug into the turf and the bottom of the stick is pushed into the earth. The information is then passed on to the clerk's brain, collated, and the going declared to be somewhere between hard (the stick broke) and heavy (the stick disappeared).

Despite its longevity, the system has several shortcomings. Not every clerk of the course wears the same size wellington boots, nor weighs the same, nor uses the same stick. The force with which they jab their stick into the ground varies, depending partly on their mood, as does their determination to avoid declaring the ground either horribly hard or horrendously heavy. This can result in a certain lack of confidence in the accuracy of the official going.

At its most extreme, some trainers regard some clerks of the course as being men of impeccable integrity and scrupulous honesty while viewing other clerks as not to be trusted with a shooting stick.

So, in the 1990s, a serious effort was made to adopt a more scientific, less subjective approach. This proved difficult because of the number of variables to be accommodated. The makeup of the soil varies from course to course, as does the drainage situation. Even on a single racecourse, changeable climatic conditions pose problems; and what is deemed good to soft for Flat racing might be considered good for jump racing.

The available options were limited. The Clegg Hammer, widely used in North America, had been developed primarily for use on roads, and was therefore suitable for dirt rather than turf tracks except, possibly, at Bath.

The penetrometer, used in France and elsewhere, was a more likely candidate. It produced a reading based on the depth that a sharp, tapered rod penetrated the surface when struck by a weight dropped from the height of a metre.

The penetrometer was trialled at a number of British racecourses but it only measured surface hardness and was not felt to be accurate across the full range of going. Numerical readings at one course, used to generate a going description, were not necessarily comparable with the same readings obtained at other courses.

Technology takes on a walking stick.

So, in 1999, the Jockey Club began a dialogue with TurfTrax, a Cambridgeshire-based company supplying data for sporting events based on advanced technology. This led, the following year, to the Smart Stick, subsequently called the GoingStick. During 2001 and 2002, in conjunction with Cranfield University, several prototypes were developed, tested and refined. More than 60,000 readings were taken on a wide range of soil types, going and climatic conditions. No one could say they didn't try.

At the end of that year, 20 GoingSticks were distributed to the Jockey Club Inspectorate and to a dozen major racecourses for further trials. Eventually, in 2003, the Jockey Club announced the phased introduction of the GoingStick, initially at 15 racecourses, starting at Sandown Park.

Tony Goodhew, the Jockey Club's Director of Racecourse Licensing and Standards, said, "We're aware that there have been a number of false dawns in the past." As the GoingStick had been in development for three years at a reported cost of about £500,000, there was more praying for success, especially at TurfTrax Racing Data Limited.

Once described as a "curious cross between a spade and some weird electronic gizmo," the GoingStick is an electro-mechanical device that measures both the amount of force taken to push the tip of the rod into the ground and the energy needed to pull the handle back from vertical to an angle of 45 degrees, replicating the force exerted on the ground by the horse's hoof.

In 2003, it was anticipated that the GoingStick would yield numerical results on a scale from 1 to 15 that could be equated with the official going descriptions of hard, firm, good to firm, good, good to soft, soft and heavy. At one extreme, a reading of between 1.0 and 2.9 would indicate heavy going while one of 13.0 to 15.0 would translate as hard.

In 2007, the use of the GoingStick became mandatory and in 2009 it became a requirement of the Rules of Racing that its readings be made available for every fixture both at the declaration stage and on each raceday. However, the readings would not replace the going descriptions issued by the clerk of the course by traditional means but be published alongside them.

When the British Horseracing Authority published a set of mean average readings for all fixtures at all racecourses from 2008 to 2013, placed alongside the clerks' official going descriptions, the readings fell within the range of 5.2 to 10.0. The extremes on the GoingStick scale of 1 to 15 were rarely, if ever, encountered.

The BHA emphasised that the two sets of information, the clerks' and the GoingStick readings, were to be viewed independently. GoingStick readings were specific to individual courses and "most valuable when considered in the context of historical readings at that course." The readings needed to be interpreted carefully.

A huge amount of time, effort and money continues to be invested in the GoingStick, and taking readings is now a daily part of a clerk of the course's work. At each meeting, at declaration stage and again on the evening before raceday or that morning, at least 30 'penetration' and 'shear' readings are taken at various points around a track.

Despite becoming the most widely used device of its type, having been adopted by many major international racing authorities, the GoingStick has not proved to be a panacea on home soil. The challenge presented by Britain's rich variety of racecourses is too great for that. Like the clerk of the course's boots and stick, the GoingStick is a guide, less subjective but still imperfect.

53 ALEC CAN'T TELL THE TIME

It was 21 November 1969 when seven runners set off to see which of them would win the Valley Gardens Handicap Hurdle at Ascot. Two and a half miles later, the answer was Pinehurst Park, who won by three lengths, at 13-2.

Trainer Alan Oughton was pleased, and so was Charles Youngman, Pinehurst Park's owner. John Jenkins was more pleased than either because Jenkins was still a 7lb claiming conditional jockey and he had just ridden the winner. The 22-year-old had a particular affection for Pinehurst Park because the previous February Jenkins had ridden his first-ever winner on him, and another that October. Later there would be two more.

But at Ascot the winning group's joy was short-lived. Neither Pinehurst Park nor Jenkins had done anything wrong. There was no tack missing nor obstacles unjumped, no riding offences nor failure to weigh in; nothing at all. Pinehurst Park wasn't disqualified, nor his rider reprimanded. Yet Pinehurst Park was not the official winner, nor were any of his rivals.

Jenkins distinctly remembers standing in the winner's circle. "I was a young boy and had ridden a winner at Ascot," he says. "We'd come from last to first. Everyone was happy. Then the loudspeaker announced that the race had been declared void."

The race was scheduled to start at 3.35pm but Alec Marsh, the Jockey Club's senior starter, sent them on their way at 3.32pm. Maybe his watch was fast. A short note in the Form Book reads, "Race declared void due to being started before advertised time – all bets off." That included mine, at 8-1.

No one apologised, either to Jenkins or me. "It was a bit annoying at the time," he says, in a considerable understatement. "When I go racing people still come up to me and remember that race. There was a lot of publicity – I've still got newspaper cuttings."

It was over 50 years ago but so was the Second World War and we haven't forgiven Hitler, have we?

Marsh was not the only senior starter to secure a place in punters' memories by supplying them with a hard luck story. Captain Keith Brown had a good stab at it in 1993, in the infamous case of the Grand National that wasn't (see curiosity 34). Then there was Captain Michael Sayers and the 1986 Portland Handicap at Doncaster.

The day after the race, if Sayers was a reader of the *Daily Mirror* (highly unlikely), he would have seen the single word headline – SHAMBLES.

The shambles had its origins earlier in the afternoon, when a metal support for one of the wheels on a set of starting stalls broke. With 23 runners for the Portland, all three sets of stalls were needed. Sayers decided that the race would have to be started by flag.

There was a false start but five horses shot off towards the winning post, five and a half furlongs away, followed by the starter's forlorn cry of, "No, no, no! Come back you buggers!"

They didn't come back but passed the winning post, which not only disqualified them from taking any further part but, as they had come under starter's orders, also meant that any bets on them were losers. It was particularly unfortunate for the person who had a bet of £10,000 to £800 (about £2,360 today) on Meeson King, ridden by Willie Carson.

Under the headline, 'Anger after start chaos,' the *Irish Independent* reported, "The Portland Handicap, one of the season's top sprints, developed into a shambles at Doncaster yesterday, and angry punters lost their cash on five horses." After they had been withdrawn, "The scene was set for the most astonishing fiasco on a racecourse this year."

The first false start was followed by another although, mercifully, there were no more mishaps. The race finally started 13 minutes late and Felipe Toro, the favourite, won easily.

The five miscreant jockeys – Carson, Richard Fox, Paul Cook, Alan Mackay and Tony Culhane – argued that the first false start wasn't one or shouldn't have been. Sayers disagreed. "There was nothing controversial about it," he said. "It was a thoroughly bad show. I talked to all the jockeys before the race and stressed I would not have them coming in at a gallop. Several of them did, and it would have been most unfair to let that first start stand."

At the subsequent inquiry, the stewards blamed the jockeys and ruled, "The false start was caused by jockeys crowding and anticipating the start."

54 IT'S TIME FOR CHIPS

New Year's Day 1999 was an important one in the history of chips. From that day every thoroughbred foal registered in Britain and Ireland was required to have an individually numbered microchip implanted in its neck as a lifelong, failsafe means of identification. A special hand-held device could check a horse's identity in seconds.

Peter Barrie, the 'King of the Ringers' (see curiosity 82), would have been appalled. His criminal career was founded on the laxity of the systems for identifying racehorses in both Britain and the USA.

In Barrie's heyday, after the First World War in Britain and in the 1920s and early 1930s in America and Cuba, there were no systematic identity checks. If two horses looked similar, unless their teeth were examined, a three-year-old could pass for a well developed two-year-old and a four-year-old for a three-year-old. To prepare himself for a horse's teeth being examined, Barrie sometimes amended them.

In the USA, a rash of ringers after the Second World War contributed to the establishment of the Thoroughbred Racing Protective Bureau in 1946 and, from 1947, the use of tattooed lips for identification.

The Jockey Club didn't follow America's example although in 1928 the Royal College of Veterinary Surgeons set up a committee to prepare a system of identification based on horses' colours and markings. Two years later their work resulted in a booklet for vets, which went through several editions and eventually led to the introduction of passports for every registered thoroughbred.

Successive refinements failed to eliminate incidents in which one horse ran in the name of another, although human error rather than nefarious intent was usually to blame.

On 1 September 1995, trainer Brian Pearce bought two three-year-old bay geldings, Ela-Ment and Hong Kong Dollar. Unfortunately, he failed to examine their passports properly, with the result that Ela-Ment twice ran in the name of Hong Kong Dollar, at Lingfield later in September and at Wolverhampton the following month.

The Jockey Club was keen to stress that there was nothing sinister about it. Their spokesman said, "This is not a ringer inquiry. The trainer has admitted he got the two horses muddled up. There is no skulduggery involved." Pearce was fined £750.

A few months later, at Southwell, Reg Hollinshead's three-year-old Loch Style ran in the name of four-year-old stablemate Taniyar in a maiden race over one and a half miles. He was supposed to be running an hour later, in a selling race over seven furlongs. Starting at 5-2 second favourite, Loch Style, unsurprisingly, was tailed off.

Hollinshead and two of his staff had become confused. The trainer explained, "They are both bay geldings and of a similar size and shape. I'm afraid the three of us did not realise we had saddled the wrong horse."

Two years later, in 1998, there were two more mix-ups. In August, at Hamilton, Jack Berry's two-year-old colt Perigeux ran as his three-year-old stablemate Royal Dream in a race for fillies. Starting as 7-2 second favourite, the two-year-old finished tailed off last.

A stable groom had brought the wrong horse from the racecourse stables.

Two months later, David Evans twice ran the bay two-year-old filly Oriel Star in the name of Slightly Dusty, also a bay juvenile filly. Evans explained that they had been mixed up as yearlings, and was fined £400.

The arrival of microchipping promised to end such mishaps, backed up by the continued use of passports. In 2004, the Horse Passports (England) Regulations required that all horses have a passport containing an accurate set of markings. The requirement, linked to the possible fate of horses for eating purposes, provoked a lively Parliamentary debate.

In the House of Lords, Viscount Falkland pointed out, "There is always an emotional response in this country to the eating of horses. We do not really like it. We recognise that others do it but we rather despise them for it. Personally, I do not eat horses, at least, not knowingly. It is possible that my cat eats horses but I certainly do not."

The latest, 2008, edition of the booklet laying out the information to be supplied in passports, issued by Weatherbys in conjunction with the RCVS and BEVA (British Equine Veterinary Association), was very detailed. Body colours, markings on 45 different parts of the horse, with additional details on features of the head, whorls and where microchips should be implanted – normally in or adjacent to the nuchal ligament at the top of the left mid-crest.

Yet neither detailed passports nor microchips were enough to counter human failures.

In 2017, Charlie McBride was pleasantly surprised to see his two-year-old Mandarin Princess win at Yarmouth at 50-1, until realising that he had sent out the three-year-old Millie's Kiss by mistake. McBride was fined £1,500.

The BHA was less pleased and introduced new microchip scanning procedures. As well as scanning horses on their arrival at the racecourse, they were to be scanned as they moved from the racecourse stables to the saddling boxes prior to each race.

It still wasn't enough. A few months later, in January 2018 at Southwell, Ivan Furtado ran Scribner Creek in the race which stablemate African Trader was due to run in, while African Trader ran in the race earmarked for Scribner Creek.

The horses had been accidentally mixed up before they arrived at the course. The BHA accepted that there was no deliberate intention to deceive but its patience had run out. "This is the second time in six months when there has been an incident in which an incorrect horse has competed in a race," it complained. "This is simply unacceptable. The BHA is now going to take measures to improve the robustness of the identification processes and reduce the risk of human error." Furtado was fined £2,000.

Yet human frailty could still foil the BHA's best efforts. At Newmarket in 2020, the mix-up involved horses trained by the highly respected and highly successful Aidan O'Brien in the Group 1 bet365 Fillies Mile. Mother Earth was supposed to carry the number 5 cloth and be ridden by William Buick, while Snowfall was due to carry the number 9 cloth and be ridden by James Doyle. Unfortunately, the horses carried the wrong number cloths and wrong jockeys.

O'Brien explained, "What happened was that our lads put the wrong saddles on the wrong fillies." Snowfall, actually Mother Earth, finished third and Mother Earth, actually Snowfall, finished eighth. O'Brien was fined £4,000. The BHA announced that there would be additional identity checks.

By then plans were already being drawn up for a new, digital passport designed to facilitate the free movement of horses between Britain and Europe after Brexit. Good luck.

Chapter

11

Prizes

In which the Countess
graces the whip • the
Ascot Gold Cup goes
overboard • sausages
are prized • Gareth
opens a box.

THE COUNTESS GRACES THE WHIP

The whip, a very old one, lies venerably in a glass case in the Jockey Club Rooms in Newmarket. It is so old that no one is sure exactly how old it is. It was the same with people, until the civil registration of births, marriages and deaths came into force in 1837. If it had been introduced earlier, the claim that Methuselah was 969 when he died would surely have foundered.

The whip has a silver head with a coat of arms engraved upon it, the arms of Barbara Villiers, alias Countess Castlemaine. Villiers was King Charles II's mistress and had five children with him. She wasn't alone. Charles had many mistresses and, applying a version of the saying, "What is sauce for the goose is sauce for the gander," Villiers had many lovers.

Unfortunately, from a dating point of view, the style of the engraving suggests a date later than the Countess's heyday, in the 1660s.

The Challenge Whip was certainly in play by 1756, when it was designated as a trophy to be raced for by horses belonging to members of the Jockey Club Rooms, whether or not also members of the Jockey Club.

In that year, the appropriately named Matchem, owned by William Fenwick of Bywell Hall in Northumberland, faced Mr Bowles's Trajan in a match.

The match was prompted by a race at Newmarket the previous year. Matchem was the champion of the North, where he was unbeaten in 1753 and 1754. At Newmarket, Bowles felt confident that Trajan was the better horse but Matchem beat him and other runners easily.

Bowles, believing that Trajan had failed due to a poor preparation, challenged Matchem's owner to a match.

The *Sporting Magazine*, looking back, in September 1840, on the memorable day, recorded that the race was run on the Beacon Course, over a distance just beyond four miles, "for 200 guineas and the Whip or Championship of

The Newmarket Challenge Whip.

Newmarket, weight 10st each. The odds at starting were 2 to 1 on Matchem, who was ridden by John Singleton.

"In running over the Flat, Matchem, who waited on his fiery competitor, appeared to have so much the worse of the race, that 5-1 was betted against him: at the Turn of the Lands, about three miles and a quarter, he went up to the lead, and the odds were soon 100-1 against Trajan, Matchem winning very easily." Fenwick won the money and also "became intituled to the Whip."

According to tradition, the plaited loop of horsehair at the top of the whip and the now depleted lash at the bottom came from the mighty Eclipse. Not in 1756, for Eclipse was not born until 1764, with his spectacular unbroken run of 18 victories achieved in 1769 and 1770.

What gives the suggestion some credence is the fact that, in 1786, Dennis O'Kelly, Eclipse's owner, won the Challenge Whip with Dungannon. Perhaps O'Kelly arranged for a portion of Eclipse's hair to be attached to the whip before his own death in 1787 and that of Eclipse two years later.

For a period from 1764, the race was run on a regular basis, boasting Gimcrack, in 1770, as one of its winners. Later, challenges for the whip dried up and when a race was staged, walkovers were common. From 1982 until 2003 the race was restricted to maidens and there was no prize money, which helps to explain the paucity of runners. With only rare exceptions the races, run over one mile, were matches.

In 2003, after Thingmebob strolled home by 10 lengths against a single opponent, at 5-1 on, Newmarket seriously considered scrapping the historic race. Michael Prosser, the clerk of the course, acknowledged that the race was, "not only part of Newmarket's heritage, but also racing's heritage, but on the other hand we want to be putting on competitive racing. The Challenge Whip was uncompetitive; it only had two runners and was not a spectacle."

The race was saved but in an attempt to attract more runners it was moved from the Guineas meeting in the spring to the autumn and converted to a handicap over one mile two furlongs.

Field sizes improved but were still small. Between 2004 and 2019 they ranged from two (2009) to 11 (2014), with an average of 5.4.

When Felix beat five opponents in 2019 there was still no prize money but the trophy was reported to be worth £20,000. In 2020, Lord Derby's Zoran beat four opponents to win what had become a footnote at the end of the opening day of Newmarket's autumn meeting.

56 THE ASCOT GOLD CUP GOES OVERBOARD

On 19 June 1907, *The Sporting Life* proclaimed, 'An Ascot Sensation. The Gold Cup Stolen.' Readers of the same day's *Times* were told that the newspaper had been "informed by Messrs. R. and S. Garrard, goldsmiths to the Crown, that the Ascot Gold Cup was stolen yesterday afternoon. The Cup was being shown on the usual table on the lawn at the back of the grandstand at Ascot, and was in charge of a representative of Messrs. Garrard and Co., who are the makers of the Cup, and a policeman. Their attention was diverted, presumably by an accomplice of the thief or thieves, and directly afterwards the Cup was missed from its gold pedestal. The Cup, which is of 20 carat gold, is egg-shaped, with richly-chased serpent handles and borders, after the style of Flaxman. It is 13in. in height and 6in. in diameter, and weighs 68oz."

The Cup was stolen during the running of the 4.30pm race but while *The Sporting Life* reported that the theft caused "great consternation," within a day *The Times* casually remarked that "nothing has been discovered as to the thief, and already the affair is almost forgotten at Ascot."

That was unlikely, not least because the Cup had been donated by King Edward VII. On 20 June, Gold Cup day, Garrard and Co. advertised a £50 reward "to any person giving such information as will lead to the apprehension

A different looking Royal Ascot. The White Knight went on to win the Gold Cup while Bridge Of Canny was promoted to third place after Eider's disqualification.

and conviction of the thief or thieves and the recovery of the property, or in proportion to the amount of such property recovered."

The race was as dramatic as the Cup's theft, with The White Knight and Eider engaging in a ding-dong battle that ended with both horses trying to bite each other as they passed the winning post. The judge declared a dead-heat, upon which Bill Halsey, The White Knight's rider, lodged an objection. "I object to the jockey of Eider," Halsey declared, "for bumping and boring and catching hold of my leg and trying to push me off."

The stewards sustained the objection in relation to Eider's jockey George Stern having bumped his opponent but exonerated Stern from having tried to catch hold of Halsey's leg. Eider was disqualified and The White Knight declared the winner.

There was no Cup for owners Colonel Tom Kirkwood and William Wyndham, the son of Baron Leconfield. Nor was there any fruitful response to Garrard's offer of a reward for information leading to the conviction of the thieves and the Cup's recovery. In August, the reward was doubled to £100, but it failed to unearth the culprits.

The White Knight won the Ascot Gold Cup again the following year but many more years passed without any news on the fate of the 1907 trophy. Then, in 1931, former Scotland Yard detective Edwin Thomas Woodhall, a prolific writer of crime stories, claimed to know the answer to the mystery of the Cup's disappearance. With two of the principal participants dead and the third living abroad under an assumed name, Woodhall felt free to "tell the inside story of why and how the Cup was stolen."

A few years later, in *Secrets of Scotland Yard* (1936), he gave a full account, true or imagined, of the theft, "the result of an absurd joke – a wager."

After leaving Scotland Yard, Woodhall had worked in the intelligence service. On one occasion during the First World War, in France, he located an army deserter and returned him to his unit. When he searched the deserter, he found a signed photograph "of a scion of one of our oldest houses of nobility, one who had been killed in action, gallantly leading his men."

In 1929, at the Cafe Royal, an immacutely dressed man approached Woodhall; it was the deserter. The man, whose first name was Thomas, remembered the kind treatment he had received from Woodhall and had traced him in order to tell him his story before leaving Britain and starting a new life under a new name.

"I am the only living man," he told Woodhall, "who knows the secret of the stolen Ascot Gold Cup." Thomas had been the loyal manservant of Lord X, whose photograph Woodhall had seen when he detained the deserter. Lord X had been killed in action, his close friend Lord Z was also dead, as was Lady

X, pursued by both men. She had died abroad before the War. All three had been involved in racing.

In 1907, two or three days before Royal Ascot, the three had a lively dinner party, waited on by Lord X's manservant. During the evening, Lady X said that "she would never die content unless the Ascot Gold Cup was hers, by fair means or foul."

The two noblemen had been drinking, "not wisely, but well," when Lord X exclaimed, "You shall have the Gold Cup, darling." Lord Z then challenged his friend to a £5,000 wager, betting that Lord X would not obtain the Cup.

The next day Thomas tried to persuade Lord X to cancel the bet, made while drunk, but Lord X insisted on honouring it, despite the fact that neither he nor Lady X had a runner in the race. When his master reiterated his unshakeable determination to "borrow" the Cup, Thomas agreed to help him.

On Gold Cup day, Thomas told Woodhall, he was lucky. "All the afternoon I passed and repassed the alluring object, waiting for my favourable moment to lift it off its pedestal, but it was too risky. It was too well guarded. Suddenly, my chance came. Just before the 4.30 race I saw the plain clothes man walk off towards the grandstand, but the policeman was still on guard."

Thomas was near the table on which the Gold Cup stood when three ladies came up and asked the policeman a question. He bent over their racecards, giving Thomas his chance. "I lifted the Gold Cup off its pedestal. Walking leisurely away, I wrapped it in my mackintosh that was slung across my arm. Any amount of people were around me, yet no one saw a stranger pick up the Gold Cup. The 4.30 race occupied all eyes."

Thomas got into Lord X's car, waiting at the entrance, and set off for his master's London flat. Lord Z settled his bet with Lord X but "the public outcry was too much for their nerves to stand, so the Ascot Gold Cup was given to me to hide."

Woodhall's story then enters one of its least credible episodes. Without further ado, he continued, "Two months afterwards Lord Z and Lady X were on my master's yacht," presumably with Lord X also on board. "It was a lovely moonlight night."

"'Thomas, have you got the Gladstone bag?'
'Yes, sir.'
'Have you placed that 56lb weight inside it?'
'Yes, sir.'
'Very well, let me help you heave it overboard.'
Splash!"
In the bag, with the 56lb weight, was the Ascot Gold Cup.
True or false?

SAUSAGES ARE PRIZED

Cast your mind back to 1665. If Queen Elizabeth II had been on the throne (she wasn't), she might have described it as an *annus horribilis*. King Charles II, who was on the throne, may well have said the same thing.

The trouble with 1665 was that it brought the Great Plague of London to London, killing an unhealthy proportion of the city's population and, in July, persuading Charles that he and his attendants would be better off in Salisbury. When the plague arrived in Salisbury, he and his court moved to Oxford.

Charles returned to London in February 1666, giving him the chance to settle down in time for the Great Fire of London, that September. Charles liked to enjoy himself and as neither the bubonic plague nor a raging inferno were much fun, he turned his mind to Newmarket and his passion for racing.

In 1665 the King came up with the idea of a 'Twelve Stone Plate' and it was

Miss Alwen Thrale winning the 1937 Newmarket Town Plate on Jimmy's Pet.

"ordered by his Majestie to be observed by all persons that put in horses to run for the Plate, the new Round-heate at Newmarket, set out the 16th day of October in the 17th year of our Sovereign Lord King Charles II. Which Plate is to be rid for yearly, the seconde Thursday in October, for ever."

As Charles II ascended the throne in 1660 and had his coronation the year after, it might seem strange that he was said to be in the 17th year of his reign. However, royalists, of whom Charles was one, preferred to erase the unpleasantness of the era of the Commonwealth and Protectorate and regard Charles II's reign as having begun shortly after his father's execution, in 1649. To make their feelings known, Oliver Cromwell's body was exhumed in 1661 and his head chopped off. Best to be on the safe side.

So, on Thursday 11 October 1666 the Newmarket Town Plate was run for the first time, on the newly laid out Round Course, over three miles six furlongs 93 yards. Little else is known about the inaugural running, nor about many subsequent runnings. Much that is known is thanks to the dogged research of Jim Fuller, who began his exploration in 2011 and has kept up the difficult search ever since.

Runners in the 1666 race were to carry 12st, "besides bridle and saddle", and to be ready for a one o'clock start. There would be three heats, with half an hour breaks between them. Race-riding behaviour could clearly be unseemly, as it was felt necessary to warn that, "Every rider that layeth hold on, or striketh any of the riders, shall win no plate or prize."

The winner's identity and the prize received are not known but whatever the prize was worth, the recipient was required to make contributions of his own. The conditions stated, "Whosoever winneth the plate or prize shall give to the Clerk of the Course twenty shillings, to be distributed to the poor on both sides of Newmarket, and twenty shillings to the Clerk of the Race; for which he is to keep the course plain and free from cart roots."

From the winner's point of view, the more runners the better because another stipulation was that every runner must "deposit twenty shillings for every heat, which the winning horse shall have; and the last horse of every heat shall pay the second horse's stakes and his own, which stakes are likewise to be deposited into the Clerk of the Race's hands before the horses start, to pay the winning horse his stakes every heat."

As racing at Newmarket was the preserve of a small number of privileged individuals, fields for the new Plate were invariably small and often reduced to a match or walkover. In 1671, a newsletter dated 17 October, reproduced in *The Manuscripts of S.H. Le Fleming, Esq., of Rydal Hall* (1890), reported, "On Thursday last, the plate, being a flagon of 32 price, was run for at Newmarket, which his Majesty won, there rid besides him the Duke of Monmouth, Mr Thin and Eliot."

In 1675, King Charles II won the race again and, 20 years later, King William III owned and perhaps rode the so far anonymous winner. From the 1720s, there is a much fuller list of the names of the winning horses and owners and, from the 1760s, of riders.

In 1774, King George III decreed that in future there would be only one heat, which must have come as a relief to the horses.

For most participants, winning was a simple task, as the commonest field size was one. In 22 of the 25 years from 1726 to 1750, there was a walkover and in the other three years, there were only two runners. A similar pattern persisted until into the twentieth century and it was only from the early 1920s that bigger fields were seen.

Small fields facilitated runs of success by a small number of riders. Between 1903 and 1921 Mr Frank Augustus Simpson won the Town Plate 13 times and when he didn't win it, Mr C W Stevens did. Simpson's dominance was achieved by beating a total of just nine opponents. Things became harder after 1921; nevertheless, Simpson landed another hat-trick of successes from 1929 to 1931.

A double figure field was reached for the first time in 1932, by which time lady riders were regularly victorious. Miss Tanner pioneered female participation when finishing third of five in 1923 and two years later Miss Eileen Joel, on Hogier, became the first lady rider to win the race.

During the eighteenth century, the race was generally worth £20 or 20 guineas but later its value slipped and did not exceed that sum until the mid-1920s, spasmodically reaching £40 during the 1930s.

After the Second World War, the race was dominated by lady riders. From 1946 to 1975, every winner was ridden by a woman. Until 1972, when Meriel Tufnell won the first race for women under Jockey Club rules, the Town Plate provided the only opportunity for them to compete in Flat races. Marie Tinkler and Carolyn Mercer, both dual winners of the Town Plate in the early 1970s, were subsequently champion amateur lady riders.

The Town Plate also provided an opening for precocious young riders. In 1964 Diana Thomson Jones, Eileen Joel's great niece, won the race on Stem Turn when she was barely 13. Two years later Marilyn Calvert, aged 12, finished second and in 1971 Nigel Tinkler, Marie Tinkler's son and later a successful jump jockey and trainer, took part when also aged 12. The following year Carolyn Mercer, the 14-year-old daughter of jockey 'Manny' Mercer, won the race on Greenacre.

Judged by the number of runners, the historic race's popularity has grown considerably over the last 60 years. It took over 260 years for the race to attract a field of more than nine but from the 1950s field sizes were often more than 20 and in 1985 reached 36.

Despite facing more opponents than most of his predecessors, Sea Buck won the race five years in a row, from 1994 to 1998. Trained by Henry Candy, Sea Buck was first ridden by his sister, Carolyn Poland, and then by his daughters, Sophie and Emma.

The race has often been supported by well known and less well known trainers. In 2004 Sheena West won on It's Wallace and in 2011 local trainer John Berry owned, trained and rode Kadouchski to success. Five years later, Sheikh Fahad Al Thani, a member of the ruling family of Qatar, with a passion for racing, rode Almagest to victory.

The attraction was not the prize money but the opportunity to ride competitively in the oldest as well as the longest Flat race in the world. It was not until the late 1970s that prize money regularly reached £100 or more and the silver cups, silver fruit dishes, silver tea services and silver whips that variously formed part of the reward, must have been treasured.

In 1951 Horace Hawes contributed a box of his Newmarket pork sausages to the mix. His business later became Powters and their sausages have become a traditional part of the winner's prize.

So too, since the 1970s, has the Goldings Perpetual Challenge Plate, sponsored by Golding's Newmarket High Street clothes store.

Covid-19 forced the race's abandonment in 2020, the first abandonment since the Second World War, but the Newmarket Town Plate's unique history and the affection felt for it makes its future assured. Well, for the time being.

58 GARETH OPENS A BOX

Early in June 2008 Gareth Hunt picked up a large square cardboard box and placed it on a table. He removed the lid and took out an old, rectangular leather case. Inside the case was a strange-looking, circular silver piece from the circumference of which hung a ring of engraved shields.

Hunt, South Lanarkshire's senior museum officer, then turned his attention to a small, square wooden box from which he carefully removed a silver bell, 12.5cm across and 10.2cm high. He placed the bell on top of the circular silver stand, ready for the Lanark Silver Bell's first public appearance for over 30 years.

Tradition suggested that the bell had been given to the people of Lanark by King William I of Scotland in 1166, William having hunted in the area, but evidence from the bell's markings suggests that the one in the box dates from the late 16th or early 17th centuries. The stand dates from 1896 while the oldest of the shields attached to it bears the inscription, 'Won by me, Sir John Hamilton of Trabroun, 1628.'

The Lanark Silver Bell, resurrected at Hamilton in 2008, 31 years after the closure of Lanark racecourse.

The next shield bears the date 1852 after which there is a run of shields, ending in 1977. That year, the race for the Lanark Silver Bell, run at Lanark racecourse, was won by Border River, owned and trained by Clifford Watts and ridden by 'Dandy' Nicholls.

The racecourse closed later that year and the Silver Bell went into storage, where it remained until 2008, when the race was resurrected at Hamilton racecourse. Some racegoers made a special pilgrimage to celebrate the historic race's revival and 7,000 people attended that evening meeting on 11 June, when £150,000 was raised for the Cash For Kids charity, to help needy children in the west of Scotland.

Tifernati, trained by William Haggas and ridden by Liam Jones, became the first in a fresh line of winners of the Lanark Silver Bell, which was displayed in a glass cabinet behind the winner's podium.

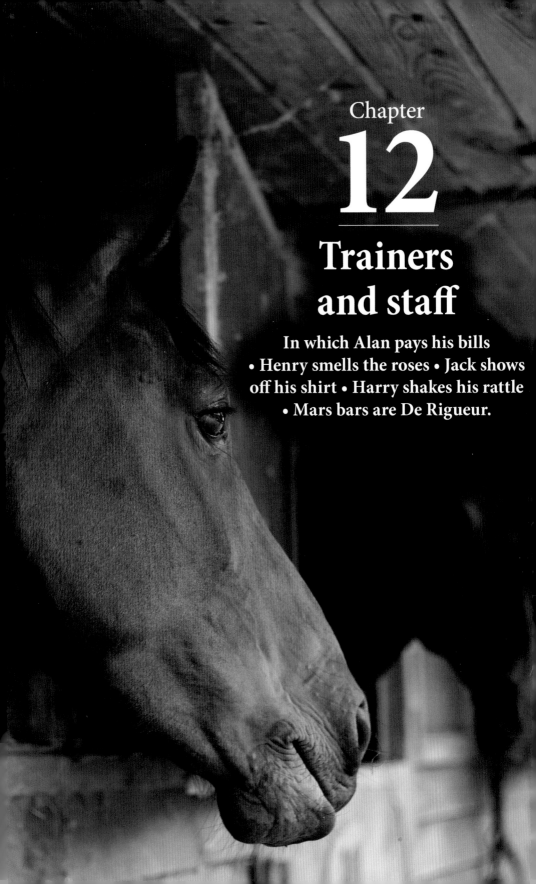

Chapter
12

Trainers and staff

**In which Alan pays his bills
• Henry smells the roses • Jack shows
off his shirt • Harry shakes his rattle
• Mars bars are De Rigueur.**

59 ALAN PAYS HIS BILLS

Early in 1994, the bills were sitting on trainer Alan Bailey's table, some of them final demands. Luckily for Bailey, Sheikh Mohammed was better placed.

Both could look back on the 1993 Flat season with some satisfaction. Mentalasanythin, the star of Bailey's stable at Tarporley in Cheshire, had won six times, peaking with victory in a Class 3 Handicap at Wolverhampton worth £8,656 to the winner. Sheikh Mohammed, based in Dubai, had his own stable star, Opera House, who had won the Group 1 Coronation Cup, Coral Eclipse Stakes and King George VI and Queen Elizabeth Diamond Stakes, together worth over half a million pounds.

Bailey's bills were perfectly timed, for Sheikh Mohammed was about to turn his dream of training horses in Dubai then racing them in Europe and around the world into reality. The horses would race under the banner of Godolphin, named after the Godolphin Arabian, one of the three founding stallions of modern thoroughbreds.

Godolphin's now world-famous royal blue colours first seen on a British racecourse in 1994.

An ambitious enterprise demanded striking colours and Sheikh Mohammed's search team found them at Bailey's small stable. Bailey had been collecting plain colours for his owners and had three sets, red, mauve and royal blue. He had lent the red and mauve colours to owners but it was the royal blue ones that Sheikh Mohammed wanted.

Bailey recalled, "Simon Crisford [Sheikh Mohammed's assistant] offered me £500. He must have known I was skint but I told him I wouldn't even lend them to him for that. We talked about it over about three weeks and, in the end, I sold them for £26,000. They were cheap at the price. I was going to hold out for more but there were a few final demands sitting on my table. They are the best colours there are. What I should have done was said, 'You can have them for £500 and give me £5,000 every time you have a Group winner.'"

Godolphin's colours were registered in Britain on 22 April 1994 and, at Newmarket six days later, Seismograph, ridden by Pat Eddery and officially trained by Hilal Ibrahim, became the first horse to win in Godolphin's trademark royal blue. Shortly afterwards, Balanchine carried the colours to victory in the Oaks and Irish Derby. By 2020, Godolphin had won 321 Group 1 races. Yes, Bailey should have asked for more.

60 HENRY SMELLS THE ROSES

Henry Cecil once said, "In life, people go through times when it's not a bed of roses."

At the time, the much-loved Newmarket trainer was suffering from the stomach cancer that would eventually kill him but he was also still smelling the roses. Horses, and one horse in particular, buoyed Cecil up but roses were always there in the garden at Warren Place, where Cecil had trained since 1976.

In some ways Cecil was an unlikely recipient of such widespread affection, a patrician figure from a privileged background. Languid, somewhat foppish, Henry Richard Amherst Cecil confessed to being an avid clothes shopper with a collection of 200 shoes. That was considerably fewer than the notorious Imelda Marcos, who also only had two feet, but it was still quite a lot.

He had distinctive mannerisms, quizzical, cocking his head to one side, speaking in staccato bursts, answering questions with a question mark in return, gentlemanly but also fiercely competitive.

Not everything was rosy. Five weeks before Cecil made his debut, in January 1943, his father, Henry Kerr Auchmuty Cecil, brother of Lord Amherst, was killed in action. His mother, Rohays Cecil, the daughter of the Baronet of Leys, subsequently married Sir Cecil Boyd-Rochfort, five times champion Flat trainer, whose patrons included King George VI and Queen Elizabeth II.

Like his stepfather, Henry Cecil was destined for Eton but claimed to be the only boy at his prep school ever to have failed the entrance exam. He once said, "I'm qualified to do nothing."

So it was fortunate that he found his metier training racehorses, first as his stepfather's assistant and, from 1969, in his own right. His success was almost immediate and over the decades Cecil earned a reputation for possessing an affinity and instinctive skill with horses.

Henry Cecil with a cherished rose.

With the backing of a string of wealthy owners, Cecil accumulated an impressive record, ultimately training the winners of 25 English Classics, including four Derbys, winning 75 races at Royal Ascot and being declared champion trainer 10 times.

Yet his road was rocky both professionally and personally, embracing a dramatic fall from grace, followed by an extraordinary resurrection. In 1989, after over 20 years married to Julie Murless, Cecil took up with Natalie Payne, who was working at Warren Place. A year later he and Julie were divorced and in 1992 Cecil, aged 48, married Natalie, aged 23.

It didn't go down well in Newmarket society, nor with Sheikh Mohammed, one of Cecil's main patrons, who felt that Natalie had too much influence on the training operation. In 1995, when Sheikh Mohammed believed that Cecil had withheld information about an injury to one of his horses, he took all 40 of them away.

Worse was to come. In 1999, the *News of the World* proclaimed that, during a visit to Ireland, Natalie had a one night stand with a leading jockey. Cecil promptly sacked Kieren Fallon, his stable jockey, who denied that he was the jockey involved. Before long, it was Cecil's turn to appear on the front page of the *News of the World*, under the headline "Top Trainer Cecil and the £800 Vice Girl." The trainer had been visited at the Grand Hotel in Brighton by a prostitute.

If things could get worse, they did. In 2000 Cecil's twin brother David died, aged 57, and Cecil was banned from driving for five years after running into an elderly couple while drunk. Two years earlier, over 100 horses had raced from Warren Place, winning 100 races, including three Group 1 events. In 1999, Cecil won the Derby and Oaks with Oath and Ramruma but thereafter the downward slide seemed terminal. In 2005 Cecil raced only 36 horses, winning just a dozen races, none of them above Listed class. The following year, he was diagnosed with stomach cancer. Aged 63, major patrons dead or departed, ill and troubled, Cecil's career teetered on the brink.

Crucially, Prince Khalid Abdullah stuck with Cecil. In 2005, he supplied eight of the trainer's meagre total of 12 winners and owned 12 of the 36 horses raced from Warren Place that year. Cecil clawed his way back to respectability. In 2009, he won 63 races, including the Group 1 Champion Stakes with Twice Over and Nassau Stakes and Breeders' Cup Filly & Mare Turf with Midday, both owned by Prince Khalid.

Appropriately, it was Prince Khalid who gave Cecil salvation and a powerful reason to defy cancer for as long as he did. In 2009 a yearling named Frankel arrived at Warren Place.

Three years later Cecil, frail, his voice a whisper, watched Frankel win the Champion Stakes at Ascot and told the eager media, "He's the best I've ever had, the best I've ever seen. I'd be very surprised if there's ever been a better."

Few disagreed, for Frankel was a dominant presence, a genuine superstar who retired unbeaten in 14 races, including 10 Group 1 events. Increasingly gaunt and ravaged, Cecil seemed to be kept alive by Frankel, the trainer determined not to miss a race of the horse's greatness.

As well as Frankel, there was the support of his third wife, Jane McKeown, who he married in 2008, and the comfort of his roses.

When Cecil and Julie moved into Warren Place, they planted hundreds of French, English and Chinese roses, helped by their gardener for over 25 years, Gordon Harvey. Cecil liked to show them to visitors, to cut and arrange blooms for the house and to give them as presents. The horses weren't forgotten. A hedge of rugosa roses lined the fillies' yard and instead of giving them peppermints, as a treat Cecil gave them rose hips.

He died in June 2013, aged 70, two years after being knighted for services to horseracing and less than eight months after Frankel's final race. Fittingly, a rose was named after him, the Sir Henry Cecil rose, with a fragrant white bloom with a cream back.

When the inaugural Sir Henry Cecil Stakes was run, on the first day of Newmarket's July meeting in 2014, the winning connections were presented with the trainer's rose, as a button-hole.

JACK SHOWS OFF HIS SHIRT

Jack Berry was born into one of those families, common in Leeds in the 1930s and 1940s, where there were a lot of children, eight in Jack's case, and not much money. There were spoons but a complete absence of silver ones. All that he has achieved in life, Berry has worked hard for. He is what used to be called 'the salt of the earth.'

As you know, the origin of the expression is often said to be found in Matthew 5:13, "Ye are the salt of the earth but if the salt have lost his savour, wherewith shall it be salted? It is thenceforth good for nothing but to be cast out and to be trodden under foot of men." That sounds like a mixed blessing and if P G Wodehouse had written the Bible, it would have been much funnier and Jack would have been described, more satisfactorily, as "a good egg," indisputably, a good egg.

Having achieved his ambition to be a jockey, Berry started an exciting competition to see whether he could win more races than he broke bones.

The much loved Jack Berry in his trademark red shirt.

It was a close thing but, to his great credit, he did, winning 47 races while breaking only 46 bones.

In danger of running out of bones, in 1969, aged 32, Berry began training from a small yard near Doncaster. That December he won his first race as a trainer with Camasco, in a selling hurdle at Kelso.

Before long he had moved to "the most dilapidated farm you ever did see," at Cockerham in Lancashire. With the help of sleeping partners and a lot of hard work, Berry flattened the buildings and gradually turned Moss Side Racing Stables into a successful operation, with a focus on two-year-olds and sprinters.

Berry had a burning ambition, one different from most jockeys and trainers. His dream, from when he was a teenager, was not to win the Derby or Grand National but the Ayr Gold Cup, a prestigious and valuable sprint handicap with a long history but not generally ranked among the sport's most glittering prizes. Still, it takes all sorts.

In 1978, Berry ran his prolific winner I Don't Mind in the race of his dreams, only for overnight rain to turn the ground against him; I Don't Mind finished fourth. Three years later it was Touch Boy's turn; he didn't see out the full six furlongs. Another three years passed before Clantime also returned home without the Cup.

There were plenty of compensating successes. Between 1978 and 1983, Bri-Eden won 19 times, an achievement topped by O.I. Oyston, who amassed 22 wins on the Flat, the last in 1989 when aged 13, plus two over hurdles.

One day, while still a jockey, Berry went shopping before racing at Ayr and bought a red shirt. That afternoon he experienced a fairly unfamiliar feeling, that of riding a winner. For some reason, possibly supernatural, Jack sensed that the red shirt and the winner's enclosure were linked.

"From then on," he wrote in his autobiography, *It's Tougher At The Bottom* (1991), "whenever I rode a fancied horse, I put the red shirt on as a lucky omen. Even when I started training, the red shirt was worn on the same basis. It began to arouse suspicion that when we had a winner, I was invariably wearing a red shirt. People often ask me if I've only got the one; this was once the case, but I've got lots now. In fact, people actually send me them. These days, I always wear a red shirt at the races, as we seem to be running more and more fancied horses."

So, inevitably, Berry was sporting a red shirt when, in 1988, So Careful became Berry's fourth stab at winning the Ayr Gold Cup. As there were 29 runners and So Careful was 33-1, it was a formidable task. Carrying only 7st 7lb, So Careful gave his trainer bliss.

"I have never been so chuffed in all my life!" he rhapsodied. "To win the Ayr Gold Cup, after waiting for so many years, was the ultimate. Without the shadow of a doubt it was the happiest day of my life." Possibly as a result, Berry declared Ayr to be "the greatest racecourse in Britain."

For Jack Berry, Friday 16 September 1988 was the pinnacle of his career but it was far from being the end. When he gave up training, in 1999, he had sent out over 100 winners in each of his final 10 seasons and in 1998 won three races at Royal Ascot.

It was an achievement to be proud of but Berry, already widely admired, earned even more respect and affection in another role, that of indefatigable fund raiser, particularly for the Injured Jockeys Fund.

In the space of four months straddling 1963/1964, jockeys Tim Brookshaw and Paddy Farrell were paralysed as a result of falls, Farrell's in the 1964 Grand National. Earlier in their careers, Farrell and Berry had worked together for several years at Charlie Hall's yard and Farrell's plight deeply affected Berry.

The desire to provide better help for Brookshaw and Farrell than was then available led to the creation of the Injured Jockeys Fund, which developed into a wonderful source of support. Berry was ceaseless in his fund raising and a key figure in the provision of annual holidays in Tenerife for groups of the IJF's beneficiaries.

In 1996 he was awarded an MBE for his fundraising work and in 2015, when Berry's inspirational efforts were at the heart of raising £3.5 million for a fitness and rehabilitation centre in Malton, it was fittingly named Jack Berry House, complete with a statue of Berry, wearing a trilby and red shirt.

Jack Berry House complements similar facilities at Oaksey House in Lambourn, opened in 2009, and the Peter O'Sullevan House, opened in Newmarket in 2019.

Jack's red shirts live on, still worn by their owner, who is Vice President of the Injured Jockeys Fund. Since 1995 Pontefract has staged an annual Red Shirt Night charity meeting to raise money for 'The House That Jack Built.' 2019 marked the 25th Red Shirt Night.

A toast to Jack's red shirt.

62 HARRY SHAKES HIS RATTLE

When 1931 arrived, so did Ballyscanlon, with a reputation for stubbornness. Epsom trainer Harry Hedges had just bought the recalcitrant seven-year-old for 105 guineas, a sum generally regarded as too much.

"All the other trainers laughed at me," Hedges recalled. "They didn't think I could make a good racehorse out of Ballyscanlon when others had failed. But I have a motto which was handed to me by my father, and that is, 'Frighten, not punish.'"

The early signs were unpromising. According to his new trainer, when Ballyscanlon arrived, "he would not jump and he would not run." Yet, applying his father's dictum, by the end of September Ballyscanlon had won five races on the Flat and over hurdles, and approaching £3,000 in prize money.

As reported in the *Coventry Evening Telegraph* (23 September 1931), Hedges explained, "As soon as I had him we took him on Epsom Downs and rigged up an amateur starting post. Two men held a long piece of elastic in front of the horse and as they let it go I gave him a whack on the flank with the 'rattle.' He was wearing blinkers, so couldn't see where the noise came from. It gave him a fright, and off he went like a streak of lightning. Since then, just the noise of the rattle has been enough to get him going."

Harry Hedges with his rattle, ready to gee-up Ballyscanlon.

When Hedges moved the experiment from the gallops to the racecourse, he kept the method secret for as long as possible, surreptitiously exchanging the whip for the rattle, particularly when Tony Escott was on board.

Inevitably, the noise of the rattle attracted attention. "As the jockey got more excited," Hedges told the *Daily Mirror* (22 March 1934), "he used to rattle the can louder and louder until, at the end of the race, there was a terrible din, but it was all quite legal."

His father's method was to bang two tin trays together but that was unsuitable for racing, so Harry used "an old condensed milk tin filled with stones and tied on to a stick." On other occasions, Hedges described the rattle as "an old metal polish tin, filled with small stones," attached to the end of a whip.

Ballyscanlon won at least one race without the benefit of the rattle when, in September 1931, the 15 year old champion apprentice Fred Rickaby rode him to victory in the Stayers' Handicap at Gatwick.

Eventually, Ballyscanlon became an unwilling participant, with or without the rattle, and in 1934, under the headline 'Good-Bye To His Rattle,' the *Daily Mirror* reported that, now an 11-year-old, Ballyscanlon was to be retired. It was a celebrity retirement, with Ballyscanlon joining 13 year-old Megan Taylor, who was already the British Figure Skating Champion and had recently finished runner-up in the World Figure Skating Championship, an event she went on to win in 1938 and 1939. Together, Ballyscanlon and the precocious 'Ice Queen' were to be seen early each morning exercising on the South Downs before Taylor began her rigorous ice skating training.

In 1935, Hedges resurrected the rattle to liven up another uncooperative inmate, Speed On. Its use may have contributed to Speed On's success that August in the Lympne Selling Handicap at Folkestone, in the hands of jockey J.Hickey.

Belatedly, Hedges' rattle stirred the local stewards into action. They summoned Hedges and Hickey and examined the possibly offending object, which included "a small tin containing a marble." Hedges maintained that "it was more humane to use a rattle than a whip" and it appeared that there was "no rule of racing that states clearly what a jockey may carry."

The Folkestone stewards referred the matter, along with the rattle, to the stewards of the Jockey Club. At the end of August, the rattle was returned to Hedges, together with the instruction that "Instruments of this kind must not be used." Hedges' rattle was silenced.

The following year he won the Cesarewitch with the curiously named Fet before a spell as licensee of the George Hotel in Epsom. Hedges died, aged 64, in 1948.

63 MARS BARS ARE DE RIGUEUR

Ascot's meeting on Saturday 27 September 1986 was a cracker. The Queen Elizabeth II Stakes was followed by the Royal Lodge Stakes, Diadem Stakes and Balmoral Handicap. The Balmoral was the least prestigious and valuable of the four but it was still worth the royal sum of £10,394.40 (about £37,000 today) to the winner, which was De Rigueur, at 20-1.

Unfortunately, stable girl Tanya Mayne had shared her Mars bar with De Rigueur the previous evening and, although De Rigueur was pleased, the urine sample he provided after the race was less satisfactory. It contained traces of theobromine, a chemical found in chocolate, regarded as a stimulant and banned by the Jockey Club.

Disqualification was automatic, enabling *The Guardian* to display a front page headline reading, 'Mars bars De Rigueur from £10,000 win" (7 January 1987). The owner forfeited the prize money, the jockey and trainer their share of it and the trainer was fined £575. That was the minimum allowed under the Jockey Club's Rules but trainer James Bethell still felt aggrieved.

"I thought Tanya would have known about it," he said. "She was with another trainer before me and also with the apprentice trainers' school. It's ridiculous that they don't teach them that sort of thing. It has cost me over £1,000 as a percentage of the prize-money and on top of that I have been fined £575 for something that I couldn't prevent. If I had known the night before I would have withdrawn him. Hopefully he will go on to win the Lincoln." Perhaps prudently, Mayne was reported to be away for a few days.

De Rigueur didn't win the Lincoln, although he finished a creditable fourth to Star Of A Gunner. The owner, Mrs C. Heath, bore the brunt of the financial loss but from that point of view, it was a mere pin-prick. Maggie Heath was married to Christopher Heath, the driving force behind Baring Securities who, in 1986, was reported to have a salary of £3 million (about £8.9 million today), making him the highest paid British businessman, plus a share of the profits.

Heath had already made a fortune selling undervalued Japanese stocks to British investors before Baring Brothers set up Baring Securities in 1984 and put him in charge. In 1986 the new operation made a profit of £10 million, rising to £60 million two years later. Having started with a staff of 15, by 1991 Baring Securities had 19 offices worldwide and 1,100 staff.

According to Jeff Randall, "his income was astronomical, and so too was his spending. He lived the high life, especially racehorses." (*The Telegraph* 28 October 2008).

An analyst of Baring's spectacular collapse in 1995 wrote of Heath, "He owned massively expensive houses; antique furniture and paintings; vintage cars, a yacht; racehorses, and had to be dissuaded by his wife from buying a helicopter and an aeroplane.

"He was not only a big spender but – with a penchant for horseracing – also a passionate gambler." (Mark Stein, 'The Risk Taker As Shadow: A Psychoanalytic View of The Collapse of Barings Bank', *Journal of Management Studies* 37, 8 December 2000.)

Racing in his own or his wife's name, in the late 1980s and early 1990s Heath owned some high class jumpers, among them Rebel Song, The West Awake and Cruising Altitude.

But there was tension between the tradionally-minded, conservative bank executives at Baring Brothers and the more aggressive approach encouraged by Heath at Baring Securities. When the latter reported its first monthly loss in 1992, although still recording a profit that year of £10.8 million, Heath was reined in and, the following year, asked to leave.

By that time Nick Leeson, who joined Baring Securities in 1989, aged 22, had established himself in their offices in Singapore and, fatally unchecked, ran riot with the company's money.

He managed to convince the firm that he was a spectacular success when in fact he was a disastrous failure, concealing his losses from insufficiently prying eyes. In one final, desperate day, 23 February 1995, Leeson lost £143 million. Barings was forced into administration, with losses of £827 million. Meanwhile, Heath withdrew from British racing.

But I digress. De Rigueur was not the first horse to suffer from a Mars bar. On 21 April 1979 No Bombs won the Sean Memorial Handicap Hurdle at Worcester. His post-race urine sample contained traces of theobromine and caffeine and, like De Rigueur, No Bombs was disqualified. He was said to have snatched a Mars bar from his groom's pocket.

Trainer Peter Easterby said, ruefully, "That's the most expensive Mars bar ever. It cost me £4,046 in prize money." At least the stewards waived a fine, and No Bombs went on to be a prolific winner.

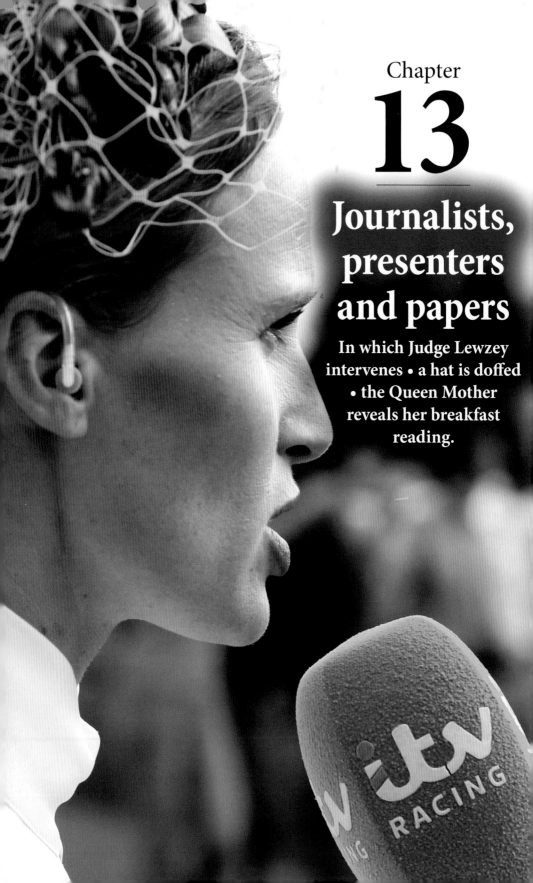

Chapter

13

Journalists, presenters and papers

In which Judge Lewzey intervenes • a hat is doffed • the Queen Mother reveals her breakfast reading.

64 JUDGE LEWZEY INTERVENES

Extraordinary even when dead, John 'Big Mac' McCririck posthumously attracted the attention of those who were already dead themselves. In 2019, McCririck having died, aged 79, *The Guardian* exhumed Julian Wilson, who had died five years earlier, to write his obituary.

Their shared death didn't improve Wilson's opinion of McCririck but gave him an after-time opportunity to express his disdain for his fellow Old Harrovian. A snob as well as a very knowledgeable if wooden BBC TV racing presenter, Wilson was appalled by a lot of things; 'Big Mac' was one of them.

Wilson was far from alone. McCririck was a fine example of someone who people felt strongly about, one camp lauding him, an opposing camp loathing him, with only a small camp occupying the middle ground. What no one could do was ignore him. He was noisy, intrusive, flamboyant, opinionated, irritating, engaging, and large. On duty, he dressed loudly, bejewelled and with a range of hats covering his largely bald head.

A few months after McCririck's death, some of his outfits were put on display at the National Horseracing Museum in Newmarket while others were put up for auction at Rowley's Antiques and Fine Art Auctioneers in Ely. The collection of clothes, watches, rings and cigars fetched around £30,000, with a diamond set horseshoe ring in 14 karat gold leading the field at £5,500.

There were a range of hats, including an oriental-style cream silk embroidered and blue velvet

John 'Big Mac' McCririck emerges from an extraordinary performance at an Employment Tribunal.

smoking cap and several baseball caps of the kind McCririck wore during television appearances at the Breeders' Cup in the USA. What was missing was his deerstalker hat, which had been displayed at the Museum but not at Rowley's salesroom. Does the hat live on, on someone else's head? Has it been found? Was it ever missing?

McCririck was several contradictory things, some of them simultaneously. Although famous and infamous as a television celebrity, latterly in lucrative but unedifying appearances on reality TV shows, he made his name as an investigative journalist with *The Sporting Life*, and a very good one. In 1978 he was voted Specialist Writer of the Year in the British Press Awards; in 1979, the Campaigning Journalist of the Year.

In the former year, McCririck exposed a sting based on the fact that Extel's greyhound service, broadcast into betting shops, gave race off-times in minutes without the refinement of seconds. By briefly delaying broadcasts, conspirators were able to bet after a race had started. The same year, McCririck led the way in covering the Rochester greyhound coup, which would have won its architects £350,000, if bookmakers had condescended to pay out.

In 1979, McCririck hit the jackpot with 'Totegate.' His persistence exposed the Tote's practice of putting winning off-course bets into racecourse pools after the race result was known. Eventually McCririck forced a reluctant Home Secretary, Willie Whitelaw, to set up an independent inquiry from which Woodrow Wyatt, the Tote chairman, was lucky to escape with his job.

'Big Mac's move into television in the 1980s put him centre stage, his deliberately provocative, sometimes sexist, always opinionated appearances, notably as a member of the Channel 4 racing team, brought him to the attention of a wider audience. Few figures in racing are familiar to those outside the sport; McCririck was one of the few.

He was a showman but a very well informed one, with a deep understanding of horseracing as a betting medium. At a time when most racing presenters were either not equipped or not inclined to ask challenging questions, McCririck knew what questions needed to be asked and was not afraid to ask them.

Time did what it always does and moved on. In 2012, by which time McCririck was 72, Channel 4 announced that it was dropping him from their racing team. McCririck, for whom the spotlight's attention was still important, accused Channel 4 of dispensing with him because of his age.

There can never have been an employment tribunal hearing remotely like the one that considered McCririck's allegation of ageism. Judge Alison Lewzey and her two lay assistants, David Buckley and Alison Mitchell, must have doubted their own ears when McCririck testified that journalist Camilla Long's breasts were not big enough for his liking and that he had high hopes of sex with Kate Winslet and/or Dawn French, without believing it likely to happen.

Judge Lewzey was obliged to intervene. "Try to answer the questions that are being put to you, Mr McCririck," she pleaded. "You are making a speech, and that is not the purpose of this examination." Among his speeches was one on religious beliefs, with particular reference to their foolishness and the harm they caused.

Several days later, the tribunal concluded that Channel 4's decision not to employ McCririck was not based on his age but on his unacceptable persona, made less palatable by his appearances on Big Brother and Wife Swap.

And the deerstalker hat? I expect McCririck's wife Jenny has it.

65 A HAT IS DOFFED

As you get older you remember things, inaccurately, that younger people often aren't interested in hearing about. Older people often aren't interested in hearing about them, either.

The genial and courteous John Rickman, trilby raised.

That is why books are sometimes preferable to people because you can put a book down or skip pages but it's harder to get someone to shut up. So, if you don't want to know about John Rickman's trilby, then don't. If it comes up in a quiz you'll regret it but it's up to you.

Anyway, in 1965 ITV launched the World of Sport as a Saturday afternoon rival to the BBC's Grandstand. At first it was presented by the suave Eamonn Andrews and then, from 1965 until its death in 1985, by the suave Dickie Davies, who took a lot of trouble with his hair.

Horseracing was a core part of the programme, popularised by the novelty of showing races from two courses rather than one and, especially, by the introduction of the ITV Seven bet. Around the nation, people watched to see if their attempt to pick the seven winners of the seven televised races and thereby win a fortune, succeeded. It didn't. Sometimes, when only six or five races were shown, there was an ITV Six or ITV Five. Success was still elusive.

The man introducing the afternoon's racing was John Rickman, who was racing by birth. His great-grandfather, Tom Jennings, trained Gladiateur to win the Triple Crown in 1865 and the Ascot Gold Cup the year after, while Jenning's son, also Tom Jennings (couldn't he think of another name?) trained the winners of the 1897 and 1912 Oaks, and 1900 1000 Guineas.

Not only that but Rickman's father, Eric Rickman, covered racing for the *Daily Mail* from 1929 until 1949, under the alias of Robin Goodfellow. When Eric stepped down, his son stepped in.

Rickman was a diligent and frequently successful newspaper tipster but it was his appearances on World of Sport that made him a familiar name, face, voice and hat.

Tall, well dressed, with a neat moustache, Rickman had an easy charm and affable manner. The raising of his trilby at the start of each broadcast became his trademark. He doffed his hat and welcomed his audience – "Good afternoon from Sandown Park," or elsewhere.

He was genial, gracious and courteous, his old fashioned manners unlikely to ruffle any of racing society's feathers. "I don't believe in all this bullying questioning," he once said. "Simply isn't on with me. Anyway, you get better results by trying to be civil."

Viewers were fond of him although as he grew older, moving into his 60s in the early 1970s, so did his style, and his trilby. In the 1980s ITV reduced their racing coverage and in 1985 the World of Sport drew to a close, with Channel 4 taking the reins, armed with a new set of presenters.

Even so, let's raise our hats, if any, to John Rickman.

THE QUEEN MOTHER REVEALS HER BREAKFAST READING

The Sporting Life newspaper was a symbol of horseracing, seen in films and television programmes, often signalling a betting storyline.

Actor Sid James, a punter in real life, was a devotee of the *Life*. In *Carry On at your Convenience* (1971), playing Sid Plummer, he is married to Beattie, played by Hattie Jacques. She dotes on her pet budgerigar, Joey, who remains resolutely mute until Sid, armed with *The Sporting Life*, discovers that the bird has a mystical ability to pick winners. When Sid reads out the runners, Joey tweets when the winning name is reached. Sid did very well out of it.

Moving up the social scale, Hercule Poirot's assistant, Captain Arthur Hastings, in the long running television series, Agatha Christie's *Poirot*, was a

Sid James seeks Joey the budgerigar's help in picking winners.

regular reader of the *Life*. So, too, was the Queen Mother, whose enthusiasm for the paper as well as the sport was seized on for marketing purposes.

In 1987, when asked if she read the paper, the Queen Mother replied, "Of course I read *The Sporting Life*." The *Life* was soon advertising T-shirts bearing her words. The Queen herself is heavily involved in racing, as an owner-breeder, and appeared in puppet form in *Spitting Image*, reading *The Sporting Life* at breakfast.

The paper was part of British culture, instantly recognisable, symbolic, sometimes influential, and produced by a team with a profound passion and affection for the paper. For many who worked at the *Life*, it was a way of life and its demise, in 1998, was emotionally wrenching, as well as financially threatening.

That was reflected in James Lambie's *The Story of Your Life: A history of The Sporting Life newspaper (1859-1998)* (2010), a fascinating labour of love by the *Life*'s long-serving chief northern correspondent, although his love did not extend to the paper's last editor.

During its long history, *The Sporting Life* survived several crises, getting off to a spectacularly bad start by trumpeting the date of its debut, 23 March 1859, but failing to appear until the day after.

Launched as *Penny Bells Life and Sporting News*, and costing one penny compared with five pence for its established rival, *Bell's Life in London*, the new venture promptly faced court action by the latter, which applied for an injunction to prevent the new title using a version of its own title.

With more bravado than consideration of the odds, editor Harry Feist went into battle, which resulted in a hefty legal bill and, from 30 April 1859, a new title of *The Sporting Life*. It was money well wasted, for the new title was better than the previous one.

Although racing was a key ingredient, the paper's early success owed a lot to its coverage of prizefighting. In April 1860, when Tom Sayers and John Heenan fought for the right to be called world champion, a special edition sold 360,000 copies and, three years later, when Heenan fought Tom King, the figure was 370,000. If correct, they were remarkable figures, especially as the population of the UK in 1861 was 29 million compared with 67 million today.

Initially published twice weekly, and four pages long, in 1883 the *Life* became a daily, covering an extraordinary range of events, including billiards, coursing, rowing, athletics, pigeon racing, lacrosse, angling, clog dancing and bottle carrying, as well as cricket, rugby and the increasingly popular football.

The National Anti-Gambling League, founded in 1890, did its best to rid the country of both bookmaking and horseracing but ultimately failed, as did the First World War. When the Second World War arrived, the paper took a vow of silence on the unwelcome intrusion, although on the eve of the start of the football season in August 1939, a week before Germany invaded Poland, the front page carried an announcement by the Football League – "Saturday's matches will take place unless there is war."

The D-Day landings in 1944 passed without mention in *The Sporting Life* (they were probably racing at Newmarket that week) which, with most racing suspended, switched from appearing daily to weekly, reverting to a daily in 1946.

The post-war years brought large crowds to racecourses but the sport was bedevilled by doping, cheating and the complacency of the Jockey Club.

In 1965 the former MP Sir David Llewellyn appeared as a columnist under the guise of Jack Logan and used his Friday column to campaign for, among other things, better conditions for stable staff and action to make riding racehorses less dangerous. The lethal concrete posts used to support wooden running rails came under attack, as did the lack of compulsion in wearing hard hats.

Logan was a pioneer, and an influential one, in taking on the all-powerful Jockey Club. He endured, whereas a very different pioneer, Jeffrey Bernard, made a lasting impression during an exciting but brief appearance.

Bernard's first column appeared on 3 October 1970. He lasted for exactly a year, with occasional breaks marked by the announcement, "Jeffrey Bernard is ill. It is hoped that his column will be resumed shortly." The illness was usually acquired in the Coach and Horses pub in Soho.

Bernard wrote about racing in a way that no one else did, irreverently, as a losing punter. He wrote about the things he liked – women, drinking, gambling – and about the things he disliked, including trainers who took themselves too seriously. Not all his pieces were good but Bernard could be, and often was, very funny.

He was happier at the racecourse, where admirers bought him drinks and he could pursue women, than at racing's headquarters. After two days at Newmarket, Bernard lamented, "It's always very depressing to discover that the best racing crumpet is usually accompanied by racehorse trainers and/or millionaires." Reflecting on the fact that Fred Archer was at home in Newmarket when he shot himself, Bernard observed, "Knowing the place pretty well, I suspect he was trying to attract the attention of the staff in the Rutland Hotel."

During the year, he offended a lot of trainers but Fred Winter, multiple champion jump jockey and trainer, showed that he could match Bernard's wit. Having been shown round Winter's Lambourn yard, and wanting to say the right thing, Bernard ventured, "Your horses look healthy." "Yes," replied Winter. "They don't stay up all night playing cards and drinking vodka."

The end came in October 1971, when Bernard was due to speak at the annual point-to-point dinner and present the Sporting Life Cup to the leading lady rider, Sue Aston. After a day devoted to acquiring Dutch courage, Bernard did well to arrive but badly thereafter. The more likely reports stated that he fell asleep on a settee in the hotel lobby and was then escorted to his bedroom; the more interesting ones that he stood up to speak then fell head first into his soup.

Bernard went on to write a longer lasting column, under the heading Low Life, at *The Spectator*, and in 1989 Keith Waterhouse wrote a successful play, *Jeffrey Bernard is Unwell*. Peter O'Toole was magnificent as Bernard, who gets locked in the Coach and Horses for the night, with his reminiscences, a bottle of vodka, and a collection of ghosts from the past. Bernard was just well enough to see the play himself.

In the late 1970s, John McCririck was an award-winning investigative reporter with the paper (see curiosity 64), which was afflicted with restrictive practices by the print unions but managed to survive the affliction and remain afloat when, in 1991, Mirror Group Newspapers' boss, bully and fraudster, Robert Maxwell, fell off his yacht.

By then an even more serious problem had arrived, in the form of the *Racing Post*. It was launched in 1986 with the bottomless pockets of Sheikh Mohammed for support. Under Monty Court's editorship *The Sporting Life* waged a doughty battle with the newcomer, introducing colour into the paper in 1989 and displaying owners' colours in racecards the following year.

In 1990 Court retired, to be succeeded by Mike Gallemore, who was replaced three years later by Tom Clarke, formerly sports editor at *The Times*. The rivalry between the two papers was intense and in 1996 the *Life* relaunched as a 'Reader-Friendly' paper intended to please the public but which ignored the needs of betting shops. It opened the way for a deal between the *Racing Post* and the Big Three bookmakers, William Hill, Ladbrokes and Coral, to supply tailor-made display sheets for their shops. Average daily sales of *The Sporting Life* slumped from over 67,000 in 1996 to less than 48,000 the following year. For the first time, the *Racing Post* became the market leader.

Yet while the staff at the *Racing Post* were celebrating and those at *The Sporting Life* generally finding Clarke guilty, a deal was negotiated under which MGN bought the *Racing Post* for £1 but with the proviso that the *Racing Post*'s publication was guaranteed for 10 years. With room in the market place for only one racing daily, it meant the death of *The Sporting Life*. On 12 May 1998, the final edition was published.

Lambie scathingly wrote that the *Life* had "succumbed to the incompetence of its management" and been "stabbed in the back by its own proprietor." The new regime, with Alan Byrne as editor, built a team drawn from both papers, inevitably involving redundancies at both.

Tipping, Information and Betting

In which Groucho Marx meets Prince Monolulu • Elis makes mischief • Lord George wins a lot of money • Phil loses his teeth • Timeform squiggles • Agnes does her ironing • Sam signs a cheque • the Butterfly flies off • Benny O'Hanlon makes a phone call • James loses his bottom.

GROUCHO MARX MEETS PRINCE MONOLULU

The lion's claws were made into a necklace that hung from Ras Prince Monolulu's neck. When Groucho Marx asked Prince Monolulu about them he told him that he was awarded the claws for his prowess hunting with a spear and bows and arrows. Like a lot of stories told by Peter McKay, the Prince's real name, it wasn't true but it was colourful.

His true story was remarkable enough and long before Prince Monolulu appeared on Marx's popular American television show, 'You Bet

Groucho Marx meets Prince Monolulu. Prince Monolulu is the one on the right.

Your Life,' in 1957, he was an established celebrity on British racecourses and beyond.

According to Prince Monolulu, he was chief of the Fatasha tribe in Abyssinia (Ethiopia). He never actually visited the country, although he claimed to have met its leader, Haile Selassie. "Do you know Haile Selassie?" Marx asked. "Yes, I met him in Bath," Prince Monolulu replied.

McKay was born on the island of St Croix, now part of the Virgin Islands, in about 1881. Some of his family were horsemen and his brother owned a racehorse. St Croix was economically poor and McKay was an energetic, extrovert young man, wanting adventure. In 1902 he stowed away on a ship to Europe, went to his first Derby in 1903 and then survived on a diet of circus work, modeling, shows and anything else that came along.

When the First World War broke out, in 1914, McKay happened to be in Germany and spent the rest of the War in an internment camp situated on a racecourse at Ruhleben, near Berlin. At the end of the war he returned to Britain and in 1920 made himself known by tipping and backing Spion Kop to win the Derby, at 100-6. Prince Monolulu was said to have won £8,000, equivalent to over £300,000 today.

His striking appearance made Prince Monolulu an unmissable figure and if his looks failed to attract attention, his loud, flamboyant showmanship did the trick. He was very tall, spectacularly dressed and black; black at a time when most British people had only ever seen white.

When television arrived, Prince Monolulu was the first black man to appear on it.

On his head, Prince Monolulo wore a headdress of red and blue ostrich feathers. His ready smile revealed gold teeth and beneath his lion's claw necklace was a brightly embroidered tunic. Around his waist he wore a Scottish tartan scarf above a pair of baggy trousers. In his hand he held a shooting stick umbrella.

He was charismatic, a Pied Piper trailed by adults and children alike, brilliant at marketing himself but also by nature a jovial and kindly man. Prince Monolulu was to be found at Petticoat Lane and other London markets as well as at Speakers' Corner in Hyde Park but the racecourse was where he was famed.

At courses large and small but above all on Derby day, the showman tipster, encircled by fascinated racegoers, shouted his famous catchphrase, "I've gotta horse!" When Prince Monolulu's memoirs, as told to Sidney H. White, were published in 1950, that was the book's title.

But he had other stock sayings. "Who gave you cocoa? The black man. Who gave you rock and roll? The black man. Who give you the winner? Prince Monolulu. Black man for luck."

Then again, "Good old England. Roast beef, two veg, Yorkshire pudding. I've got a horse to beat the favourite."

Its name could be discovered by paying for one of the brown envelopes Prince Monolulu tempted his audience to buy – and they often did. Prince Monolulu would whisper a warning in recipients' ears, "If you tell anyone, the horse will lose."

Then he might shout, "God made the bees, the bees made the honey, you have a bet and the bookies take your money."

The bookies often took it anyway, from those who had bought Prince Monolulu's tips as well as from those who hadn't, for his heyday coincided with golden years for racecourse bookmakers, when crowds were large and punters unsophisticated.

Yet those who came into contact with this unique character were often pleased to be able to say that they had once watched him perform and opened one of his brown envelopes.

"The first of June was my birthday," Prince Monolulu would exclaim. "That's why they call it the Glorious First of June."

He was a bright memory in many people's lives. In 2020, Bryan Payne recalled that his earliest racing memory was of Prince Monolulu's ostrich feather headdress, when Payne, aged four, was at the 1957 Derby. "I was terrified and hid behind my father in abject fear until the 'Prince' picked me up and proclaimed to the large crowd 'I got a baby!!'"

The tipster backed horses as well as tipping them. In 1958 he rose on the back of Ballymoss, a top class three-year-old the previous year who, as a four-year-old, won the Coronation Cup, Eclipse Stakes, King George VI and Queen Elizabeth Stakes and Prix de l'Arc de Triomphe. Awash with winnings, Prince Monolulu crossed the Atlantic to watch and back Ballymoss in the Washington DC International at Laurel Park, Maryland. Ballymoss started favourite but finished third. Prince Monolulu said that he lost all he had previously won.

He was not rich and for many years lived in a sparsely furnished flat in Cleveland Street, Fitzrovia, where he was a popular local figure. The source of stories to the end, in 1965 Prince Monolulu was visited in hospital by the well known journalist Jeffrey Bernard (see curiosity 66).

According to Bernard, himself not always a reliable source, when Bernard put a strawberry cream chocolate into the patient's mouth, Prince Monolulu choked to death.

Much later, the Prince Monolulu pub opened at 28 Maple Street, Fitzrovia, not far from where its namesake once lived. The pub is no longer there but Prince Monolulu's jacket lives on at the National Horse Racing Museum in Newmarket.

68 ELIS MAKES MISCHIEF

A single wooden wheel stands in the Jockey Club Rooms in Newmarket, long detached from the strange vehicle which, in 1836, aroused great curiosity on its maiden voyage from Goodwood to Doncaster.

The vehicle was invented by Lord George Bentinck, who hoped to make a fortune from it, not by selling his novel creation but by using it to transport two racehorses, Elis and The Drummer. Bentinck was a prodigious gambler and his objective was not merely to win the St Leger with Elis but simultaneously to land an enormous betting coup. The 'horse van' was vital to the coup's successful execution.

Bentinck, who owned Elis in association with Lord Lichfield, recruited a Mr Herring, a coachbuilder based in Covent Garden, to construct a purpose-built horsebox, the first to take racehorses to race meetings.

Although equipped with padded walls and a cushioned floor, the horse van's body was high off the ground and liable to give its occupants a bumpy, swaying ride. Nevertheless, it represented an improvement on the conventional method of racehorse transport, which left all the work to the horse. As Doncaster racecourse was 250 miles from Goodwood, where Elis and The Drummer were trained, this would have taken a fortnight and probably left Bentinck's St Leger candidate in less than tip-top condition.

A wheel – there were others – from the horse van that carried Elis from Goodwood to Doncaster to land the 1836 St Leger and win Lord George Bentinck a lot of money.

Elis's racing history made him a prime candidate for the season's final Classic. Resilient as well as talented, Elis had rattled off a series of impressive successes as a two-year-old. As a three-year-old, he was narrowly defeated by Bay Middleton, the subsequent Derby winner, in the 2000 Guineas, won the Drawing Room Stakes at Goodwood and, two days later, finished second in the Goodwood Cup over two and a half miles. Amazingly, but not unusually in that era, Elis ran again the same day, winning the Racing Stakes. A dozen days later, on 10 August, he won the Lewes Stakes when giving 21lb to the runner-up, Hock.

Elis's obvious qualifications had a depressing effect on his ante-post price for the St Leger. Bentinck was a clever tactician and had devised a plan. He made it known that he wished to stake 1,000 sovereigns on Elis but would not run the horse unless bookmakers offered better odds than were then available. That was unlikely if bookmakers learnt of Bentinck's horse van, so those engaged in building it were sworn to secrecy and kept in ignorance of its mission.

As the days rolled by and the big day drew nearer, it seemed that Elis's connections had left it too late to get the favourite to Doncaster in time for the race. Elis's price drifted and Bentinck was able to get his money on at about 12-1.

The design of the horsebox made loading the horses difficult but was eventually achieved. Six horses were harnessed to the van and they set off, accompanied by three colourfully liveried postilions and a supply of the racehorses' usual feed.

At every town they passed through, the horse van attracted curiosity and speculation as to its contents – a dangerous criminal on his way to prison, perhaps? At Lichfield, they stopped off and worked Elis and The Drummer, his lead horse, on the racecourse. In three days, the horsebox reached Doncaster and the horses were stabled at the Turf Tavern in St James's Street, not far from the racecourse.

Betting on the St Leger had been prodigious. According to *Bell's Life in London and Sporting Chronicle* (25 September 1836), "It was not, like the generality of Legers, confined to Newmarket, Manchester and York but spread like a contagious disease through almost every town in the Kingdom. Nor were our neighbours in France uninterested lookers on, many thousands of francs having been sported by the members of the Paris Jockey Club. In short, we cannot recall to memory a race which took so great a hold of the public mind."

Gladiator, runner-up in the Derby, was the early favourite but persistent lameness forced his withdrawal and retirement. Attention was then drawn to Scroggins, bought by Bill Scott for 990 guineas. Scott raced in partnership with his brother John, Bill doing the riding and John the training. They were a formidable team. By 1836 John had already trained five St Leger winners and

Bill ridden four. Bill's reaction to the arrival of Elis was that his connections "meant mischief but they would find plenty to do – van and all!"

On St Leger day, Tuesday 20 September, "The crowd on the race-ground," according to the *Yorkshire Gazette*, "was immense. Every spot from which a glimpse of the horses could be obtained was covered, all the minor stands were full and the grand one crowded to excess, its spacious balconies teeming with beauty and fashion and its roof trembling beneath the weight of those who were awaiting, with throbbing hearts, the eventful race, big with the fate of thousands."

After two false starts, the field of 14 set off at a brisk pace, Scroggins starting as the 6-4 favourite and Elis, ridden by John Day, at 7-2. Twenty years later, *The Sportsman* looked back, with a vivid imagination, on a memorable race. As the duo made ground together, "one watching the other with determined spirit .... Scott seemed resolutely determined to stick to his opponent as closely as possible and never, on any former occasion, appeared to be animated with more energy. In this respect, John Day was not behind his opponent and a terrific race hushed the multitude."

Elis took up the running, pursued by Scroggins and Beeswing. "The speed was tremendous. Elis, with his splendid action, looked most admirable, going with comparative ease and nicely handled by his rider while Scott, still eyeing the 'van-horse,' as he called Elis, looked more resolute than before."

As they approached the furlong mark, "Scott roused his horse with a master's hand and the whole energies of Bob Johnson were applied to Beeswing. Elis held himself gallantly onwards and got quite clear of his two opponents." Maintaining his lead, Elis won by two lengths with Scroggins narrowly resisting Beeswing's challenge for second place.

Lord Lichfield, officially the owner of the winner, received news of his victory while at the theatre. It must have improved his enjoyment of the play as, according to *The New Sporting Magazine*, "Lord Lichfield wins about £6,000 above the stakes and his noble confederate [Lord George Bentinck] nearly thrice as much."

Whatever sum Bentinck won, it was a considerable one and a great deal more than it would have been without his clever use of the horse-van. There were many more betting coups to come.

69 LORD GEORGE WINS A LOT OF MONEY

The names of John Kent's pigeons are not known but on 1 May 1844 the trainer attached a message to a pigeon's leg and sent the pigeon on its way from Chester racecourse to Goodwood House, a distance as the pigeon flies of 185 miles. To make sure, Kent sent another pigeon in its wake.

Lord George Bentinck. A highly influential figure in racing and a formidable gambler.

Shortly after 8.00pm that evening, the 5th Duke of Richmond received the message he was hoping for. It told him that Red Deer, trained by Kent and wearing the Duke's colours, had won the Tradesmen's Cup, the forerunner of the prestigious Chester Cup.

The Duke was a popular figure in West Sussex and when Red Deer arrived at Fareham Station, at that time the nearest station to Goodwood, Kent recalled that "the owner's colours were displayed in the greatest profusion and along the line the people cheered vociferously. Indeed, the demonstration could not have been of a more enthusiastic nature had the subject been the victory at Waterloo."

If Kent and the Duke of Richmond were delighted, Lord George Bentinck must have been ecstatic, for he had just won a fortune.

Bentinck, a highly influential figure in racing, ran the stables at Goodwood and his conviction that Red Deer would win the Tradesmen's Cup had a long gestation.

Kent, in his *Racing Life of Lord George Cavendish Bentinck MP and other reminiscences* (1892), recalled that the previous year Red Deer had run so poorly on his sole run as a two-year-old that the Duke "desired that he might be disposed of on any terms whatever. At not even a nominal price could a purchaser be found for him. A great, overgrown, leggy colt, no one would look at him a second time." So he remained at Goodwood.

That autumn Red Deer improved physically and in trials over distances beyond two miles proved a revelation, comfortably beating top two-year-olds. It was decided that he should be aimed at the Tradesmen's Cup.

No three-year-old had ever won the race since its inception in 1824 and until 1842 no three-year-old had even contested the Cup. It was regarded as beyond their reach. Yet when the weights were announced, in those days at the nomination stage, Kent and Bentinck's confidence soared. Red Deer had been allotted bottom weight of just 4st. At the other end of the handicap, Alice Hawthorn, the winner in 1842, was set to carry 9st 8lb.

In a letter to Kent dated 13 January 1844, Bentinck wrote, "I am glad to see Red Deer in at 4st for the Chester Cup, for if Kitchener can get Red Deer out and if he is the horse over a distance of ground that you tried him to be, I don't see how he can be beaten."

Sam Kitchener was an inexperienced 14-year-old jockey who weighed only 3st 4lb but had won the previous year's Stewards' Cup at Goodwood on Bentinck's Yorkshire Lady.

As Kent observed, "with his Lordship's love for heavy speculation it may be easily imagined to what extent he would bet on a race of this description. During the winter Lord George was able to get on a large stake in small sums by backing the three-year-olds [as a group – 13 of the 118 nominated horses were three-year-olds], Kent's lot and Red Deer outright, without directing attention to the horse."

On 24 February 1844, Bentinck wrote, "At present all I have done is to get 700 to 100 about [Kent's] lot for the Chester Cup. I wish I had had the luck to get the odds about the three-year-olds. I have desired my commissioners to be on the look-out for any repetition of such offers."

On 19 March Bentinck reported progress. "I am very glad to hear Kitchener seems to manage Red Deer so well," he wrote. "I have now got on the odds to £285 about the lot at 7-1 and the odds to £75 outright about Red Deer, which averages about 24-1. It has been very hard work to get on, all in £10 bets."

Bentinck continued to back Red Deer and lay his opponents, including Bramble, a four-year-old Bentinck owned himself. When Bramble beat The Caster in a match, he was made favourite for the Tradesmen's Cup, for which he was due to carry 7st 9lb. Kent assured Bentinck that Bramble "had no earthly chance of giving the weight to Red Deer, unless the latter fell down."

In mid-April, Red Deer won the Somersetshire Stakes at Bath, albeit after a run-off following a dead-heat. Heavily backed for the Tradesmen's Cup, by raceday Red Deer was 7-2 favourite in a field of 26.

Kent and Bentinck were confident that Red Deer had the beating of his opponents. Their biggest concern was that Chester's tight track would not suit Red Deer and that the strong pulling colt might run away with his tiny rider.

The trainer led Red Deer to the start himself but struggled to restrain the headstrong horse. Bentinck himself was the official starter and, with such a big field, arranged them in two rows, with Red Deer in the second row. Kitchener had him placed behind two stablemates, Bramble and Best Bower.

According to Kent, "When the start was effected at last, Red Deer went into his bridle with a vengeance. He gave two or three violent plunges, rushed between Bramble and Best Bower and took up the running at a strong pace, increasing his lead the further he went. Red Deer ultimately won by a considerable distance, going on by the Dee-side turn before Kitchener could pull him up." Alice Hawthorn, giving the winner a massive 78lb, finished an honourable second.

The Sporting Magazine remarked that the result "proved again that weight levels all distinction." It also provoked criticism of the handicapping system. In 1857 *The Sporting Review* asserted that "the ruinous lightweight system began with the victory of Red Deer at Chester in 1844 and from that time the disease took steady root and soon drove all heavyweight crack jockeys out of the vast majority of handicaps."

Lord George Bentinck was usually reticent about his betting profits and losses and Kent wrote, "What sum Lord George actually won I do not know but in a letter he wrote me some time after, he stated, 'I received every farthing due to me, much to my surprise, as on no previous occasion have I escaped loss from defaulters when I betted on the same scale.'"

Whatever the sum, it was a big one. The following year, when Bentinck's horses won 58 races, was spectacularly profitable. Kent wrote, "Lord George's winnings by betting during the year 1845 must have amounted to close upon £100,000," a sum equivalent, on a conservative calculation, to £10 million today.

70 PHIL LOSES HIS TEETH

He was short, just over 5ft 5ins, bearded, bespectacled and gnome-like. In 1952, when he was 42, he had all his teeth removed and subsequently made do with gums. Almost 20 years later he informed one of his many correspondents, "I don't have any teeth, natural or artificial."

Phil Bull's appearance was curious, yet dapper. On display, at the racecourse, he was smartly dressed in suit and tie, or bow-tie, and although he sometimes clutched a pipe between his gums, it was a cigar that completed his outfit. He smoked 15 of them a day.

Bull was not like other people and nor were his days. In his prime, in the 1940s and 1950s, his day started in the middle of the afternoon, with breakfast at 4.00pm. He often then played snooker until lunch at about 7.00pm or 8.00pm, followed by a bout of writing, followed by several hours of study, two

Phil Bull (right) with bookmaker William Hill.

or three of which might be spent in the bath, accompanied by a cigar. Along the way, he got through a couple of bottles of wine.

From 1946 Bull lived at The Hollins, on the outskirts of Halifax, bought from the proceeds of a level of betting success other punters could only fantasise about.

Having left university with a degree in mathematics, Bull took the conventional route into teaching, followed by an unconventional route into gambling. Applying his mathematical expertise to the study of racehorses and races, Bull developed an approach based on a sophisticated analysis of race times that translated into a substantial, sustained, tax-free income.

His arrival at The Hollins followed a £14,000 payout consequent on Dante winning the 1945 Derby. As £14,000 then equates to roughly half a million pounds now, it was a very satisfactory outcome.

Bull became used to satisfactory outcomes, as his betting records reveal. From 1943 to 1952 his average annual profit was about £22,000 (over £700,000 today). It was not made by finding long priced winners but short-priced ones, when he considered their price, albeit short, represented good value.

Although espousing socialist ideology, Bull embraced a capitalist lifestyle. His explanation was, "when in Rome, one does as the Romans do, at least until the Roman Empire falls." It was the same in Halifax. He arrived at racecourses in a Rolls-Royce, owned a string of racehorses and in 1947 set up the Hollins Stud, where he bred, then sold, Romulus, winner of the 1962 Sussex Stakes and Queen Elizabeth II Stakes.

In the 1940s Bull produced a quickly respected series of annuals, starting with *Best Horses of 1942*. In 1948, these were succeeded by the iconic *Racehorses of ....* annuals. Working with Dick Whitford, Bull married time and form analysis to produce assessments of each horse's merit, presented in clear prose accompanied by a Timeform handicap rating.

After 1947 Bull passed the writing responsibilities to others and from 1964 did the same with the management of Timeform, with Reg Griffin emerging as the day-to-day manager of what became a thriving business. Bull was a demanding and sometimes difficult leader but he also established a culture that gained Timeform a reputation for integrity and high standards.

As he became less intimately involved in the business he owned, Bull also reduced his betting activity. This was largely because of the impact of the reintroduction of betting tax in 1966, and also because an increasing number of subscribers to Timeform were backing the horses Bull himself had his eye on.

In 1966 betting tax was set at 2.5% of turnover, doubled to 5% two years later. In 1970 the tax was increased to 6% on off-course turnover; in 1972 the on-course tax was reduced to 4% while in 1974 the off-course tax was raised again, to 7.5%. It was a heavy burden for both bookmakers and punters.

In 1967 Bull lost over £25,000 (about £450,000 now). Nevertheless, between 1943 and 1974, when he gave up serious betting, Bull made £300,000 (about £4.7 million today), with 24 winning and 8 losing years.

With more time to pursue other ambitions, Bull presented the case for reforms that recognised racing's role as entertainment and betting's importance for funding the sport. In the mid-1970s he called for the introduction of evening and Sunday racing, with betting shops allowed to open for both. It was hard going. Promoting reform was one thing, persuading the Jockey Club to embrace change, quite another. It was not until 1993 that betting shops could open after 6.30pm while Sunday racing did not arrive until 1992, with betting to accompany it in 1995.

Bull's attitude to the undemocratic, elitist Jockey Club was inevitably hostile. In 1976 he accepted an invitation from the Racegoers' Club to represent racegoers and punters on the newly created Racing Industry Liaison Committee. Set up by the Jockey Club, with no executive powers and chaired by the Jockey Club's Senior Steward, it soon became apparent that RILC's role was to offer advice which neither the Jockey Club nor the Levy Board felt any obligation to accept.

With hope rather than expectation, in 1980 Bull became chairman of the newly-formed Horseracing Advisory Council. This was to be independent, with the chairman given one of the Jockey Club's three seats on the Levy Board and allowed to attend the Club's monthly meetings. In August 1980 Bull resigned, describing HAC as "a cosmetic charade."

The following year he told trainer Vincent O'Brien that he left HAC because his time was too valuable "to be wasted on idiots who can't think and don't want to know about anything that doesn't suit them." Diplomacy was not his strong point but would probably not have helped.

In 1983 Bull condemned the Jockey Club as "an elite, private establishment body. The essential qualifications for membership are social and financial, not intellectual, and not at all to do with competence, experience or achievement in racing .... Nothing is going to change if the Jockey Club can help it."

Bull was the subject of an illuminating biography by Howard Wright, *Bull The Biography* (1995). Among many other things, it points out that Bull's often quoted reference to horseracing as "the great triviality" is a misquote; he actually said, "in the context of life as a whole, racing is a mere triviality." A pity, "the great triviality" is better.

Bull died in 1989, aged 79. A committed atheist, trenchantly dismissive of all religious beliefs, it was Bull's conviction that, as far as existence in any form was concerned, that was definitely that.

72 TIMEFORM SQUIGGLES

Founded by Phil Bull in 1948, Timeform and its publications soon became an integral part of the racing scene; the annual *Racehorses of....* eagerly awaited and highly respected. With entries for every horse raced on the Flat during the relevant year, it was the racing aficionado's Bible. The publication of Timeform's *Chasers & Hurdlers 1975/76* marked the launch of companion volumes for jump racing.

For both punters and racing professionals the annuals were valued works of reference and for those whose livelihoods depended on breeding, buying and selling thoroughbreds, Timeform's verdicts could be financially significant.

Some readers tended to be less appreciative when the squiggle or double squiggle – known as "the dreaded double squiggle" – appeared beside the name of a horse they owned or trained, for a Timeform squiggle was not a badge of honour but of shame.

A single § denoted "a horse who is somewhat ungenerous, faint-hearted or a bit of a coward; one who may give his running on occasions but cannot be relied upon to do so."

A double §§ was uncompromising in its characterisation of the recipient – "an arrant rogue or a thorough jade; so temperamentally unsatisfactory as to be not worth a rating."

As the law does not provide legal redress for the defamation of a horse, Timeform could be rude with impunity or, as Bull observed, "you can't libel a horse." In most squiggle cases a defence of truth, honest opinion or fair comment would, in any event, have ensured acquittal.

Yet, over the decades, the definition of single and later double squiggles became less fierce. From 1981/82 to 1991/92, while the definition of a double squiggle remained unchanged, that for a single § was amended to "a horse of somewhat unsatisfactory temperament; one who may give his running on occasions but cannot be relied upon to do so."

For 1992/93 the single squiggle undertook another small modification, being for "a horse who is unreliable, either for temperamental or for other reasons; one who may run up to its rating on occasions but cannot be trusted to do so."

In 1993/94 there was a further tweak, with a single squiggle denoting "a horse who is unreliable (for temperamental or other reasons)." Rather sadly, the double squiggle's long association with "an arrant rogue or thorough jade" came to end. Instead, a double squiggle confined itself to the verdict, "so temperamentally unsatisfactory as to be not worth a rating."

Just as people have their favourite singers, so they have their favourite squigglers, with Vodkatini high up on many enthusiasts' blacklists.

Vodkatini's celebrity rested partly on his ability, which was considerable, when he chose to display it. During the 1987/88 jumps season, Vodkatini won five chases, including the Grand Annual Chase at the Cheltenham Festival, and in 1988/89 won a further three times.

This was not the record of a recalcitrant yet the warning signs were already clear. Two of Vodkatini's victories were achieved after, in one case, bolting to the start and, in the other, whipping round at the start and losing 20 lengths. Having started as favourite for both the Tingle Creek Chase at Sandown and the Captain Morgan Chase at Aintree, Vodkatini declined to start in either. This trait was not popular with favourite backers and earned Vodkatini a single squiggle.

Chasers & Hurdlers 1988/89 observed, "The career of Vodkatini reminds one of the little girl in the nursery rhyme of whom it was said 'when she was good she was very very good, but when she was bad she was horrid.'"

Unashamed, Vodkatini raced on, sometimes, but didn't win again and in 1990/91 was demoted to a double squiggle. In his defence, although he never deigned to offer one, Vodkatini could have pointed out that he won 13 times, which was 13 times more than most racehorses manage.

Vodkatini showed that the squiggle was not the preserve only of those near the bottom of the equine pile but was within reach of those at the top. On the Flat, the 1994 and 1996 St Leger winners Moonax and Shantou both later joined the squigglers Club.

Moonax was once described as "the world's naughtiest horse," quite a claim in such a competitive field but one unlikely to be contested by anyone at trainer Barry Hills's yard, apart from Joyce Wallsgrave, Moonax's faithful groom.

According to Hills, "Joyce got on very well with him but we had to be careful when she had weekends off. He'd take a piece out of anyone." A sign on his box warned visitors against entering, as Moonax had a habit of biting, kicking and crushing intruders against a wall.

Jockey Darryll Holland recalled, "Joyce had the patience of a saint. They had this great rapport, so he was good with her even though he was terrible with everyone else."

There was a lot to forgive but in 1994 it was worth it because, having won the St Leger, Moonax went on to win the Prix Royal-Oak and be proclaimed champion stayer in that year's Cartier Awards.

Moonax won twice more and finished runner-up in five more Group 1 races before a dramatic switch to hurdles. Less than two months after a narrow defeat in the 1996 Prix Royal-Oak, he appeared in a novice hurdle at Huntingdon. Understandably sent off as the odds-on favourite, Moonax finished second again. After two more hurdling defeats, in May 1997 Moonax was sent to Chester, for the Group 3 Ormonde Stakes.

By then his temper had taken a turn for the worse. Holland had been "warned to expect something different" and couldn't help noticing that Wallsgrave was wearing a body protector and heavily padded arm guards. The special rapport between horse and groom had apparently come under strain.

Moonax sent showers of saliva flying over his mane and refused to leave the parade ring. When he finally did, he walked out backwards. Once at the start, he declined to enter the stalls until a blindfold was fitted. The battle between man and beast wasn't quite over. As Holland remembered, "when we were loaded into the stalls, he went down and splayed his legs to try and lie down on the grass. He jumped off fine, though, and ran well for me to finish third."

Vodkatini, Moonax and Shantou were not the only talented recipients of the Timeform squiggle and Moonax was not the only horse dangerous to know.

Ubedizzy was a very capable sprinter but prone to use his teeth as well as his legs. Andrew Crook, later a trainer but then a groom at Steve Nesbitt's yard in Middleham, started work with the standard 10 fingers but by the time Ubedizzy left the yard Crook was down to nine and a half while Ubedizzy was up to two squiggles. Crook said later, "If I was offered £1,000 a week to do him now, I wouldn't do it. The times I used to come out of his box with a leg missing off my trousers or my shirt torn to bits."

Even in a muzzle, Ubedizzy was dangerous. After finishing second in the 1978 Abernant Stakes, he knocked Crook over, pinned him to the ground and tried to bite him. Crook must have been relieved when the Jockey Club banned Ubedizzy from racing again in Britain.

Sent to race abroad, in 1979 he won a Listed race in Sweden.

Centurius was better behaved but in his own way, equally frustrating. Being the brother of Grundy, winner of the 1975 Derby, great things were expected of him and great things would have been achieved if Centurius had been willing.

Early in 1981, Walter Swinburn considered Centurius to be his likely Derby mount. "I was dreaming about Centurius rather than Shergar," Swinburn recalled. "I had won the Mornington Stakes at Ascot on him and he was a horse with a high cruising speed, impressive to ride."

When Shergar won the Guardian Newspaper Classic Trial at Sandown by 10 lengths, then the Chester Vase by an imperious dozen lengths, Swinburn changed his mind. It was just as well because while Shergar went on to win the Derby, Centurius went on to drive connections mad.

The expression "found nothing" was made for him. Lobbing along on the bridle with victory seemingly a formality, Swinburn would press the accelerator and Centurius would apply the brakes. Awarding him a squiggle, Timeform's *Racehorses of 1981* remarked, "He races genuinely until he finds himself near the front, whereupon he gives up." Among the races Centurius could have won had he wanted to was the King Edward VII Stakes at Royal Ascot.

Of all the talented delinquents my own favourite is Knockroe but as I've written about him several times before, I'll leave it to you to discover his foibles. You can't expect me to do everything for you.

Most of those on whom the Timeform squiggle was bestowed lived in the equine basement, from where Broxadella merits special mention.

In 1983, at Wolverhampton on her first appearance as a three-year-old, Broxadella "swerved badly left start, took no part." At Ayr, she "swerved badly left start" again and was "always behind." On her final run of the season, at Beverley, racegoers showed they were willing to forgive and forget by making Broxadella second favourite. The form book recorded, "swerved left and unseated rider start, took no part."

In 1984, unreformed, Broxadella was unruly and refused to race at Warwick before being banned from Flat racing after visiting Pontefract, where she "whipped round start" and "took no part."

The award of a double squiggle was a formality, with Timeform opining that Broxadella "has gone completely the wrong way temperamentally and must be left severely alone."

Trainer Arthur Jones doubtless heaved a sigh of relief and wished Tony Brisbourne well as Brisbourne prepared Broxadella for an unlikely career over hurdles.

Making her jumps debut at Bangor in 1987 it took three helpers to get jockey Mark Brisbourne on board, after which Broxadella tried to lie down. Initially in last place, by the time the partnership reached the second hurdle they were 20 lengths clear, after which Broxadella resigned and finished last.

Transferred to Peter Davis's yard, in 1989 Broxadella's potential as a chaser was explored, at Southwell. She refused to race. Finally, consistent if nothing else, Broxadella bolted before her hurdling swansong at Nottingham and was then tailed off and pulled up.

As time passed, so did double squiggles. In 2006 Greg Wood of *The Guardian* complained that, to obtain one, "a horse pretty much needs to be banned by the Horseracing Regulatory Authority for refusing to race."

Timeform explained that "the double squiggle is a victim of too much racing. These days there are so many utterly appalling contests that even a double squiggle horse might pop up in one that it had a chance of winning."

Wood agreed. "At the bottom end of the racing scale, utter hopelessness has become the norm," he wrote. "The horses are an indistinguishable, lumpen mass. When they are all as bad as each other, it becomes rather pointless to distinguish between degrees of ineptitude."

A pity, really.

72 AGNES DOES HER IRONING

On the morning of 27 January 2007, Agnes Haddock sat next to an ironing board in The Ironing Board in the Cheshire town of Northwich, as she did every Saturday, and decided what to do.

The 50-year-old owner of The Ironing Board had to decide which horses to put on her Scoop6 coupon when she went to the local Betfred betting shop, as she did every Saturday.

The Scoop6 was the Tote's 'Superbet', introduced in 1999 to attract customers with the lure of becoming rich by risking very little. Each Saturday, punters faced the awesome challenge of picking the winners of six televised races. Participants were betting into a pool and if, one week, no one was successful, the pool was carried forward to the following week.

That Saturday, £228,734 had been carried forward. By the time the first Scoop6 race started, at 2.25pm, the pool had swollen to £410,332. Some of the money came from small punters with bigger sums speculated by professional gamblers. The latter put time and knowledge into making their selections and combined them in carefully considered permutations.

Agnes's approach was less sophisticated. She picked one horse in each race for the minimum total stake of £2. In the first race she chose Simon because she had once worked with a nice lad called Simon. In the second she chose Exotic Dancer because he had finished second when she had chosen him a month earlier. For the third race she chose Clouding Over because, when she went into the betting shop, it was.

The fourth race was different because it was won by Katchit, who wasn't the horse that Agnes had selected. The horse she selected was a non-runner and under the Tote's rules, her selection was replaced by the favourite, Katchit. It was ironic, because Agnes didn't usually back favourites. That left two races; Agnes went for Haggle Twins because she liked the trainer, Charlie Mann, and in the final leg chose Whispered Secret for the very good reason that she liked his name.

The races were all shown on Channel 4 and, from start to finish, were scheduled to take less than two hours; three races from unfashionable Southwell alternating with three from jump racing's Mecca, Cheltenham. Agnes watched at the splendidly named Royal Antediluvian Order of Buffaloes Club in Northwich.

"It was nerve-wracking to say the least," she said. "There were about 30 of us at the Club and when the final race came on, I was jumping up and down so much that I missed half of it."

The fingernail biting finale was a 13 runner chase over two miles five furlongs at Cheltenham. Supposed to start at 3.55pm, the race began 15 minutes late,

Agnes Haddock about to give up her ironing job.

with the low sun causing four fences to be omitted. It meant that the run-in was almost half a mile long.

Whispered Secret was trained by David Pipe, as was the favourite, Vodka Bleu. By the time they reached the long run-in, Vodka Bleu was well behind while his stablemate held a narrow lead from New Alco. Rodi Greene on Whispered Secret and Graham Lee on New Alco battled it out, with Agnes's future clinging on to win by half a length.

"When I saw my horse pass the winning post everyone started cheering and I just stood there, gobsmacked. I couldn't believe it," said Agnes. "I bought drinks all round and spent £192 on the most expensive round of my life."

There were 26 live tickets when the race began but only one survived, that of Agnes Haddock. As the *Mirror* predictably yet still satisfyingly proclaimed, 'Haddock Chips In to Batter Bookies.' She had won £410,332.

It put ironing in the shade and a week later it got even better. The win fund was the main pool but there was also a bonus fund, reserved for winners of the win fund. To scoop that, participants had to find the winner of one of the following week's Scoop6 races, the race to be chosen by the Tote.

Before racing on 27 January, the bonus fund held £200,460, swollen to £278,288 that day. Potentially, it could make Agnes's bumper win even more bumper but the Tote had a habit of choosing the most difficult race possible. On Saturday 3 February Agnes faced the challenge of picking the winner of the totescoop6 Sandown Handicap Hurdle, a hotly contested 16 runner puzzle.

It must have been tempting to opt for Whispered Secret, running again after his vital contribution the previous week but Agnes plumped instead for the favourite, Taranis, trained by champion trainer Paul Nicholls and ridden by the brilliant Irish champion jockey, Ruby Walsh.

As the two and three quarter mile contest reached its climax, Taranis held a narrow lead from Whispered Secret and preserved it to the line. When Mrs Haddock had longed for Whispered Secret to win, he had, by half a length, and when she wanted him to lose, he had, by half a length. Instead of winning £410,332, Agnes had won £688,620.

Big winners often say that it won't change their lives and two months later she assured the *Northwich Guardian* that "Everything is just the same as it was. I've still got the business and I've no plans to sell up." Yet in September she sold The Ironing Board, explaining, "my accountant advised me to sell my business. It was with great regret that I sold it."

Agnes bought property locally and set up Aggie's Nags Club, an online syndicate at aggiesnags.com which charged members £20 for eight weeks participation in joint Scoop6 ventures. On 21 December 2009, with over £500,000 in the win fund, the syndicate held one of the 21 winning coupons. Each was worth almost £24,000 but with 270 members, the Club's participants had fun rather than fortunes.

73 SAM SIGNS A CHEQUE

One Monday morning in about 1880, George Lambton made his way along Cork Street in the West End of London and knocked on the door of number 17. The son of Lord Durham was shown into an office where he saw "a little fat man with a bald head sitting at a desk smoking a big cigar." It was Lambton's first meeting but not his last with Samuel Lewis, moneylender.

Sons of wealthy aristocrats, with prospects of wealth to come, had a habit of spending, especially gambling, beyond their current means. Lambton's visit was prompted by an expensive week at Manchester races and his reluctance to make yet another appearance at the office of his lawyer, who held the keys to £10,000 but made Lambton feel "that I was a boy at school up before the headmaster."

Lewis asked Lambton what he wanted and Lambton replied, "I want a thousand pounds this morning." The request was urgent because it was settlement day for the losing bets he had struck at Manchester. As £1,000

Samuel Lewis, moneylender to the aristocracy.

translates into about £80,000 today, it was a bold request.

When he told Lewis of the £10,000 held by his lawyer, Lewis advised him to overcome his reluctance because the lawyer would charge only five per cent for his compliance whereas Lewis's charges would be considerably more.

How much more would depend on the security Lambton was able to offer, the period of the loan and Lewis's confidence in being repaid. The urgency of his customer's request was also likely to feature in the calculation.

Lewis had an impressive list of aristocratic clients and regularly charged interest at a rate of 40 per cent to 60 per cent. After his death, the *McCook Tribune* recalled that he was known as "the greatest and meannest of modern day Shylocks." Moneylenders, especially Jewish ones, like Lewis, were generally disliked. Sir George Lewis, a prominent lawyer who was also Jewish, pilloried his namesake as a prime example of a moneylender who was "a curse to society and a danger to the community."

Lambton's opinion was considerably more favourable, encouraged by the fact that, at the end of their first conversation, Sam Lewis wrote out a cheque for £1,000, to be repaid in three months time. "I walked out of his house treading upon air," Lambton remembered, "thinking how splendid this was, that life would be quite simple as I could get £1,000 as easily as picking a gooseberry off a bush."

In Lambton's classic work, *Men and Horses I Have Known* (1924), he recalled Lewis with affection and respect; neither Shylock nor a curse to society but "the best and straightest moneylender of all time. He naturally drove a hard bargain but in all his dealings he was as straight as a die. I could tell many stories of his good nature and kindness to men who were really down. There is no doubt that several prominent owners of racehorses were in the hands of Sam Lewis but never did he use this power to his own advantage."

During the hearing of a case brought by Lewis in 1897, Lord Chief Justice Russell endorsed Lambton's good opinion of the moneylender, stating that "he has conducted his affairs in an honest and straightforward manner and his word is as much to be credited as that of any other man of business."

Lambton regarded Lewis as a friend and wrote, "curious as it may seem, the majority of his clients were also his friends." Together, they often visited Sam to enjoy his quick wit and hear the latest gossip.

One particular kindness, albeit also to Lewis's own advantage, spared Lambton the need to emigrate to Canada. Lambton's elder brother regularly bailed him out but the time came, in the mid-1880s, when he declined to do so again. Instead, he arranged for Lambton to join the staff of their uncle, Lord Lansdowne, who was Canada's Governor-General. Lambton hated the prospect.

As he waited in Liverpool to board a ship, he was arrested and taken to Holloway prison. Lewis had obtained a writ preventing Lambton from leaving the country. As Lewis was Lambton's main creditor, he assumed that the moneylender was acting to protect his money but it emerged that, having established from Lord Marcus Beresford, a friend of Lambton's, that the sea voyage was unwelcome, Lewis acted to save Lambton from a future in Canada.

Lewis himself was susceptible to gambling ventures, particularly at the casinos in Monte Carlo and Ostend, without which, he told Lambton, "I don't know how I should get rid of [my wealth.]"

Lambton was a sound client but although Lewis became a wealthy man by lending money to impecunious aristocrats, it was a risky business. In 1893, the spectacularly stupid 4th Marquis of Ailesbury, inheritor of the Savernake Estate and 40,000 acres, owed Lewis £256,000, which was unfortunate for Lewis, as Ailesbury died the following year, aged 31.

When it was Lewis's turn to die, in 1901, aged 63, the 20th Earl of Shrewsbury owed him £370,000; General Owen Williams, equerry to the Prince of Wales and founder of Sandown Park, owed £143,000; Lord Rosslyn £78,000; Lord Essex £55,000 and the Marquis of Anglesey and Lord Lurgan £52,000 each.

Nevertheless, Lewis left £2.7 million, equivalent to roughly £210 million today, the majority of which was bequeathed to charities, payable after his wife Ada's death, which occurred in 1906. During the interval, she was known as "the wealthiest widow in England."

Perhaps uniquely, Samuel himself was described as "moneylender and philanthropist." Asked what he would like as his epitaph, Lewis replied, "I lend to the Lord and give to the poor."

He gave £670,000 (roughly £52 million today) to provide cheap accommodation for the poor and £250,000 to the Prince of Wales's Hospital Fund. In all, Lewis bequeathed £750,000 to various hospitals while over 50 charities benefited from Samuel and Ada's bequests.

The Samuel Lewis Housing Trust became an active builder and manager of housing estates in London. In 2001 its name was changed to the Southern Housing Group. It now describes itself as "a business with social objectives, one of the largest housing associations in the south-east of England," owning and managing over 28,000 homes with 72,000 occupants. All this because of wealthy nineteenth century aristocrats' gambling debts.

74 THE BUTTERFLY FLIES OFF

It was late May in 1965 when John Mort Green asked the janitor at the White House near Regents Park if he could borrow his overalls. The Butterfly, as Green was nicknamed, would have tipped him generously, as he always did.

Tall, slim and dapper, The Butterfly dirtied his hands, pulled a hat down over his eyes, and set off. In those days, there were more betting shops than today and more of them were owned by small independent bookmakers. The Butterfly flitted from shop to shop, looking like a workman, never staking more than £8. By the end of a long day, he had laid out £860, all at around 20-1, betting that Sea Bird II would win the Derby.

£860 was a lot of money in 1965 (equal to about £15,000 today) and house prices were considerably lower. That year, the average price of a new house nationally was £3,800. If Sea Bird II won the Derby, The Butterfly stood to win four houses and a sum equivalent to roughly £300,000 today.

Known as Papillon in France and Cho Chosan in Japan, The Butterfly was described by the respected author Richard Onslow as "the best known professional gambler on horses in the world today." (Great Racing Gambles & Frauds 2, ed. Richard Onslow (1992), p 176).

In Britain, he had a big advantage over other gamblers – he was Australian.

The son of a bookmaker, Mort, as he was also known, discovered the nature of the relationship between some bookmakers and some jockeys, evidenced by particular bookmakers offering relatively generous odds about particular mounts of particular jockeys, always losing.

"If they operated on me," Mort said, "they'd find a stomach full of ears." It was a time when many bets were lost before a race had started because not all the jockeys were trying. You needed to know what most punters didn't, which jockeys were trying to win and which to lose.

Mort studied the form and the jockeys. He was good with people, engaging, funny, full of life, and observant. "Horses don't talk but jockeys do," he'd say. "They were my bread and butter. I pride myself on one thing, I'm never on dead meat."

Mort did well or, as he once told me, "Situation is, I've never done a day's work in my life." It wasn't true. He worked diligently, studying the form, getting to know people, paying for information.

In 1963, when he was 33, Mort flew to London and moved into a luxury apartment in the White House. A chauffeur drove him to the races in a Rolls Royce from which Mort emerged wearing an expensive suit, hand-made shoes and a Pierre Cardin hat, with a butterfly on the back. "I'm full of money," he'd announce. "Racecourses during the day for business, Mayfair at night for pleasure."

Mort wasn't the only Australian to arrive at British racecourses in the 1960s. Several top Australian jockeys were based in Europe – Bill Williamson, Bill Pyers, George Moore, Russ Maddock, Scobie Breasley, Ron Hutchinson, Garnie Bougoure and Pat Glennon. Mort was a familiar, friendly face in a sometimes hostile environment. He was told things that others were not.

In 1965, French trainer Etienne Pollet had a star three-year-old in his Chantilly stable, Sea Bird II. Pat Glennon, the horse's regular partner, would later say that Sea Bird II was "the best horse I have ridden and the best horse I have ever seen." But Sea Bird II was fractious and Glennon told Mort that, for that reason, the plan was to run him in the French Derby rather than make the journey across the Channel.

Then, less than two weeks before the Epsom Derby, Glennon phoned Mort. "I galloped him today," Glennon told him, "and they've changed their minds. We're coming to England."

In those days, French racing received scant coverage in the English press. Peter O'Sullevan, a celebrated race commentator and journalist – later known as the 'Voice of Racing' – was the first to break the news, but by then The Butterfly had flown.

Believing that Sea Bird II would not run in the Derby, bookmakers had offered the 20-1 that Mort scooped up. By the time the race started, on 2 June, Sea Bird II was the 7/4 favourite in a field of 22.

Glennon's only worry was that his mount might overheat in the preliminaries. "If I can get him down to the start okay," he told Mort, "he won't be beaten." Sea Bird II went down like a lamb and came back a champion. His victory was imperious. As *Timeform*, not given to hyperbole, put it, "Sea Bird's performance had to be seen to be believed. He beat twenty-one opponents without coming off the bit."

Later, he would win the Prix de l'Arc de Triomphe equally majestically against formidable opponents, leading *Timeform* to give Sea Bird II a rating unequalled until Frankel reached his peak in 2012. For many, including John Randall and Tony Morris in their book *A Century of Champions* (1999), Sea Bird II was the greatest racehorse of the 20th century.

By the time the Arc was run, *Sports Illustrated* (9 August 1965) had devoted a double-page spread to The Butterfly and the subject of their article had gone to sea. The Derby won, Mort repeated his tour of London's betting shops and deposited the money with the Bank of America. Later, he took out £22,000, went to the Thomas Cook travel agency and booked a six month luxury cruise around the world on the *Queen Mary*.

When he got back, Mort wrote a book called *Come Fly With The Butterfly* (1969), revealing his ten secrets of successful gambling.

John Mort Green wasn't a saint but neither was he a serious sinner. He was a one-off, full of life, full of stories, full of sayings. One of his favourites was, "Laugh often, it is life's lubricant," and he did, reaching 85 before he died, in 2014.

John Mort Green, the Butterfly. One of racing's great characters.

75 BENNY O'HANLON MAKES A PHONE CALL

It was a Telefon box, green and white, and just the one. The enterprise relied on there being just the one telephone box at Bellewstown racecourse, and it being occupied by Benny O'Hanlon.

O'Hanlon was a big, tough man and on that Wednesday afternoon, 25 June 1975, no one was going to get him to leave that telephone box. As Barney Curley put it, "To get him off the phone it would need a man to take out a gun and shoot him." It was Curley, of course, who put him there.

Curley himself was hiding in some bushes near the second last hurdle, waiting for the runners in the Mount Hanover Amateur Riders' Handicap Hurdle to pass by before he joined the racecourse crowd. As he walked into the racecourse enclosure, a man said to him, "Well done, Barney," and then Curley knew for sure that Yellow Sam had won.

Everyone is different but Curley was more different, training to be a Jesuit priest before graduating as an iconic gambler; a man for whom secrecy, loyalty, patience, planning and knowledge were core ingredients of success.

Yet even the best gamblers sit on sharp knife edges, winning never a certainty. Curley could vouch for that because in 1975, aged 35, he was in financial trouble and needed Yellow Sam to win to settle some hefty debts, including the £20,000 he owed his friend and bookmaker Sean Graham.

The horses Curley owned weren't very good, Yellow Sam amongst them. In two seasons racing, he had yet to finish in the first seven, although conditions had been against him, which perhaps suited Curley. As summer approached, trainer Liam Brennan told him that Yellow Sam, a five-year-old, had improved. He was paceless but jumped well and would be suited by switching to faster ground. Brennan thought that Yellow Sam could win a small race.

The Mount Hanover Amateur Riders' Handicap Hurdle was suitably weak and Yellow Sam had the benefit of a top amateur rider, Michael Furlong, and firm ground. Several weeks earlier, Furlong had been asked not to accept a ride in the race. So he waited, but when told that it was Yellow Sam he was to partner, Furlong was not thrilled at the prospect. "Why the hell does he want me riding this?" he thought. "His form was terrible."

It was no surprise that Yellow Sam was chalked up at 20-1 on the Bellewstown bookmakers' boards but getting 20-1 for more than loose change was going to be difficult. It required sound planning and skilful execution.

Times were different then. Except for high profile races, bookmakers didn't offer ante-post or early, day of the race, prices. If you bet off-course, you were paid out at Starting Price, the price ruling in the betting ring when the race started. An off-course bookmaker might take your bet but if it meant risking a big payout, especially if fellow bookmakers reported similar interest in an outsider,

Barney Curley (left), Benny O'Hanlon and the Telefon box at Bellewstown racecourse, vital to the Yellow Sam coup.

action would be taken to shorten the horse's Starting Price. Bookmakers would back Yellow Sam on-course and the offer of 20-1 would quickly disappear. It wouldn't take a lot of money to shrink the odds dramatically.

Curley had gathered about IR£15,000 (at that time the Irish pound was linked to sterling; today's equivalent value is about £115,000) to put on Yellow Sam. It was going to be difficult but some features of the betting market were helpful. The major bookmakers controlled a smaller proportion of betting shops than they do today and the systems for warning bookmakers, particularly small independent shops, of a potential gambling coup were less sophisticated. If alarm bells started to ring, how were bookmakers to get money into the racecourse betting ring to cut Yellow Sam's price? There were no mobile phones or personal computers and at Bellewstown, crucially, there was just that one telephone kiosk.

Curley assembled a team of 100 trusted individuals and allocated them to a group of team leaders. The team leaders were not told what to do until the day of the race. At 1.45pm, they were told to prepare their men for action. About an hour later, the men were despatched to about 300 betting shops, with instructions to place bets of between IR£50 and IR£300. Sean Graham's shops were spared.

O'Hanlon was already ensconced, immovable and implacable, explaining to impatient protesters outside the kiosk that he was on the phone to a hospital to hear the possibly last words of his beloved but fading aunt. Neither the hospital nor the aunt existed.

Shortly before three o'clock, Brennan gave Furlong his riding instructions. He was to bide his time in the two and a half mile race and hit the front when he thought the time was right. As he legged the jockey up, Brennan said, "This fella will win."

Plans often go wrong, especially when there are obstacles between the start and finish of a race, but nothing went wrong. Yellow Sam won readily, by two and a half lengths. A total of IR£15,300 was staked and the odds stood still, at 20-1. Curley had won more than IR£300,000. How much that equates to today depends on which method of conversion you choose. Let's say about £2 million.

Winning is one thing, being paid another, but in the end every bookmaker paid. It helped that no one shop had to pay out more than IR£6,000 and that Curley had done nothing illegal or against the rules.

As an amateur rider, Furlong could not be paid but he could be given a present, and he was. A week or two after the great day, Curley drove him to a Dublin garage, where Furlong was handed the keys to a new BMW.

The team leaders were each paid IR£1,000 and the troops IR£200. Yellow Sam was given a warm welcome when he arrived home and won his next race before joining Ken Oliver's yard in Scotland. Sadly, he was killed in a fall the following year.

His name lived on and in 2014 the Yellow Sam Bar was opened at Bellewstown racecourse. The following year, to mark the 40th anniversary of Curley's triumph, Colm Maher wrote a One Act comedy – 'Yellow Sam. The Greatest Gamble in Racing History.' Padraic McCintyre played Curley and Gerard Adlum played everyone else, including Benny O'Hanlon.

There were four performances, before racing on 26 and 27 August, and again after racing.

Curley and Furlong were there to see the play, and to pose for photographs beside the telephone box.

Nick Townsend was also there, as he had provided the playwright with helpful information. Townsend's book, *The Sure Thing. The Greatest Coup In Horse Racing History* (2014) has informed this piece, too. It's well worth reading, not least because the Yellow Sam coup was not the only or even the biggest or most controversial of Curley's stings. In 2010 he masterminded a coup that won £4 million.

By then, his imagination had turned to a more philanthropic project. In 1996, after the tragic death of his son Charlie in a car accident, Curley founded the Direct Aid For Africa charity to support the underprivileged in Zambia.

When he finally told his life story, in collaboration with Townsend, Curley called the book *Giving A Little Back* (1998).

Some of the money won in 2010 was used to help fund DAFA and in 2020, aged 80, Curley reflected, "My days as a gambler are over; I have moved on. A wise man once said, 'It is in the giving, we receive.' I believe he was 100 per cent correct. I have never been happier and running DAFA is the best thing by far that I have done in my life."

Barney Curley was no saint but in later life he had a good go at becoming one.

76 JAMES LOSES HIS BOTTOM

Dave Nevison is RacingTV's large charactered, life-embracing pundit who worked in the City as a foreign exchange trader before becoming a professional punter.

That was in 1993 and, having been used to dealing in very large sums, Nevison was surprised to discover that, in horseracing, professional punters and racecourse bookmakers generally dealt in much smaller ones.

Dave Nevison and the unluckiest bet of all.

Fellow professional Eddie 'The Shoe' Fremantle supplied him with a passport to success by teaching Nevison the virtues of constructing his own 'tissue.' This meant allocating odds to each horse in a race based on his judgment of every horse's chance of winning.

Each horse's price accounts for a percentage of the 100 per cent 'book' being constructed. So, odds of 2-1 translate into 33.3 per cent (100 ÷ 3), whereas 9-1 equates to 10 per cent (100 ÷ 10).

The odds offered by bookmakers will generally be shorter than in the punter's tissue because, in order to make a profit, their book on the same race will be constructed to make up to, say, 115 per cent.

When significantly better odds are available in the betting market than those the punter has alloted to a particular horse, a bet beckons. It might result in backing several horses in the same race.

This approach is radically different from that of most punters, who look at a race and search for the winner, with less focus on each runner's price.

If Nevison was asked, as he often was, what he fancied in a race, the answer was that he didn't fancy anything until he knew what price it was. He was betting according to the odds rather than on selections.

It sounds fairly straightforward but to convert your tissue into a sustained profit requires sound judgment when allocating odds and nimbleness in exploiting the opportunities presented.

The approach suited Nevison well and for a long time he was very successful. By the late 1990s he was making about £50,000 a year, tax-free, and during the next few years, even more. In 2003, with his betting partner Mark Smith, he made £260,000, followed by £325,000, followed, in 2005, by £4,000; yes, £4,000, before expenses.

It was never easy, always hard work and while there were plenty of big wins there were testing setbacks, too. In the last four months of 2005, Nevison lost £250,000.

Betfair's arrival, in 2000, gradually made his method less profitable because the Betfair exchange model produced a market where the odds represented a truer indication of each horse's chance of winning than the traditional fixed odds market. There were fewer exploitable differences between the market's odds and those in Nevison's tissue, and margins were smaller.

He and Smith also enjoyed plenty of success with Tote Jackpot and Scoop6 bets, including a Jackpot win of £268,643 at Haydock in 2004 and £96,645 from a Scoop6 bet in 2006. By 2007, although Nevison still anticipated further healthy profits from his established approach, he and Smith decided to concentrate more on the big pools. One attraction was that, while Betfair was populated with knowledgeable punters, many of those betting into the Tote's pools were less sophisticated or, as Nevison might have put it, mug punters.

In the long run he might well have bagged another monster pot but, as the economist John Maynard Keynes pointed out, "In the long run, we are all dead." There were plenty of crossbars hit but between March and September 2007, Nevison won £60,000 on fixed odds bets but lost £140,000 going for gold on the Tote.

Along the way, he experienced all the ecstasies and agonies that are an inescapable part of gambling, with the sums won and sums narrowly denied being many times greater than for casual punters. He told his story, with me assisting, in *A Bloody Good Winner* (2007) and its sequel, *No Easy Money* (2008). The former is better than the latter.

Although Nevison branched out into the bloodstock business as well as his existing journalism and broadcasting, the lure of a life-changing win had not disappeared. On 15 January 2009 there was a rollover of £450,000 in the Tote Super7. Picking all seven winners was a formidable challenge but enough punters had a stab at it to boost the pool to £583,837.

Nevison's and Smith's betting was not going well and they staked a modest £84. All four of their bankers won and by the time the final leg arrived, the 3.50pm at Taunton, only six tickets had survived, two of which, including theirs, were on Topless.

Eight horses set out for the three mile three furlong chase but when the final fence was reached, only four were still running and Topless was leading them. The mare only had to jump the last fence to win, and she did.

James Davies and Topless set off for the winning line. All the jockey had to do was keep going while Nevison and Smith waited a few more seconds for ecstasy to arrive. Then, incredibly, 20 yards from the finish, Topless stepped innocuously to her right, Davies lost his balance and his bottom departed from the saddle and fell to the ground, along with the rest of him. Nevison went for a very long run.

Six years later he told the *Racing Post*'s Peter Thomas (2 July 2015), "I still think about it once a week or so. It could have paid off the mortgage and I'd have been in a totally different situation. I'll never forget that moment and I can't really look back at it and laugh. It's not the kind of thing I can go into a pub and say, 'You'll never guess what happened to me.'"

If you are tempted to say, "I know how he felt," I doubt it.

The finish of that Carlsberg UK Handicap Chase not only put Nevison off diving into Tote pools, it also put him off betting altogether for quite a long time. "I no longer do the big jackpots," he said. "It's too long between drinks and I can't stand the stress. I've accepted I'll never be a millionaire. I'd rather just get a winner now and get in the payout queue."

Chapter

15

Bookmakers, punters and betting shops

In which the 1986 Revolution arrives • pens are pocketed • Gary wishes he was in Worcester • Mr Saucy Squirrel meets a minister • Churchill views stunted tyrants.

THE 1986 REVOLUTION ARRIVES

An enormous amount has been written about the French Revolution of 1789, as also about the 1917 Russian Revolution. Fair enough, they were jolly important, but so was the arrival of televisions into betting shops, and that hardly gets a mention.

To appreciate the magnitude of the French and Russian Revolutions it is important to know what the state of play was before. It is the same with the Betting Shop Television Revolution of 1986. Try to pay attention – it might come up in a quiz.

In 1960, the Betting and Gaming Act legalised betting shops, which then multiplied like rabbits. By 1968, there were almost 16,000 betting shops in Britain. They were made lawful, not to encourage gambling but in recognition of the impossibility of suppressing it. Better to legalise gambling and regulate it than wage a hopeless war against it.

Subsequently, successive governments subscribed to the increasingly strained principle of 'unstimulated demand.' Bookmakers were allowed to meet the existing demand for betting but prohibited from doing anything to stimulate it, such as providing a cup of tea.

The early betting shops were not situated on High Streets, as they are today, but tucked away, almost clandestinely, in side streets. Advertising a shop's location was illegal and so was anything else that might tempt potential customers.

Bookmakers were not permitted to have shop fronts that allowed those outside to see inside, which was a blessing for customers wishing to remain anonymous. To enter a betting shop, you either really wanted to bet or were badly in need of a free pencil.

Conditions were basic and spartan, the walls stained with nicotine, entry a socially dubious activity and even seats in short supply, as they might encourage punters to loiter. Loitering was to be discouraged. There were no refreshments and no televisions, although plenty of cigarette smoke, so that your clothes still reeked of it when you got home, to be greeted by, "You've been to the betting shop again, then?"

'Rab' Butler, Home Secretary during the passage of the 1960 Act, later reflected, "the House of Commons was so intent on making betting shops as sad as possible, in order not to deprave the young, that they ended up more like undertakers' premises."

Even when racing was shown on the BBC and ITV, betting shops were not allowed to show it. Instead, a company called Extel (Exchange Telegraph Company Limited) supplied audio commentaries of dubious accuracy, designed to make finishes sound exciting.

The final furlong tended to take a long time and involve dramatic changes of fortune, with "and the favourite's finishing fast," a favourite of Extel commentators. Favourite backers were often disappointed to discover that the favourite had not finished as fast as they had been led to believe. On other occasions, a horse that had got the better of a close finish turned out to have won by several lengths, hard held.

Sometimes, when at the races, I would stand near the racecourse betting shop and compare what I was watching live on the track with Extel's commentary, broadcast into the shop. They were often very different, although the eventual winner was the same.

On occasions, a commentary would be interrupted by the announcement, "telephonic interruption to Ayr", or Bangor, or Chepstow, or wherever the horse you'd backed and was in the lead was running. When telephonic connection had been reestablished and the result announced, the horse had disappeared.

The absence of pictures did not prevent punters from engaging in animated debates over the performance of participating jockeys and the likely outcome of stewards' enquiries. There was plenty of time for that because, in those days, horse and greyhound races dominated betting shops and there were far fewer races than today, none of them 'virtual.'

Then, in 1986, the Revolution arrived. The government softened its position sufficiently to allow televisions into betting shops, as well as limited refreshments and more comfortable facilities. The following year, SIS (Satellite Information Services) began to broadcast live coverage of horse and dog racing. Soon, the Revolution spread throughout the nation.

For me, the reality of the Revolution came in a Coral's betting shop in Bury St Edmunds in February 1988, a shop where SIS had arrived. There, in front of me, was The Bury St Edmunds Television.

Later, deregulation gathered pace. In 1993, betting shops were allowed to open in the evening during the summer; in 1995, coinciding with the arrival of Sunday racing, they could open on Sundays.

The National Lottery, launched in 1994, posed a potential threat to betting shops but in reality opened up new possibilities, as gambling became a more acceptable activity and restrictions were relaxed further.

Dingy sidestreet dives were transformed into bright High Street retail outlets, with batteries of television screens, gaming machines, and non-stop betting opportunities, promoted non-stop. The selection of products was much wider, consumer protection greater. I suppose it was for the better. Well, not the gaming machines.

78 PENS ARE POCKETED

Pens came later. In the beginning, when the first betting shops opened, in 1961, it was pencils. Often, pencils on a string, to protect bookmakers from pencil thieves. Later, as Britain became more advanced, pens started to appear.

They were short, unreliable pens, with a short lifespan. Sometimes this was because, from a writing point of view, they were dead on arrival, sometimes it was because their ink supply was tiny, and sometimes it was because they had already left the shop in a customer's pocket.

For all three reasons, for better or worse, many a bet failed to reach the counter in time for victory or defeat. A pen that worked was a prized possession, sometimes argued over, a bit like the Crimea, but with fewer deaths.

Pocketing a pen was theft but it was forgiveable theft, a trivial consolation for a losing afternoon, for which a plea of 'justifiable stealing' deserved to be viewed compassionately. Since Ladbrokes had taken your money, it only seemed fair that you should be allowed to take one of their small red pens. As far as I know, no cases ever reached court.

Possessors of a pen, perhaps the only working specimen in the shop, were reluctant to relinquish possession, even if they showed no sign of using the pen to write out a bet.

There were other uses, as one regular customer demonstrated by using the pen (I think it was a blue William Hill one) to stab holes in *The Sporting Life* on the shop wall. One hole was created in the racecard for the 2.45 at Brighton, another in the form for a horse in the 3.30 at Catterick, followed by an angry line through the name of the horse he had just backed, without success. Confronting him would have been unwise, as he might have mistaken you for another recently backed loser, and stabbed you in the eye.

Pens were vital for writing out your bet but before televisions arrived in betting shops, starting in 1986, they were also useful when listening to the commentary.

I liked to fold my betting slip in half and, along the top edge, mark the appropriate number of furlongs, ending with the winning line, then track my selection's progress as the commentary progressed. It was satisfying moving from zero, through numbers such as 4 or 2, to finally write the number 1 beneath the winning line. A pity it didn't happen more often.

The pen is still a visible part of every betting shop's daily life, less elusive and more reliable than in the past, but for many customers, betting online or at a machine, life without a betting shop pen is now a reality. The pen is past its prime.

79 GARY WISHES HE WAS IN WORCESTER

There were two cars to choose from, parked in front of Gary Wiltshire's large house near Towcester, and both were Mercedes E320 convertibles. On the morning of Saturday 28 September 1996, Wiltshire got into one of them and set off for Worcester racecourse.

Wiltshire was always setting off for racecourses, a habit that had served the characterful bookmaker well; so well that, as well as the house near Towcester, he owned a cottage in Norfolk, a villa in Portugal and half of another house in Buckinghamshire.

Wiltshire started young, being taken to Harringay dogs in his pram at a time when his parents lived opposite a betting shop in Islington, opened by Harry Barham in 1961, the first year that betting shops were lawful.

Although only six, Wiltshire was fascinated by the shop. Later, this might have supplied a warning of the dangers of bookmaking, as in 1972 Barham was murdered. At the time, his shops in Islington and Holborn were said to have recently lost £50,000 and he was awaiting trial for the fraudulent evasion of £123,000 (about £1.7m today) in betting duty.

The murder remains unsolved and in 2014 I submitted a freedom of information request to have the Metropolitan Police files on the case, held at the National Archives in Kew, made available. My application was turned down and if anyone wants to see them, they'll have to wait until 2061, which is a bit late for me.

At school, the 11 year-old Wiltshire made the mistake of laying Charlottown to his fellow pupils in the 1966 Derby but a few years later, on holiday with his parents at Combe Haven caravan park, near Hastings, he was more successful, betting on the Donkey Derbys on the beach.

Wiltshire left school at 16 with two 'O' levels, in gambling and finding fish and chip shops, both of which were to be important parts of Wiltshire's life, and body. His grandfather had sold flowers at Leather Lane market in Camden and Gary followed him into daffodils while also continuing to develop a gambling addiction.

When he was 18, he became a boardman at a Hector Macdonald's betting shop, turned down the chance to become a shop manager, worked as a clerk to a bookmaker at Walthamstow greyhounds, and attended Gamblers' Anonymous, but only briefly.

In the snakes and ladders of Wiltshire's eventful life, the next few years were dire but by 1978 he had scrambled his way back up the hill far enough to obtain a bookmaker's licence.

He first set up his pitch at a flapping track at Hinckley, in Leicestershire; flapping being a branch of greyhound racing not regulated by the National Greyhound Racing Club, and associated with untoward practices.

Wiltshire owned a greyhound called Exclusive Native who himself was sometimes involved with unseemliness. When Exclusive Native was not required to win, he was fed a sausage with an aspirin inside. It helped cure any headache the dog might have had but wasn't conducive to winning races.

Hinckley raced on Wednesday and Saturday evenings at a time when there was no competition from betting shops, which were not yet allowed to open in the evenings. That left the novice bookmaker with plenty of time for other initiatives. As well as branching out to greyhound tracks at Warwick, Leicester, Oxford and Milton Keynes, specialising in betting without the favourite, Wiltshire continued to work on market stalls.

From dogs, he moved to horses, standing first at Perth, then at Folkestone and Ayr, enabling him to use the slogan, "From Folkestone to Ayr, Wiltshire's there."

As the journeys got longer, Wiltshire got larger, the result of stopping off for fish and chips, hamburgers and Chinese take-aways. On the way back from point-to-point meetings, he was prone to indulge in prawn cocktails, sirloin steak and Black Forest gateau.

Along the way there were some setbacks but also some triumphs, not least in 1990, when Wiltshire had £1,000 each-way on Norton's Coin for the Cheltenham Gold Cup, at 200-1. That led to the purchase of his villa in Portugal.

Gary Wiltshire, a player of life's Snakes and Ladders.

Holes in one at golf tournaments were also lucrative, since other bookmakers tended to assume that the odds against there being one were long when the statistics showed that they were short. To help things along, before the 1992 Open Golf tournament, Wiltshire and his collaborator, Johnny Earl, supplied independent betting shops with lists of prices bearing the name of Fairway Golf. The lists included odds for a hole in one, at suitably attractive odds. Then Wiltshire and Earl took their own prices.

It meant that Gary was able to move into racehorse ownership, beginning in 1991 with Vado Via, who he claimed for £6,000. Vado Via returned the favour by winning at Bangor, then at Exeter, then Haydock – where Wiltshire had £15,000 on at about 6-1 – followed by further successes at Nottingham and Newton Abbot, twice.

There were more horses, more gambles and a tipping line and, all in all, when Wiltshire got into his Mercedes that Saturday in September 1996, life was rosy. Business was booming and his wife, Sue, was due to have their first baby.

With his bookmaker's hat on, he preferred the modest jumps card at Worcester to the tricky Festival of British Racing card at Ascot and set off along the A43 to join the M40, en route to the M42, en route to Worcester. As Wiltshire approached the M40, he saw that, northbound, it was jammed. So he pulled into a lay-by and decided the best bet was to divert to Ascot.

After four races there, Frankie Dettori had won four times and Wiltshire was about £800 up. Dettori had a huge following and many betting shop punters had backed his mounts in multiple bets, so the big off-course bookmakers' acted to reduce their potential liabilities by backing Fatefully, Dettori's next ride, into 7-4 favourite. It was an 18 runner handicap and Wiltshire judged Fatefully's chance of winning to be much less than his odds suggested. He layed Fatefully and Fatefully won.

Wiltshire ducked the sixth race, which Dettori won again, on Lochangel. What happened next you will already know because it is engraved on horseracing's history and in the public's mind. Frankie Dettori spread his fame by completing the set of seven winners on Fujiyama Crest while Gary Wiltshire became a name by losing £1 million on the same result.

It was another 18 runner handicap and, in the morning, Fujiyama Crest had been 12-1. As off-course bookmakers piled in to cut their possible losses, Dettori's mount was cut to 3-1, then 9-4, ending as 2-1 favourite.

Those prices, Wiltshire wrote in his 2011 autobiography, *Winning It Back*, "were barmy, stark staring bonkers, insane." He was an experienced and bold bookmaker and this was a rare chance to lay a horse at about 3-1 when it should have been four or five times that price. "It was a licence to print money, I thought as I took our first bet, £5,000 at 4-1 from bookmaker Roy Christie."

Then it was Coral's turn, £40,000 at 7-2 and another £20,000 at the same price, with more to come. When other rails bookmakers were offering as low as 6-4, Wiltshire was taking on all comers at 3-1. Defeat, except for Fujiyama Crest, was not in his mind. Instead he was thinking, "At the end of all this I'm going to have half a million pounds wrapped round my bollocks to play with for the rest of my life. I'm not kidding, it felt fantastic."

Wiltshire may have had reason on his side but not fate. Fujiyama Crest won by a neck. When Wiltshire reached his car and studied his ledger with his clerk, Peter Houghton, it revealed that he owed Coral £487,500 and over £1 million in total.

Determined to show that, although down he was not out, Wiltshire returned to Ascot the next day but wrote, "the chill I felt that Sunday morning as I got closer and closer to the track is repeated every time I go there, even fifteen years after the event. I don't think that feeling of dread will ever go away."

"It was even money whether I wanted to live or die," he said, but soon resolved that he was going to pay everything he owed. Coral's trading director Trevor Beaumont gave him time when some others did not and Wiltshire set about selling assets. The two Mercedes went, so did the house at Little Horwood, the cottage in Norfolk, the villa in Portugal and the house near Towcester, which he and Sue had only recently moved into. They moved into Sue's small house near Birmingham.

With the exception of Vado Via, who was with her first foal at stud, Wiltshire's racehorses were sold and their former owner returned to working on market stalls as well as in the betting ring.

Wiltshire named Vado Via's foal Mi Odds and he lifted his owner's spirits by winning 15 races between 2000 and 2005.

In the ring, there were the usual ups and downs until, in 2003, the Tote approached him and bought all 46 of Wiltshire's pitches, with Wiltshire, 'The Belly from the Telly,' running their rails pitches.

The one good thing about the disaster of Dettori Day was that it made Wiltshire known and respected for having paid his debts and rebuilt his career. With his knowledge of betting, his outsize personality and endearing nature as well as his 30 stone plus presence, television producers wanted him. He became part of Sky Sports' greyhound team and of the BBC's horseracing team.

Yet life didn't become smooth and when Wiltshire brought his story up to date, in *Angels, Tears & Sinners* (2019), he looked back on a stressful and difficult time. The combination of Sue divorcing him, allegations of involvement in nefarious betting activities, losing his job with Sky Sports and reaching a dangerous weight of 37 stone resulted in an episode of serious depression. For over a year, Wiltshire was a recluse and stayed away from racecourses.

He succeeded in clearing his name over the betting allegations and, having had a gastric sleeve fitted, paid for by Fred Done, Betfred's owner, reduced his weight to 24 stone. With Sharon, his new partner, he found a measure of contentment so that, when asked if he was happy, paused then replied, "As happy now as I've been for a long time."

Both Wiltshire and his life were smaller. Sharon and he lived in a rented cottage, the television work that meant a lot to him remained elusive and although he had a lot of racecourse pitches, the scale of his betting was much reduced. In *Angels, Tears & Sinners* he revealed that, over the previous 10 years, he had done more punting than laying.

In 2019, when asked again if he was happy, Wiltshire replied, "When I used to sell flowers down the market, I was happier."

The good news was that he had found happiness with Sharon and among most racing people there was a fund of goodwill towards him. Wiltshire still regularly wears the familiar smile that brought a matching smile to other people's faces and he remains a characterful, endearing, very human presence.

80 MR SAUCY SQUIRREL MEETS A MINISTER

1976 was a big year for Woodrow Wyatt. *The Exploits of Mr Saucy Squirrel* was published and he was appointed Chairman of the Horseracing Totalisator Board. Wyatt, 57, had no obvious qualifications for the latter position, although the same could be said of several of his predecessors.

The first chairman of what was then the Racecourse Betting Control Board, established in 1928, was Sir Clement Hindley. A distinguished civil engineer, Hindley had spent the previous 30 years working on the railway system in India, where he was Chief Commissioner of Railways.

If it had been the Railways Control Board, he would have been ideal but on his appointment to the RBCB Hindley declared, frankly, "I am not what you would call a great racing man." Luckily for him, the post was a part-time one, enabling Hindley to occupy other positions for which he was better qualified, leading in 1939 to his appointment as President of the Institution of Civil Engineers.

In 1944 death terminated Hindley's tenure, to be replaced by Sir Reginald Blair, an accountant and former and future Conservative MP whose main claim to racing fame was that he lived at Hermit's Wood, near Chalfont St Giles, the future home of Dorothy Paget. The highly eccentric and frequently obnoxious Paget owned Golden Miller, winner of the Cheltenham Gold Cup five times in a row between 1932 and 1936, as well as the 1934 Grand National.

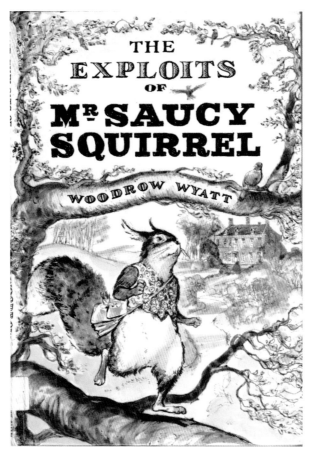

Woodrow Wyatt, chairman of the Tote and writer of children's books.

In 1947 Blair was succeeded by General Sir Miles Dempsey, freshly retired from a career in the Army, to which he returned, as Commander-in-Chief of Land Forces, in 1951. Memorably, giving evidence to the 1949-1951 Royal Commission on Betting, Lotteries and Gaming, when asked if the RBCB did less than bookmakers to encourage betting, Dempsey replied, "I do not think we do anything to encourage betting in the way of advertising or anything like that. We hope if there is betting we will get it but we do not take any practical steps to induce the public to bet with us. Our total expenditure is about £50 a year on advertising."

It was then the turn of Dingwall Bateson. In 1953, two years after his appointment, Bateson was knighted, not for his work at the RBCB but as the retiring President of the Law Society.

In 1961, when the RBCB evolved into the Horserace Totalisator Board, the Indian connection was revived in the shape of Sir Alexander Sim, formerly

Commissioner for the Port of Calcutta. He lasted until 1970, when Arthur Taylor, ex-deputy chairman of Customs and Excise, became, briefly, the first full-time chairman. Then there was Lord Mancroft (1972 to 1976), who had held minor positions in government and, while Tote chairman, followed up his earlier book, *Booking the Cooks* (1969) with *A Chinaman in my Bath, and other pieces* (1974).

Then there was Wyatt. In an age when personal connections were often the best passport to appointment, Wyatt cultivated relationships with successive Home Secretaries and Prime Ministers to first obtain and then retain his chairmanship of the Tote.

Roy Jenkins, Home Secretary at the time of Wyatt's appointment, was a friend, as successful in politics as Wyatt was not. In 20 years as a Labour MP, from 1945 to 1955 and again from 1959 to 1970, the only government office Wyatt held was that of Under-Secretary of State at the War Office, for six months in 1951.

His business ventures failed but Wyatt found his niche on television and, particularly, as a journalist. His appearances on *Panorama* during the mid-1950s put him in the public eye or, as he put it, with characteristic immodesty, "My TV appearances catapulted me into fame."

He was a columnist for the *Daily Mirror* from 1965 to 1973 and for the *Sunday Mirror* for the following 10 years but as he moved from political left to right he then found a more congenial home at the *News of the World*, under the questionable title of 'The Voice of Reason.'

His columns had a large readership and there was no danger of their author understating their impact. In 1985, Wyatt wrote, "I believe that my articles have influenced attitudes and voting patterns more than the total output of the grander and smaller circulation papers. Writing my weekly column has been for the last 20 years the most important work I have ever done."

Running the Tote for the previous nine years seemed to be less important. Reflecting on Jenkins' offer of the chairmanship, Wyatt wrote, "I had always been amused by the racing world and thought the Tote could be an interesting public office."

It received little attention in his autobiography, *Confessions of an Optimist* (1985), and for Wyatt the annual high points of the job were the opportunity to escort the Queen Mother at the Cheltenham Festival and Royal Ascot, and the Tote's annual lunch. His influence was visible in the number of government ministers in attendance. In 1991, for instance, the Home Secretary Kenneth Baker was accompanied by Foreign Secretary Douglas Hurd to hear Wyatt's typically entertaining speech. Six years later, the Prime Minister, John Major, was there to "pay tribute in person to Woodrow Wyatt, who has been such an outstanding chairman."

Wyatt was good company, ebullient and characterful as well as vain, materialistic, and a snob, something he felt did not require apology. "Snobbishness can be a virtue," he insisted. "The creative aspiration to be among the best and to be the best yourself, the most obvious manifestation of which is the general regard for the upper reaches of society and power."

At the Tote, his management style was autocratic and unscientific but he was an invigorating force. As colourful and conspicuous as his predecessors had been grey and anonymous, invariably wearing a bow tie and smoking a cigar, Wyatt gave the Tote a public personality and led it with energy and panache.

Since 1972, the Tote had been able to offer fixed odds as well as pool betting and Wyatt embraced the new, albeit still restricted, opportunities. Determined to adopt a more commercial approach, he refreshed the executive and launched a series of initiatives including, in 1977, what would be the Tote's most popular bet, the Placepot. Customers had to select horses placed in each of five races, changed to six in 1981.

Yet Wyatt was lucky to survive as Tote chairman beyond 1980. The situation was reminiscent of a scene in *The Exploits of Mr Saucy Squirrel*, when Mr Squirrel visits a government Minister. The Minister explains that politicians like to appear in newspapers when they have done something good. "They're not so keen about it," he tells Mr Squirrel, "if the newspapers want to write that they made a mistake or wasted public money or find out something they're not very proud of."

What John McCririck found out, and was published in *The Sporting Life* in July 1979, was that the Tote had been putting winning off-course bets into racecourse pools after the result of races was known. The effect was to reduce winning dividends.

On 14 July 1979 *The Sporting Life*'s front-page headline demanded – 'Resign! The Tote Boss Must Go Call by MP.' Labour MP Bruce George had tabled a Parliamentary question asking William Whitelaw, Home Secretary in the new Conservative Government, to set up an inquiry.

Three days later, Ossie Fletcher, *The Sporting Life*'s editor, penned a piece titled, 'Why Wyatt Must Go.' Fletcher wrote, "It will be a major scandal if Woodrow Wyatt survives as chairman of the Horserace Totalisator Board."

Pugnacious and hard to shame, Wyatt attempted to bluster his way out of the problem but when Sir Timothy Kitson and Bob Mellish, chairman and vice-chairman of the Parliamentary All-Party Racing and Bloodstock Committee, urged Whitelaw to set up an inquiry, and with fresh evidence of wrongdoing emerging, the Home Secretary felt obliged to act.

The inquiry, led by Francis Aglionby, a Crown Court judge, reported in February 1980. Although the government had stated that the findings would be published, only a summary of the Report was made available. It concluded that, between 1 September 1977, when Tote Credit Limited was established, and 17 July 1979, when the practice of transmitting bets after the result was known was prohibited, dividends, particularly for dual forecast bets, were sometimes reduced by "a very large amount."

Crucially, however, it found that Wyatt had no knowledge of the abuses, with blame directed at Jeff Wells, Tote Credit's managing director, and Mark Elks, its racing manager. The attempt to unseat Wyatt failed.

The full Report was revealed in 2006. Aglionby found that "abuses and malpractices did occur" and that when dividends looked particularly high, "revisions occurred from time to time, always resulting in a substantial downward movement of the dividend."

In the case of bets placed by off-course bookmakers, "from time to time, not all these trade bets were transmitted. All the winning bets were transmitted but not all the losing ones." In one example, from the 2000 Guineas Trial at Salisbury on 7 April 1979, the dual forecast dividend was reduced from £62.86 to £5.77.

According to Aglionby, the abuses took place, not with a view to personal gain but because of "misplaced enthusiasm" for the Tote's financial welfare.

During his long tenure, Wyatt developed a strong affection for the Tote and resented the stream of criticism, uninvited advice, the Jockey Club's unsupportive stance and, especially, suggestions that he was too old for the job.

The older Wyatt became, the more frustrated his critics felt. Unfortunately for them, partly through his 'Voice of Reason' column in the *News of the World*, Wyatt was a diligent scratcher of the ruling Conservative government's back.

An admirer of Margaret Thatcher to the point of sycophancy, he once told her private secretary, "I'm a little bit in love with her." During the 1986 Conservative Party Conference, he told Mrs Thatcher, "You looked beautiful, so beautiful that I fell in love with you all over again." The following year Wyatt was made a life peer and there were regular Sunday morning telephone conversations with the Prime Minister.

In 1990, with Wyatt's latest term as Tote chairman due to expire the following April, by which time he would be 72, and Home Office officials rumoured to be opposed to his reappointment, Thatcher came to his aid. In one of the final acts of her premiership, she reappointed him for two more years.

Hopes that her removal might result in his were dashed when John Major, Thatcher's successor, gave Wyatt another reprieve, until 1995. The 'Voice of Reason' busily praised Major for "holding fast to the rudder through the rough waters", dismissed the Prime Minister's critics as "silly," and predicted that Major would "lead the Tories at the next election – and win."

Wyatt, aged 77 in 1995, was still not ready to depart. He declared, "I need to carry on for at least two years." John Major obliged by reappointing him until 1997. "I don't think it makes any difference what age I am," Wyatt insisted. "Adenauer ran Germany when he was 89. It's not all that much more difficult to run the Tote."

It was a financial relief for 'The Great Survivor,' who had lamented the fact that if he was forced to retire, "I shall have nothing to live on other than my savings and a miserable £60,000 a year [about £115,000 in 2020] pension from the Tote."

In 1995 the patronage system which had served Wyatt so well suffered a serious setback when the Committee on Standards in Public Life, chaired by Lord Nolan, recommended that appointments such as the chairmanship of the Tote should be based on merit. In future there needed to be more than one candidate for the job.

In 1997, Wyatt was finally replaced by Peter Jones. By the end of the year, Wyatt was dead. There'll certainly never be another. Whatever his flaws, Wyatt could – and of course did – boast of a substantial growth in profits and contributions to racing, of a business brought from near bankruptcy to relative success.

There had even been a sequel to *The Exploits of Mr Saucy Squirrel*, namely *The Further Exploits of Mr Saucy Squirrel* (1977).

81 CHURCHILL VIEWS STUNTED TYRANTS

Not Winston Churchill but Major Seton Churchill, Vice-President of the National Anti-Gambling League and author of *Betting and Gambling* (2nd edition, 1894), a work highly recommended by the NAGL.

It is fair to say that neither Churchill nor the NAGL, founded in 1890, were enamoured of either gambling or horseracing. As Churchill put it, gambling "is a dark cloud of moral pollution," "there is great moral corruption associated with every race meeting," and "we should discourage racing." Or, as the NAGL summarised its aim, to "offer a strenuous and uncompromising opposition to every form of Betting and Gambling."

Unfortunately for racing, the NAGL's early campaigning focus was on racecourse bookmakers and the racecourses which allowed them to operate.

Churchill let fly, in particular, at bookmakers, jockeys, tipsters and newspapers. Bookmakers, alias "betting parasites," had been depressingly successful "in extending the number of worshippers at the shrine of the Goddess of Chance. Unless something is done, the disease will continue to increase in virulence."

As to what should be done, "There are some who would treat them as brothel keepers and other panderers to vice are dealt with, that is, suppressed entirely. Others there are who would tax them highly, so that at all events they shall disgorge some of their ill-gotten gains to relieve the public purse." Churchill hoped that public opinion would move in favour of prohibition but in the meantime suggested a licensing system, with magistrates adopting a stricter enforcement of the law than was currently the case.

Jockeys, referred to by Churchill as "stunted tyrants," were also sinners. "Half the mischief on the Turf," Churchill contended, "arises from the way in which these overpaid, spoilt menials can be bribed, and there are plenty of bribers ready."

Tipsters did even more harm than bookmakers. "Their very existence is a witness to the ignorance and credulity prevalent among the outer fringe of the racecourse public." Tipsters preyed on "soft-headed youths," and newspapers were guilty of allowing them to do so.

"It speaks volumes for the low morality of the sporting journals generally," Churchill railed, "that their owners allow themselves practically to be bribed to admit into their columns lies of the most barefaced character." He hoped "that the government will see its way to introduce measures for purifying our newspapers. Not only should all betting news be kept out of the paper till after the event but means could surely be found to suppress the lying advertisements of these professional gamblers."

The NAGL had some influential members, notably the Quaker industrialist and social reformer Seebohm Rowntree, who provided financial support and edited *Betting and Gambling: A National Evil* (1905), whose contributors included the future Labour Prime Minister, Ramsay MacDonald.

Rowntree himself wrote that gambling was "a national evil" which had "spread its poisonous roots throughout the length and breadth of the land, carrying with them misery, poverty, weakened character and crime." Those responsible were "an army of social parasites in the shape of bookmakers and their touts." The answer was state action and moral reform.

In the meantime, the NAGL launched a series of legal actions with the aim of outlawing betting from racecourses, en route to banning it elsewhere. In 1895, it took action against three Jockey Club stewards, the Earl of March, Earl of Ellesmere, and Lord Rendlesham, accusing them of allowing bookmakers to operate at Newmarket racecourse. The charges were dismissed but the stewards did not argue that bookmaking was legal, merely that they had not knowingly permitted it.

Uncertainty arose because of the unsatisfactory framing of the 1853 Act for the Suppression of Betting Houses. The Act declared that it was "illegal to keep or use any house, office, room or other place for betting," but were racecourse bookmakers using a 'place'? Police prosecutions sometimes reduced bookmakers to walking around racecourse enclosures, shouting the odds, without any equipment. Standing in one spot, under an umbrella, might result in a magistrate ruling that the bookmaker was using a 'place' for betting.

In 1896, the NAGL took action against Richard Dunn for betting at Hurst Park, where Dunn was a major shareholder. He had been betting on the move and the magistrates acquitted him but also sought the opinion of the Queen's Bench. The following year, five judges ruled, unanimously, that, when Parliament passed the 1853 Act, its intention was to rid the country of bookmaking, not to "afford it a sort of sanctuary in a betting ring."

Betting on racecourses was outlawed and, if it continued, racecourse directors were in danger of being prosecuted. The NAGL were delighted but racecourse owners, fearful of the impact on attendances, were not. In a risky manoeuvre, they arranged for one of the staff at Kempton Park racecourse, Charles Powell, to apply for an injunction against the racecourse to restrain it from providing betting facilities. The case was referred to the Court of Appeal, who refused the injunction and thereby effectively overturned the earlier ruling of the Queen's Bench.

It was a blow for the NAGL but when the House of Lords set up a Select Committee on Betting, in 1901, the League's influence contributed to the Committee's verdict that street betting was "a great source of evil," one that the 1906 Street Betting Act was intended to suppress. The NAGL claimed, "the Act is our child," but it was a pyrrhic victory as the Act was a failure.

After the First World War, the NAGL went into decline, finally expiring in 1948. Churchill himself expired in 1933, aged 81.

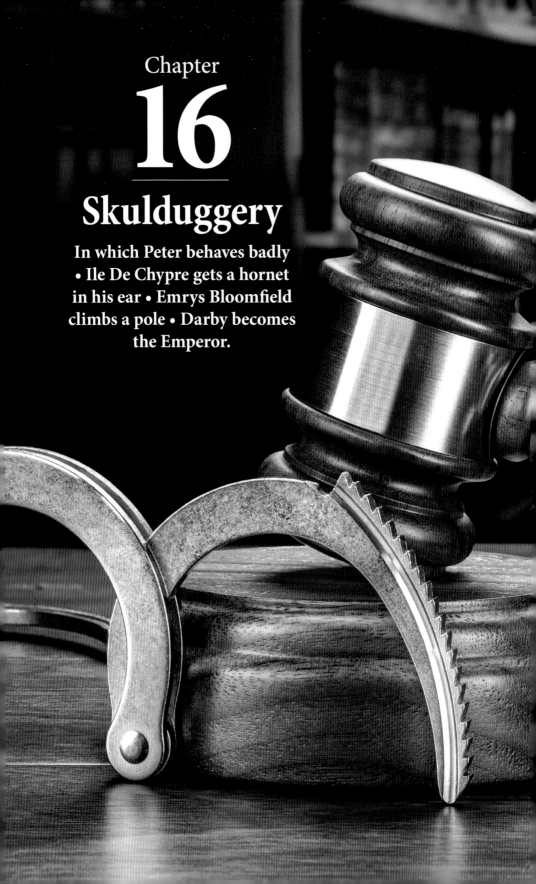

Chapter

16

Skulduggery

In which Peter behaves badly
• Ile De Chypre gets a hornet
in his ear • Emrys Bloomfield
climbs a pole • Darby becomes
the Emperor.

82 PETER BEHAVES BADLY

The label on the squat bottle read, "'Barrie Tonic' Shake bottle well 3½ hours before race and you will have a winner."

Peter Christian Barrie, the creator of the tonic, had confidence in his own product, which he called "harmless dynamite." In 1951 he claimed, "It took me 13 years of experiment to develop the Barrie Tonic and I am satisfied that in it I now have the perfect means of producing winners. I maintain that it is not doping, as defined by the authorities but, believe me, it's just as certain. Surely there is nothing wrong in turning a bad horse into a good one?"

Barrie hoped that his tonic, which he claimed was already responsible for 48 winners, would turn himself into a winner. "I am looking to this tonic to give me the fortune I intend to have before I retire to a life of ease in Australia," he wrote.

To accelerate his emigration, Barrie circulated details of his tonic to every registered owner and trainer in Britain.

Unfortunately his tipping agency, 'The Barrie Ring,' was doing badly, resulting in a lot of disgruntled subscribers and bad publicity. Things got worse when *The People* proclaimed, "Ringer Barrie's 'Harmless Tonic' is Dangerous Dope." Analysis of the dark brown, salty-tasting liquid revealed that it contained large quantities of potassium bromide, caffeine and alcohol. The bromide would produce a temporary sedative effect while the caffeine and alcohol were stimulants. *The People* condemned Barrie as "a menace to the Turf if ever there was one."

He had been a menace for a long time, not just in Britain but in America, too. Known as the 'King of the Ringers,' Barrie's speciality was painting one racehorse to look like another, inferior horse. He considered himself to be a master of his criminal craft and practiced diligently.

In 1919, in the guise of Mr Pearson, Barrie ran a horse called Coat Of Mail in a race for two-year-olds at Stockton. Backed from 25-1 to 5-2 favourite, Coat Of Mail romped home. It was no surprise to Barrie, as Coat Of Mail was actually a three-year-old called Jazz, in disguise.

Later that year he invented a horse called Silver Badge and won a race at Cheltenham with him, at 10-1, allegedly yielding a profit of £7,000. Silver Badge was actually Shining More.

In 1920, things took a turn for the worse when Barrie was arrested, tried and given a three year prison sentence. On his release, he got to know Edgar Wallace, a racing enthusiast as well as Britain's best selling writer. In 1923, Wallace ghosted Barrie's confessions for *John Bull*, a popular weekly magazine.

Too notorious for his own good in Britain, Barrie moved to Canada and then to New York. He got a job with champion trainer Sam Hildreth, befriended former champion jockey Mark Fator and devoted himself to race-fixing. In 1926, after Fator had been refused a licence, Barrie moved a small stable of horses to Cuba, for more ringing, before returning to the US the following year.

In 1931 Barrie acquired his best known ringer, Aknahton. Aknahton was a talented three-year-old while Shem was an untalented juvenile. "Considering horse-faking as an art," Barrie wrote, "then the changing of Aknahton into Shem was a masterpiece."

Aknahton, alias Shem, duly rewarded Barrie and his associates handsomely when winning at Havre de Grace, Baltimore. With newspaper reporters and racing authorities on his trail, Barrie moved Aknahton to Bowie, Maryland, raced him under the name of Hickey and triumphed again.

Cashing Aknahton in as often and quickly as possible, Barrie won with him twice at Agua Caliente in Mexico, under the alias of Gailmont. Moving on again, to Hialeah Park in Florida, Barrie's activities soon attracted the attention of the Pinkerton Detective Agency's detectives.

Peter Christian Barrie 'King of the Ringers'.

Clinging precariously to freedom, in 1932 Barrie and his glamorous girlfriend Ethel Patricia von Gerichten, both travelling under a series of false identities, went on a ringing spree that was finally halted in 1934 when Pinkerton's dogged detective, Captain Clovis Duhain, caught up with Barrie and von Gerichten at Saratoga.

In November 1934 Barrie was deported and returned to Britain "more or less broke." He promptly sold his story to *The People* and tried to resurrect his twin occupations of race-fixing and tipping. Both were unsuccessful and the 'King of the Ringers' went into a long decline.

Barrie never did return to Australia. Latterly he lived in a Lewisham Council lodging house for single men and, suffering from dementia, died in Greenwich District Hospital in 1973, aged 85. If you would like to find out more about Barrie and other disciples of 'ringing', you might enjoy my *Ringers & Rascals. A Taste of Skulduggery* (2003). I've looked on Amazon and you can get a used copy for £1.69.

Barrie died poor, alone and uncelebrated but perhaps his claim, in 1951, to have doped 100 horses played its part in persuading racecourses to tighten their security, with the stables at Hurst Park guarded "night and day, to prevent any attempts at nobbling."

In 1952 passports were issued to all persons authorised to enter racecourse stables and the Jockey Club reviewed the issue of doping. Little came of it and it was 1960 before a committee chaired by the Duke of Norfolk proposed the introduction of routine dope testing.

In 1962 the draconian treatment of trainers, previously liable to lose their licences if one of their horses was found to have been doped, with or without the trainer's knowledge, was relaxed.

83 ILE DE CHYPRE GETS A HORNET IN HIS EAR

It was the Thursday of Royal Ascot, 16 June 1988, Gold Cup day. Racegoers were debating the controversial disqualification of Royal Gait, the Gold Cup's easy winner, and some were looking forward to the traditional sing-song around the bandstand that took place after each day's final race.

Royal Gait's loss had been Sadeem's gain, for Guy Harwood's five-year-old, ridden by Greville Starkey, had been promoted from second place to first. The duo had a fine chance of doubling up in the closing King George V Handicap, for which their Ile De Chypre was 4-1 second favourite.

There were 18 runners for the mile and a half contest but as the leader entered the final furlong, there could be only one winner. Ile De Chypre was three lengths clear and going to win comfortably. Suddenly, Starkey's mount veered left, towards the stands rail. Starkey was unseated, leaving Thethingaboutitis, trained by Geoff Lewis and ridden by Tony Culhane, to take the prize.

Ile De Chypre was said to be "not straightforward" but he was straightforward enough to finish second when carrying top weight in that year's Cambridgeshire Handicap and in 1989 to finish second in the Group 1 Coronation Cup at Epsom before winning the Group 1 International Stakes at York.

Ile De Chypre's inexplicable behaviour was one more case of a horse snatching defeat from the jaws of victory. So the Ile De Chypre incident might simply have been added to the list of bizarre defeats if it had not been for James Laming's appearance at Southwark Crown Court in October 1989. Laming, a 49-year-old car dealer from Peckham, was there to be tried for allegedly conspiring with others to supply cocaine and with possessing half a kilo of the drug, worth £100,000.

Escaping conviction and prison was going to be tricky because Laming had been found in possession of bank notes containing traces of cocaine and was obliged to admit an association with the conspiracy's Mr Big – Rene Black, a Peruvian drug baron who, unfortunately for Laming, had turned Queen's evidence.

Black and his brother Rudi produced drugs on an industrial scale at a rural factory in Surrey and had a distribution warehouse near Heathrow Airport. Already awash with houses and expensive cars, they were planning to distribute drugs worth £15.5 million before the Drug Squad arrested Rene and made what was then the largest ever seizure of cocaine.

Rudi, fortuitously or presciently, was in America at the time but Rene was being held in Lewes prison. He decided to play his only card and spill the proverbial beans. With a £1 million price on their prize witness's head, the police went to extraordinary lengths to prevent him being murdered. Black was flown by helicopter from Lewes to Redhill, where he was installed in an armed van and escorted to Southwark with a helicopter hovering overhead.

For Laming, a desperate situation demanded a desperate gamble or, as his defence counsel, Jonathan Goldberg QC, put it, his client's defence was "one of the most remarkable ever presented in Crown Court."

Laming admitted involvement with Black but maintained that he was not involved in drug dealing but in a new initiative based, Goldberg told the jury, on Laming's development of "a technically brilliant ultrasonic gun." It was a conspiracy, not to distribute cocaine but "to undermine the entire system of racecourse betting and bookmaking in this country by the use of [this] device."

Black, attracted by the potential for influencing race results, successful betting and money laundering, allegedly gave Laming £10,000 to fund the device's development. It was more than enough, as Laming stated that "all the information on ultrasonics came from *Encyclopaedia Brittanica*."

The King George V Handicap was used as a trial run for the device, cleverly concealed in a pair of large binoculars. "It looks like an ordinary pair of black racing binoculars," Goldberg explained, showing the binoculars to the jury, "but take off the lens caps and you see what looks like the backside of a jet engine." The lenses had been removed and two high-powered transducers inserted.

Goldberg told the Court that the 'stun gun' emitted a high frequency sound, undetectable to humans but terrifying to animals. The effect on a passing racehorse would, Laming's counsel submitted, be "equivalent in human terms to a hideous, ear-piercing shriek."

As Ile De Chypre galloped towards victory, Laming's brother Robert, standing by the running rail, pulled the trigger with the effect, according to Laming, that Ile De Chypre would "feel like he has got a hornet or wasp in his ear."

Robert was not available to testify, having, as James put it, "legged it." In his absence, James changed his mind about where, exactly, Robert had been

Jonathan Goldberg QC faced the tricky task of defending James Laming.

standing. This became necessary, first, because it was pointed out that the spot he initially indicated was too far away from Ile De Chypre for the device to have had an effect and, second, because co-defendant Martin Cox testified that both James and Robert had been standing together, in a different spot.

Laming also struggled to explain how, exactly, bets would be placed in a way that ensured a profit.

Proceedings took a turn for the better for the defence on Monday 6 November, when Greville Starkey gave evidence about the results of tests with the 'stun gun' carried out at his stud farm that weekend.

The device was directed at three ponies and horses, described by Starkey as "bombproof." It had no effect on Dandino, his daughter Helen's pony, but had a major effect on a Welsh cob called High Flier and a hunter called Minstrel.

With Starkey on board, High Flier "suddenly took off at 100 mph" with Starkey trying in vain to stop it. "It was taking me all my strength," he said, "and I was still out of control." When Minstrel went past the 'sonic gun,' he also took off.

Sound expert Brandon McHale, in attendance, testified, "We were quite sure we were having an effect on the horses and it was quite alarming."

The jury may or may not have been persuaded of the efficacy of the beaming binoculars but they were satisfied that Laming was part of the conspiracy to supply cocaine and of possessing half a kilo of it. On 21 December, all appeals having failed, Laming was sentenced to 14 years in prison.

The case of the 'nobbling sonic gun' passed into history but cases of horses casting victory aside persisted. In a hurdle race at Exeter on 21 October 2014, Go West Young Man jumped the final hurdle in front and approached the winning line with the race won, only to suddenly veer from the far rail to the stands side rail, very much like Ile De Chypre, and lose all chance. Unlike Ile De Chypre, Go West Young Man did not go on to glory but only to confirm his waywardness, for which he didn't need encouragement from beaming binoculars.

84 EMRYS BLOOMFIELD CLIMBS A POLE

On the morning of Thursday 16 July 1953, Leonard Philipps and Emrys Bloomfield set off from Dinas, in the Rhondda Valley, and drove towards Bath. About a mile from the racecourse, in Lansdown Lane, Philipps parked his lorry and the two men manoevred a ladder against a telegraph pole.

While Philipps, a rag and scrap metal dealer, held the ladder, Bloomfield climbed to the top and used an oxyacetylene torch to burn through the telephone cable. It was about 1.30pm; the Spa Selling Stakes, the first race of the afternoon, was due off at 2.00pm.

Philipps had been employed to do the job by Gomer Charles, a South Wales bookmaker in league with a London bookmaker, Harry Kateley, who had a trade account with Charles and was the ringleader of the conspiracy. Its other members were Maurice Williams, a professional gambler who shared Kateley's bookmaker's office, William Rook, a businessman and racehorse owner who was a heavy betting client of Kateley's, and Lieutenant Colonel Victor Robert Colquhoun Dill, employed to manage a turf accountant's office in Hampstead, recently bought by Williams and trading under the name of J.Davidson & Co.

Dill had worked as a bloodstock agent in France for a while before returning to England, and unemployment, in 1952. His Eton educated voice and military credentials were perhaps useful on the phone.

Two months earlier an unraced two-year-old called Santa Amaro, bought in France for £2,000, arrived at Folkestone and was taken to Cabbage Hill Farm at Binfield, in Berkshire. Kateley arranged for a trial to be staged at Worcester

The conspirators in the Francasal case arrive at the Old Bailey. Harry Kateley (left), Victor Dill (centre) and Maurice Williams (right).

racecourse to test the horse's ability. The trial left its observers satisfied that their purchase was well up to winning a selling race.

The plan was to run Santa Amaro at Chepstow on 25 May but the conspirators' failure to get the horse registered with a licensed trainer in time forced them to abandon the plan. At the end of May, Santa Amaro was returned to France.

The following month, Dill arranged for the purchase of another French two-year-old. Francasal cost £820 and was worth no more. In six outings, all in claiming races, he had finished in the first six only once.

The two horses arrived from France on 11 July. The next day, horse transporter Sigmund Webster drove Santa Amaro to Cabbage Hill Farm and then took Francasal to his own yard at Sonning Common, 15 miles away.

Epsom trainer Percy Bailey had been told to expect a new arrival called Francasal, who was to run at Bath on 16 July. Both Francasal and Santa Amaro had already been entered for the Spa Selling Stakes and Santa Amaro had also been entered for a race at Newmarket on the same day.

On 13 July Webster delivered a horse to Bailey's yard. Bailey believed it was Francasal but in fact it was Santa Amore. Three days later, when Santa Amore left Epsom for Bath, Francasal was driven from Webster's yard at Sonning Common towards Newmarket. The horsebox driver, Sidney Bennett, had been told to stop en route and phone Kateley, who instructed him to turn around and take the horse back to Sonning Common.

Williams then telegraphed Newmarket's clerk of the course, asking him to let Willie Snaith, booked to ride Santa Amore, know that the horsebox had broken down.

Meanwhile, from the turf accountant's office in England's Lane, Hampstead, Dill placed bets totalling £3,580 on Francasal, at Starting Price, spread around 20 bookmakers. Charles, from his office in Cardiff, spread another £2,500 among seven bookmakers.

The sums involved were enormous. £1 in 1953 would be worth about £30 in 2021. Between them, Dill and Charles staked the equivalent of over £182,000 on Francasal.

Off-course bookmakers with heavy liabilities would normally have telephoned bets to the racecourse to shrink the horse's odds but the telephone line was down. In *The Sporting Life*, Francasal and Santa Amore were among '20-1 others' in the betting forecast. Neither had any known form and Billy Gilchrist, Francasal's rider, was an unfashionable jockey.

Bailey passed Kateley's riding instructions on to Gilchrist. He was to wait until the final furlong of the six furlong race before striking for home. Instead, he took up the running after a furlong and led the rest of the way, winning by one and a half lengths. At the subsequent auction, Rook bought Francasal in for 740 guineas.

Francasal's SP was 10-1. The conspirators had won the equivalent of £1.8 million.

The winning horse, actually Santa Amore, and the real Francasal, were reunited at Webster's yard at Sonning Common. The intention was to return them both to France. On 17 July Dill asked the British Bloodstock Agency to arrange for Francasal to return to France as a matter of "extreme urgency," but it was already too late.

The headline in the next day's *Sporting Life* read, 'S.P. Gamble On Francasal', followed by 'Phone Failure Helped The Odds' and 'G.P.O. Investigations Into Bath Breakdown.' The National Sporting League and National Bookmakers' Protection Association advised their members to withhold payment of winning bets pending the outcome of investigations.

The police received an anonymous tip-off, informing them that Kateley and Charles were the men they needed to interview.

On 19 July, the police seized Francasal from the yard at Sonning Common and Santa Amore from Cabbage Hill Farm. Several witnesses, including the farrier who had fitted the winning horse's racing plates, readily identified which was which.

Three days later Bath's clerk of the course sent a telegram to the Jockey Club to lodge an objection to the winner of the Spa Selling Stakes, "on ground that the winner was not Francasal."

The conspirators were soon identified, along with Leonard Phillips. He denied having been to Bath but the cutting of the telephone wire had not gone unnnoticed. William Glass, a council worker inconveniently cutting the grass nearby, had made a note of the lorry's registration number. Phillips refused to disclose the name of his accomplice or that of his paymaster. On 18 September he was sentenced to three months in prison.

The following day Kateley, Williams, Charles, Dill and Rook appeared at Bow Street Magistrates Court, charged with conspiring to commit fraud by running a 'ringer.' On 12 January 1954, their trial opened at the Old Bailey.

In the face of compelling evidence of their guilt, the defendants advanced the case that it was a legitimate betting coup. Santa Amore had run in Francasal's place but it was the result, not of a deliberate ploy but by accident. The interruption to the telephone service was crucial but the police failed to establish a link between Phillips and the defendants.

Three weeks later, on 2 February, the jury retired to consider their verdict. Jurors later revealed that verdicts of 'guilty' would quickly have been returned but for the implacable opposition of one of their number, Patrick Beason. After three and a half hours, Mr Justice Sellers was informed that the jury were unable to agree. Majority verdicts were not permitted until 1967, so Sellers ordered a retrial.

The next day, one of the jurors contacted the Director of Public Prosecutions and prosecuting counsel to let them know that a juror called Pat, who had been seated behind the jury's foreman, had talked to men sitting at the back of the court and been seen talking with some of the defendants in a nearby cafe.

Beason admitted having spoken to Williams in the cafe during the trial. The men at the back of the court were identified as Kateley's father and Israel Edelstein, a known criminal. After the trial, Beason had allegedly been paid by another criminal, Isaac Andrews.

On 9 February, prosecuting counsel received another anonymous telephone call. Williams was said to have been in the bar at Walthamstow dog track, a regular haunt, bragging about how he had got Pat, one of the jury, 'squared up.'

When the second trial opened at the Old Bailey on 16 February, fearing further attempts to contact members of the jury, the defendants were refused bail and a policeman was allocated to each member of the jury, to escort them to and from the court.

On 17 March the jury found all the defendants except Rook guilty. Kateley, described by the Judge as "quite obviously the head and brain of this conspiracy," received a three year prison sentence. Williams and Charles got two years and Dill nine months.

Yet were the conspirators' elaborate plans necessary? Why did Santa Amore not run in his own name at Bath? He was an unraced, unknown quantity whereas Francasal's lack of ability was already established but few people were aware of Francasal's form in France.

With the telephone cable cut, would Santa Amore have started at a much shorter price than he did, disguised as Francasal? The conspirators must have thought so.

A month after the trial, the stewards of the Jockey Club disqualified Francasal and awarded the race to the runner-up, Pomonaway. Both horses and all those found guilty were disqualified for life.

In 2002 Tony Morris, Phillips' son-in-law, named a two-year-old Santa Amore, with a view to running it in the Len Phillips Memorial Francasal Two-Year-Old Selling Stakes. May Phillips, Leonard's widow, was to present the trophy. Sadly, May died a few weeks before the race and the plan to run Santa Amore was abandoned after he ran poorly in preparatory races.

85 DARBY BECOMES THE EMPEROR

Unnoticed among acres of headstones, Darby Sabini's grave is in Hove Cemetery, on the Old Shoreham Road. It was the road where Sabini had lived in a small terrace house and died, in 1950, aged 62.

There would have been few mourners. By then, Sabini was forgotten. He died after his time. If it had been 25 years earlier, it would have been a different funeral.

Darby was the name on his gravestone and the name he was usually called but it was not his real name. That was Ollovia, one of six sons of an Italian immigrant who variously called himself Joseph or Octavia or Olavio or Charles Sabini, who married Eliza Handley and lived in the Little Italy area of Clerkenwell, in central London.

Darby Sabini, 5ft 8ins tall and barrel chested, was a moderately successful boxer who could lay a man out with one blow, especially with the assistance of a knuckleduster. After the First World War ended, in 1918, there was a brief economic boom, record racecourse attendances and plenty of money in punters' pockets and bookmakers' satchels.

The Sabini brothers, led by Darby, were intent on extracting some of it. Other fingers were already in the pie, notably those of the Brummagem Boys, led by Billy Kimber. They had established a lucrative racecourse business sustained by intimidation and violence.

On many racecourses, particularly in the cheaper rings and in public areas distant from the grandstands, pitches were allocated, not by right, but might. Bookmakers often had no choice but to share their profits with gangsters, and to pay for the services they offered – protection, lists of runners, chalk, sponges and buckets of water, wanted or not.

The Brummagem Boys ruled the roost. An undisciplined gang, some from Birmingham but, according to a 1922 police report, "mostly convicted London thieves of the worst type," the gang charged bookmakers as much as 50 per cent of their profits for the privilege of conducting their business unmolested.

When the Sabini gang challenged Kimber's gang for control of southern racecourse pitches, the result was bloody warfare.

In March 1921, at a trotting meeting at Greenford, Darby Sabini was threatened by members of the Birmingham gang, led by George 'Brummy' Sage, Kimber's London-based ally. Sabini produced a revolver, and fired it. No one was hurt, and the court accepted Darby's claim of self-defence. He was fined £10 for possession of a firearm.

Four days later, encouraged by Walter Beresford, a respected bookmaker, Kimber visited Sabini with a peace plan. It involved the Sabinis abandoning their claims at Ascot and Epsom, the jewels in the southern crown. Sabini's counter-proposal called for Kimber's gang to retreat to the Midlands. The meeting ended abruptly when Kimber was shot by Alfred Solomon, Sabini's associate. Kimber stuck to the gangland rule book, and declined to cooperate with the police investigation. A jury subsequently accepted Solomon's claim that it was an accident.

A few weeks later, at Epsom's Derby meeting, Andrew Towie, an associate of Kimber's, was attacked with a mallet and bottle. It was small beer compared with what followed.

On the final day of the meeting, as a party of 10 bookmakers and their assistants made their way in a Crossley tender along the London Road towards the Brick Kiln Inn at Ewell, they were ambushed. "Here come the Italian bastards," one of the ambush party yelled. "Kill the bloody lot of them."

Thirty or more men, members of the Birmingham gang, armed with hammers, iron bars, razors, spanners, hatchets and bricks, surrounded the tender, and attacked its occupants. They put several men in hospital, but they were the wrong men. The Brummagem Boys thought they were ambushing the Sabini gang. Instead, they had mistakenly attacked their own allies, from Leeds.

When they fled, the police were soon in pursuit, and confronted them at the George and Dragon pub at Kingston Hill. 28 men, all from Birmingham, were arrested and, at the Surrey Assizes, 17 were convicted of causing grievous bodily harm and given prison sentences ranging from nine months to three years. The Birmingham gang had scored a spectacular own goal.

Two months later, in August 1921, the Racecourse Bookmakers' and Backers' Protection Association was set up, with Walter Beresford as its first President. Its initial objective was to protect southern punters and layers from molestation but, with neither the racing authorities nor the police providing adequate assistance, the Association felt obliged to turn to the experts in protection, the Sabini gang. Beresford already employed Harry Sabini, Darby's brother, as his racecourse clerk.

The Association's vice-president was Edward Emmanuel, an eyebrow-raising choice. Emmanuel was a noted criminal. According to Arthur Harding, another underworld figure, he was 'the Jewish Al Capone,' with both the police and the Sabini gang allegedly on his payroll.

Several stewards were appointed to protect the Association's members. The police reported that they "were mostly well known racecourse frequenters of a pugilistic tendency." They included Darby Sabini, Alfred White, Fred Gilbert, a member of the Sabini gang later accused of betraying it, and Philip Emmanuel, a relative of the vice-president.

The new Association was soon in danger of being tainted by its choice of representatives. In February 1922, White and Alfred Solomon were among those arrested for a razor attack on Michael Sullivan and Archie Douglas, both members of the Birmingham gang. A few weeks later, Solomon was again arrested after Gilbert was attacked with a razor. The victims declined to identify their attackers.

In July, at Brighton, the Sabini gang slashed John Phillips with razors and, at Newmarket, they attacked J. M. Dick, the racing correspondent of the *Evening News*, who had condemned the gangs.

The following month, Joseph Sabini and White, described by the police as the Association's chief steward, were among those charged with shooting at Gilbert and Sage outside the Southampton Arms pub in Camden High Street. Despite the disappearance of a key witness, White and Sabini were convicted and sentenced to five years and three years in prison, respectively. Mr Justice Roche remarked that the sooner the Association was dissolved, the better.

By then, it had dispensed with the stewards' questionable services, partly because the stewards had started to levy unauthorised charges of their own. Meanwhile, the gang war took another twist, as elements in the Sabini ranks demanded a bigger share of the gang's racecourse takings.

In November 1922, at the Fratellanza Club in Clerkenwell, Darby and Harry Sabini were attacked by the four Cortesi brothers, formerly their allies but now aligned with the Birmingham gang. Harry Sabini, recently charged with assaulting George Cortesi, was shot, while Darby's false teeth were broken. At the Old Bailey in January 1923, Enrico and Augustus Cortesi were both sent to prison for three years, and the Sabinis reasserted control.

At the end of 1922, Sir Samuel Scott, the Jockey Club's senior steward, suggested a conference with senior police officers following complaints "respecting the increase of ruffianism in the rings at race meetings."

While the Jockey Club stewards, chief constables and Home Office officials pondered, the ruffians continued their ruffianly conduct. Following the 1923 Derby, Darby and Harry Sabini appeared at Epsom Police Court charged with assaulting Maurice Fireman, alias Jack Levene, during a pitch dispute on the Downs. Darby had allegedly hit Fireman with a knuckleduster, while Harry threatened to take Fireman's eye out with a knife. There was some evidence that Fireman was the aggressor, and the case was dismissed.

By then, the Sabini gang had almost won the battle for southern supremacy, and settled into a profitable routine of overcharging racecourse bookmakers for a peaceful pitch, lists of runners and other tools of the trade.

Detective Chief Superintendent Edward Greeno later recalled, "the obliging man with the large bucket and small sponge who ran up the lines wiping out the odds on the bookmakers' boards between races was not doing it for love. It cost half a crown a time, and it was no use the bookmaker trying to save his half-crown by doing it himself. Nor was it any good saying he had brought enough chalk for the day; he had to buy chalk from the man who offered it. For every race the bookmaker needed a printed list of runners. They were printed by a Mr Edward Emmanuel for maybe a farthing apiece. To the bookies they were half a crown a set. Sometimes a bookmaker with a mistaken idea of independence refused to pay, and there are still a few around with razor-scarred faces to show how foolhardy they were."

One anonymous correspondent, writing in 1923, informed the Home Office that Emmanuel was still financing the Sabinis, was still often seen in the company of friendly police officers, and that "nine racing men out of every 10 live in absolute terror of them."

Darby Sabini's power and money were evident in 1924, when Alfred Solomon, in the presence of Emmanuel, stabbed Barnett Blitz in the back of the head with a stiletto knife.

Solomon, an associate of Sabini, had been lucky. Only the theatrical persuasiveness of defence barrister Sir Edward Marshall Hall saved him from being convicted of murder rather than manslaughter. Sabini had arranged for Hall to represent Solomon.

During 1924 and 1925, on the racecourse and off it, a variety of gangs engaged in what the press depicted, often exaggerating wildly, as full scale battles, until the government and Jockey Club finally responded.

In 1925, Sir William Joynson-Hicks, the Home Secretary, declared, "It is a state of affairs that cannot be tolerated," and pledged to break up the gangs. Under Chief Inspector 'Nutty' Sharpe, the Flying Squad began to target troublesome race meetings, while the Jockey Club appointed a team of about 60 ring inspectors, mainly retired police officers, to patrol the courses.

The regionally based Bookmakers' Protection Associations, which would unite to form the National Bookmakers' Protection Association in 1932, set up pitch committees to make pitch allocation fairer, and racecourse officials became involved in pitch administration. They were only partially successful.

In 1926, Sabini denied a suggestion that he made £20,000 to £30,000 (about £1.5m in 2019) a year on racecourses but, two years later, an anonymous 'Londoner' informed the Home Secretary that, "upon the racecourse, the Sabini gang reign supreme. The police never interfere with them. It is foolish to cry, 'God save the King,' one is safer if one shouts, 'God save the Emperor, Darby Sabini,' a far more powerful monarch."

There is no doubt that some, perhaps many, police were in the pay of the Sabinis, and gang leaders who controlled teams of violent thugs were sometimes referred to in extraordinarily complimentary terms, even by senior officers.

Former Chief Inspector Tom Divall, writing in 1929, described Billy Kimber, the leader of the Birmingham gang, as "one of the best," and some of his gang as "really good fellows." In Divall's eyes, the fact that Kimber and George Sage refused to give evidence after they had been shot by members of the Sabini gang showed "what generous and brave fellows Sage and Kimber were."

Many years later, in 1940, former Detective Superintendent F. Taylor, asked for information on Darby Sabini, who Taylor claimed to have known for 20 years, confined himself to observing, "His livelihood has always been among the racing world. To me, Sabini appeared straightforward and one who would go a long way to prevent trouble." Although it was true that Sabini preferred persuasion to violence, it was a remarkably indulgent assessment of the leader of a gang that owed its success to physical intimidation, a gang made up of violent villains.

Successful prosecutions were difficult to obtain, as were witnesses prepared to give evidence in court. In 1929, 'Nutty' Sharpe, commenting on two recent assaults, observed, "assaults of this kind by desperate racecourse-frequenting criminals are not infrequent but police have the greatest possible difficulty in obtaining evidence."

When Sabini appeared in court at Brighton later that year, charged with assaulting David Isaacs, a bookmaker, following a dispute at Hove Greyhound Stadium, there was the usual distinct shortage of witnesses. Asked for an explanation, Isaacs replied, "How can I get witnesses against a man like this, when everyone goes in fear of their life of him?" Sabini was fined £5.

Darby had moved to Brighton in about 1926, while his brothers remained in London. Like Epsom, Brighton racecourse was popular with criminals, because it was not fully enclosed and difficult to police but generally gangs found their racecourse operations increasingly curtailed. The Sabinis shifted their attention to greyhound tracks.

By 1936, Darby's influence was waning and blatant intimidation of racecourse bookmakers was less common. That year, an infamous episode of gang warfare at Lewes racecourse marked the end rather than a fresh beginning of racecourse violence.

On Monday 8 June 1936, a gang of about 30 men, all armed, first walked along the row of bookmakers' pitches, scanning the bookmakers' faces. James Spinks, the gang's leader, finally spotted Alfred Solomon and Mark Frater, Solomon's clerk. The gang rushed towards them. Solomon was struck on the head but managed to escape, Frater did not and was violently attacked.

When the police arrived the gang fled, shedding weapons as they went, weapons that would soon be displayed at Lewes Assizes. Hammers, iron bars, jemmies, knuckledusters and broken billiard cues were scattered around the betting ring. Some of the gang escaped but 16 were arrested and, on 27 July, appeared before Mr Justice Hilbery, charged with maliciously wounding Frater, assaulting Solomon, and riotous assembly.

Solomon did not give evidence and, while on bail, Spinks had a drink and a chat with Frater, after which Frater disappeared. The police retrieved him in time for the trial but his evidence was useless. Terrified, Frater copied the example set by many other victims of racecourse gangs, and lost his memory.

Detective Sergeant Collyer and Detective Constable Janes hadn't lost theirs and, although all 16 defendants denied having been involved, all 16 were found guilty. They were sentenced to imprisonment for periods ranging from 18 months to five years.

What Brighton's *Evening Argus* called the 'Lewes Racecourse Fracas' was one of the inspirations for Graham Greene's 1938 novel, *Brighton Rock*, in which the gangster Colleoni is believed to have been based on Darby Sabini.

Whatever influence he still retained was lost in 1940, when Italy joined the war on Germany's side. Darby and Harry Sabini, together with many other British citizens with Italian ancestors, were both interned, as "persons of hostile origin."

Darby, by then living in Hove under the name of Fred Handley, Handley being his mother's maiden name, was arrested at Hove greyhound stadium. Local inquiries about him produced a range of responses. Hove's chief constable reported that he knew Sabini as Fred, that he stood as a bookmaker at Hove dog meetings, collected money from racecourse bookmakers in return for protection and racecards, and that "Sabini and his brother (Harry) are persons who were at one time feared among the lower type of bookmakers on horse and dog racing tracks."

Detective Inspector E.Greens was more outspoken. "He is a drunkard and a man of most violent temperament," Greens wrote, "with a heavy following and strong command of bullies of Italian origin and other undesirables. A dangerous gangster and a racketeer of the worst type."

Darby appealed against his internment and, during his examination in December 1940, testified, "It is like going to church today, on a racecourse. All that rough business is finished." For the previous three years he had been standing as a bookmaker under the name of Dan Cope, and also worked for the Bookmakers' Protection Association, selling lists of horses on a commission basis.

During a court appearance in 1929, Sabini had described himself as a printer's agent and, in a statement he made shortly after his internment, he said that he worked as the representative of a printing company. The company was the Portsea Press, whose proprietor was Edward Smith, alias Edward Emmanuel, 'the Jewish Al Capone' reputed to have controlled the Sabini gang in its early days, now producing lists of runners and betting tickets for sale to bookmakers. Emmanuel and Darby Sabini were still working together.

In February 1941, the Home Office advisory committee dealing with Sabini's appeal recommended his release. The following month, a report sent to the Home Secretary by the Brighton police made it clear that they regarded Sabini's criminal activities as a thing of the past. "There is little doubt," the report stated, "that Sabini was the head of a race gang and considerable trouble was experienced by police with this gang, and others running in opposition on various racecourses. These gangs were finally broken up and it is safe to say that gang warfare during the past few years has been practically negligible, owing to police action, whilst the Sabini gang can rightly be said to be non-existent." Contrary to Greens' opinion, he was not now regarded as a dangerous gangster or racketeer.

In 1943, Darby was sent to prison for three years for receiving stolen goods. While there, he received the news that his only son, Harry, who had joined the Royal Air Force, had been killed in action in Egypt, aged 21.

After the war, a new generation of London gangsters, led by Jack 'Spot' Comer and Billy Hill, took control. They concentrated on clubs rather than racecourses, and Hill recruited several former members of the Sabini gang.

Darby Sabini, for a while the criminal emperor of Britain's southern racecourses, lived on in quiet anonymity, his death certificate giving his occupation as turf commission agent.

After You Finish

Well done.

ACKNOWLEDGEMENTS

Working with the team at Merlin Unwin Books has been a joy. Thank you to Karen McCall, Lydia Unwin, Joanne Potter, Joanne Dovey and Merlin Unwin himself. Their enthusiasm, expertise, diligence and good humour have made it a delightful and rewarding experience. Anything that's still wrong is my fault.

Rupert Mackeson pointed me in their direction, for which I'm grateful.

Susannah Gill, the Tote's Communications and Corporate Affairs Director, was instrumental in the Tote's welcome sponsorship of the photographs in this book.

Many individuals have contributed to the content of individual curiosities. Jean O'Brien, Frank Wise's niece, kindly lent a rare photograph of her uncle after winning the 1929 Irish Grand National on Alike (curiosity 9).

Arthur Barrow shared his memories of the rags to riches story of Master Smudge (curiosity 14). Sarah Hollinshead and Berys Connop did the same for the less celebrated In The Money (curiosity 17) while John Jenkins recalled his irritating experience with Pinehurst Park (curiosity 53).

Francesca Fox, at the Jockey Club Rooms, kindly authorised the photographs of Eclipse's foot (curiosity 20), the Newmarket Challenge Whip (curiosity 55) and the Elis wheel (curiosity 68) taken by Dan Abraham.

At Heath House in Newmarket, Sir Mark Prescott supplied access to St Simon's rather revolting skin (curiosity 21) as well as many wonderfully entertaining and educational hours.

The remarkable, if remarkably destructive life of the 17th Lord Saye and Sele (curiosity 29) could not have been told without the help of Martin Fiennes, son of the 21st Lord, who kindly gave access to family records.

The celebrated photographer Pat Healy donated a splendid photograph of Killarney racecourse (curiosity 44) while Amy Starkey, formerly managing director of Kempton Park, now in charge of the Jockey Club Racecourses' East Region, provided helpful information on the appearance there of the Royal Philharmonic Orchestra (curiosity 45).

The memories and memorabilia of the centenarian Harry Green, relating to Gordon Richards' record achievements in 1933, owe their appearance (curiosity 47) to the characteristic generosity of author and journalist Chris Pitt and his wife Mary, treasure troves of obscure information.

Jim Fuller kindly shared the fruits of his research into the history of the Newmarket Town Plate (curiosity 57) while Jonathan Goldberg QC, who represented James Laming at his trial in 1989, alerted me to a contemporary cartoon of the affair (curiosity 83).

Many others deserve a mention including, alphabetically, Kim Bailey, Bill Barber, Tim Cox, Bill Eacott, Tim Hailstone, Sean Magee, Lee Mottershead, Matthew Taylor and Neil Watson. I'm bound to have missed someone out, for which I apologise.

And thanks to Patricia for putting up with it all.

SOURCES

Extensive. I feel slightly guilty for not providing a comprehensive, excessively long, list of sources. Some are indicated within the text.

Writing this has reminded me of the sadness of getting rid of books. I now have a collection of generally inferior replacements.

On the other hand, the many archives accessible through the internet, including newspaper archives such as britishnewspaperarchive.co.uk and newspapers.com, have been invaluable.

You can spend hours trying to find a small piece of information and I often have.

tote

A Word From the Tote

The Tote has been part of the fabric of British racing for nearly 100 years. In 1928 an Act of Parliament paved the way for the creation of the Tote, with the aim of providing a safe place to bet, funds for horseracing and more tax revenue for the Treasury, where Winston Churchill was Chancellor of the Exchequer. The following year the Tote served its first customers.

Winston Churchill supported the creation of the Tote when Chancellor of the Exchequer.

Very few people know more about the Tote than David, who wrote *For the Good of Racing ... the first 75 years of the tote* (2004).

Since we acquired the Tote in October 2019 we have brought in many improvements which will ensure the Tote has an exciting story to tell when it hits its century in 2028, one that David might be willing to update everyone on!

As racing's pool betting operator, the Tote provides a distinctive alternative to fixed-odds betting, with customers betting into a shared pool rather than against a bookmaker. The pool betting model means the Tote is agnostic about results so welcomes winning customers - and we all love winners in racing.

The developments we have brought to the Tote are ones that Churchill and other famous characters in the Tote's history, including its longest-serving Chairman Woodrow Wyatt, could not even have dreamt about. From Tote Guarantee, ensuring the Tote will always match or exceed the Starting Price, and an App for the digital age, to collaboration with other pool betting operators around the globe to introduce World Pool to British racing. The Tote is now very much a leader in the betting sector.

It is no surprise that Tote-related stories feature on several pages of the book, given the organisation's role in the sport and the people it has touched over the decades. We are working to ensure there are many more exciting stories to come from the Tote in the years ahead.

We are delighted to sponsor this engaging and entertaining book and we hope you enjoy reading it as much as we have done.

Best wishes from all the UK Tote Group

Photo credits

Chapter Openers all supplied by Shutterstock

Also published by Merlin Unwin Books
www.merlinunwin.co.uk

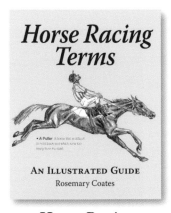

Horse Racing Terms
Rosemary Coates

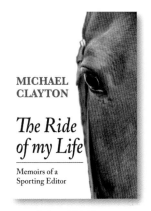

The Ride of my Life
Michael Clayton

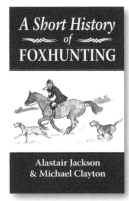

A Short History of Foxhunting
Jackson & Clayton

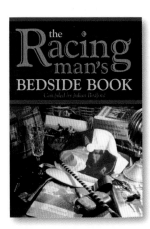

The Racingman's Bedside Book
Julian Bedford

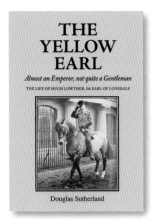

The Yellow Earl
Douglas Sutherland

A Day at the Races
Peter May

Also published by Merlin Unwin Books
www.merlinunwin.co.uk

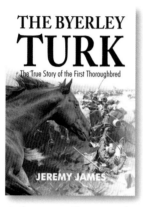

The Byerley Turk
Jeremy James

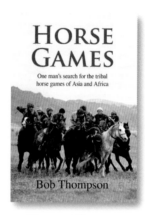

Horse Games
Bob Thompson

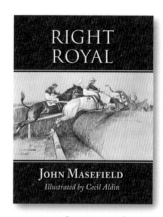

Right Royal
John Masefield

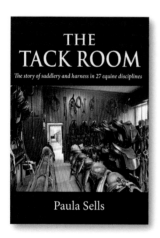

The Tack Room
Paula Sells

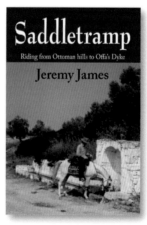

Saddletramp
Jeremy James

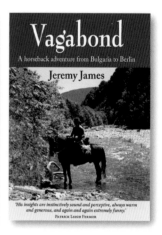

Vagabond
Jeremy James